EXPERIENCING THE SOUL

D1167233

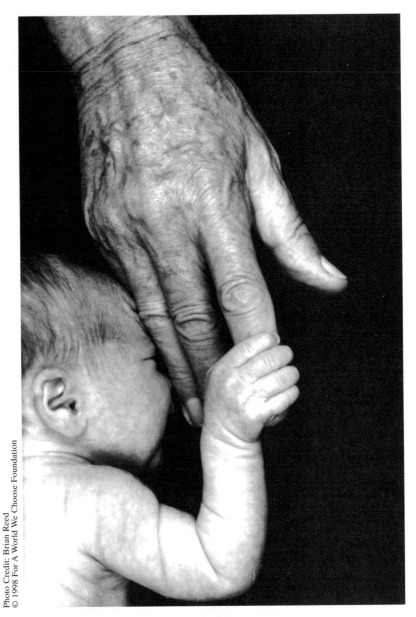

This photo of a ten-day-old infant with his 84-year-old grandfather symbolizes the polarity of birth and death. At the time of birth, the soul enters the physical world. At the time of death, the soul leaves the physical world.

EXPERIENCING THE SOUL

Before Birth, During Life, After Death

EDITED BY

ELIOT JAY ROSEN

Hay House, Inc.
Carlsbad, CA

Published and distributed in the United States by:

Hay House, Inc., P.O. Box 5100, Carlsbad, CA 92018-5100 • (800) 654-5126 • (800) 650-5115 (fax)
Editorial: Jill Kramer   *Design:* Jenny Richards

Grateful acknowledgment is made for permission to reprint from the following copyrighted material:

Inner and Outer Peace Through Meditation, by Rajinder Singh. Copyright © SK Publications 1996. Used by permission of Element Books, Inc.
Dancing in the Flames, by Marion Woodman and Elinor Dickson. Copyright © 1996. Reprinted by arrangement with Shambhala Publications Inc., Boston; and Random House of Canada Limited.
Sacred Mirrors: The Visionary Art of Alex Grey, by Alex Grey with Ken Wilber and Carlo McCormick, published by Inner Traditions International, Rochester, VT 05767. Copyright © 1990 Alex Grey.
Self-Realization magazine, Summer 1997. Copyright © 1997 Self-Realization Fellowship, Los Angeles, California, USA.
Facing Death and Finding Hope, by Christine Longaker. Copyright © 1997 by Christine Longaker and Rigpa Fellowship. Used by permission of Doubleday, a division of Bantam Doubleday Dell Publishing Group, Inc.; in the British Commonwealth (excluding Canada), Random House UK Limited, London, England.
Excerpt from the poem, "The Cry of the Soul," from *Love At Every Step—My Concept of Poetry,* by Darshan Singh. Copyright © 1989 by SK Publications, Bowling Green, Virginia.
Excerpts from the *Noetic Sciences Review* (Winter, 1994), published by the Institute of Noetic Sciences, Sausalito, California.
"Life in Hell " cartoon, 6/13/97, Acme Features Syndicate. Copyright © 1997 by Matt Groening.
Sacred Individuality, a forthcoming book by Joseph Sharp. Copyright © by Joseph Sharp 1997.
KITV-4, Hawaii Argyle Television Inc., Honolulu, Hawaii, for excerpts from a public broadcast of Betty J. Eadie.

Photo Credits: Melinda H. White for "We Are the Angels: We Are the Mortal People"; the National Hospice Organization for permission to reprint the photo entitled "Disco Harry's Last Dance," by Philip C. Leeuwen; NASA for the photo of astronaut Edgar Mitchell; Nancy Jo Gilchrist for the photo of Eliot Jay Rosen; Brian Lambert for the photo of the Dalai Lama with Eliot Jay Rosen; Anne Kramer for the photo of Max and Martin; George Saavedra and IMAGIC for their donation of photo-enhancement services.

Library of Congress Cataloging-in-Publication Data

Experiencing the soul :   before birth, during life, after death /   edited by Eliot Jay Rosen.
   p.   cm.
   Includes bibliographical references.
   ISBN 1-56170-461-X (pbk.)
   1. Spiritual life. 2. Soul.   I. Rosen, Eliot Jay.
BL624.E96   1998
129—dc21   97-51709
                                    CIP

ISBN 1-56170-461-X

01 00 99 98   4 3 2 1
First Printing, April 1998

Printed in the United States of America

Other Hay House Titles of Related Interest

As Someone Dies, by Elizabeth A. Johnson

Between Heaven & Earth, by Laura A. Huxley

The Earth Adventure, by Ron Scolastico, Ph.D.

The Experience of God, by Jonathan Robinson

"I Come As a Brother," by Bartholomew

Infinite Self, by Stuart Wilde

Life! Reflections on Your Journey, by Louise L. Hay

Practical Spirituality, by John Randolph Price

Wake-Up Calls, by Gerald G. Jampolsky, M.D., and Diane V. Cirincione

The Ways of the Mystic, by Joan Borysenko, Ph.D.

All of the above titles can be ordered by calling Hay House at:
(800) 654-5126

Please visit the Hay House Website at: **www.hayhouse.com**

To the beauty embodied in the existence
Of spiritually perfected human beings, both
Past and present, who dwell among us as scientists
Of the soul, whose grace consummates our soul's
Final homecoming, and whose mystery lies far
Beyond this beholder's eye to fathom.

CONTENTS

PART II: THE SOUL BEFORE BIRTH

PART III: THE SOUL AFTER DEATH

PART IV: THE SOUL IN THE NEAR-DEATH EXPERIENCE

PART V: EXPERIENCING THE SOUL

FOREWORD

by Academy Award®-winning actress
Ellen Burstyn

My interest in the area of the nonmaterial dimension of reality began while I was still a child, when my grandfather died. My mother and I had been out shopping. Upon our return, we went to my brother's room to see if he was home. My brother was currently staying in the room my grandfather had lived in for several months after the death of my grandmother. As we entered the room, I was startled to smell the overpowering aroma of flowers. I turned to my mother and asked, "Do you smell that?" My mother answered quietly, "Yes, it smells like flowers." Remembering my grandmother's funeral just a few years before, I said, "It smells like a funeral parlor." Just then the phone rang. My mother walked to the phone in an unnaturally measured pace and picked up the receiver in what seemed like slow motion. I watched her face crumble as she received the news of her father's sudden and unexpected death.

I could not understand this experience. I hoped some day that I might. I carried it with me like candy in my pocket waiting for the right time to eat it and digest its strange sweetness. Not only did a full explanation of that event never come, but as I grew older, my pocket filled with more candy, more events of a mysterious kind that intrigued me but brought no concrete answers. In fact, my questions deepened. Over the years, I came to realize that at the core of our reality is what Buckminster Fuller called the "a priori mystery." This mystery has led me, haunted me, fascinated throughout my life. It has defined my interests, influenced my studies, prompted my pursuits, stimulated my curiosity, and informed my every day.

In 1978, while developing the story that Lewis Carlino later wrote as the screenplay for *Resurrection,* I had been reading Elisabeth Kübler-Ross's work *On Death and Dying,* and also Raymond Moody's *Life After Life.* From Raymond Moody's reports of the near-death experience, we created the scene of my character, Edna, who found herself going through a non-physical tunnel of light after a traumatic car accident. Edna then returns to life with a deeper understanding of life's dimensions and possibilities, including the power to heal the sick.

The tunnel image is repeated later in the film when she almost dies after taking on a patient's symptoms. Edna sees her own father in the tunnel and awakens to the knowledge that her father is dying. The scene that follows with Edna and her father on his deathbed was inspired by Kübler-Ross's work with the dying, and again Moody's, when her father says, "The light, Edna, the light," as he makes the transition to the immaterial realm. I felt the ideas in the works of these two pioneers in the field were so important, I was happy we could seed them into the consciousness through the popular medium of film.

Now, 20 years after *Resurrection,* comes this wonderful anthology with articles from almost all the leaders in thanatology and related fields. There is even a description in Bill Guggenheim's chapter on "The Varieties of After-Death Communications" where he describes smelling the fragrance of flowers immediately after a loved one dies, just as I experienced when my grandfather died. This collection charts the ways in which researchers, scientists, psychologists, visionaries, and spiritual leaders have observed the manifestation of soul throughout the universe.

I pray that this book touches your heart and mind and inspires your soul on the spiritual journey.

PREFACE

This book (and the companion video series that shares the same name) is a direct result of a life-transforming, five-hour-long meditation that I experienced in July of 1994. At the time, I was working as a hospice social worker in Honolulu with people in the process of dying. One quiet Saturday morning, I gently lifted out of my body in meditation and entered a realm of Light. A "Being of Light" began a two-way, telepathic communication with my spirit-soul with these exact words: *"Society is now ready to accept that consciousness survives the death of the physical body."* It was conveyed to me that a worldwide spiritual awakening was upon us, and that humanity would soon come to accept the reality that death is only a transition to another dimension—and not the end of life. I was told that in the near future, more of us living on Earth will consciously experience ourselves as souls *during* Earth-life, and not have to wait until we leave our bodies after physical death to remember who we really are. The Being of Light proceeded to give me detailed instructions on how to create a book and video series that would help prepare us for the dawning of this new awareness.

As I had no previous training or experience in making films, without words, my spirit-soul telepathically expressed its doubts that I had the wherewithal to accomplish what was being asked of me. A part of me thought that perhaps some erring celestial administrator had "pulled the wrong file" and lifted the wrong "Rosen" out of his body. The Being of Light's compassionate replies to all my unspoken concerns were in these exact words: *"Don't worry, we will help you,"* or simply, *"Know that it will be arranged."*

To give a flavor of what transpired in those extraordinary five hours, at one point I candidly—and very much in character—asked the Being of Light, "What about the money? Who's going to pay for all this?" The Being of Light—again without words—conveyed to my spirit, *"In exactly two weeks, someone is going to offer you $5,000 to get started."*

Upon my return to my normal everyday consciousness, I wrote down as much as I could recall of the guidance and directions I was given. I immediately began contacting those individuals and organizations who I hoped would not only believe my otherworldly account, but help financially support the project.

After two weeks of following up leads and referrals, I just happened to mention to a friend in an offhand way that I'd recently had a profound spiritual experience. I shared the briefest of highlights with him, and after hearing my story, my friend could barely control his excitement. He told me that I *had* to speak to his friend Carol Lassen.

Carol was the executor of the Lassen Foundation, the charitable organization founded by world-renowned environmental artist Chris Lassen. When I eventually got a phone call through to Carol and told her my story, I could tell that she and I were definitely "on the same page of music." Carol told me that she completely understood what had happened to me "in the light" because she herself had undergone a life-transforming near-death experience many years before.

When she had finished relating her own account, she paused, and a palpable presence began to fill the silence on the other end of the phone. I knew that she was tuning in to a deep place within herself. I then heard Carol slowly speak the following words: "On behalf of our foundation, I feel guided to offer you $5,000 to get started."

Goose bumps spontaneously arose on my arms. Tears welled up in my eyes. Only at that moment did I remember the Being of Light's prediction that "in two weeks" someone would offer "$5,000 to get started." I glanced at the calendar on my desk—exactly two weeks had elapsed. Deeply moved, with a quivering, trembling voice, I was barely able to utter "thank you." Since then, other amazing events that the Being of Light predicted have also come to pass.

A "Soul's Eye" Overview of This Book

For the last three and a half years, I've been traveling around the United States, filming and interviewing people who have had profound spiritual experiences, including a broad spectrum of experts from various scientific and spiritual fields. Only 32 individuals were selected for this book—many more appear in the companion video.

To create a greater feeling of intimacy, I decided to dispense with the original question-response, interviewer-interviewee format and edit the transcribed manuscripts so that the contributors speak directly to the reader.

As you'll soon discover, these contributors have different conceptions of the soul that at times may *seem* to conflict with each other. I believe, however, that they are describing different *aspects* or *stages* in the soul's journey—not unlike the proverbial story of the blind men grabbing hold of different parts of an elephant and arguing about the essential nature of "elephantness." As the story goes, one blind man takes hold of the tail and says that the elephant is like a snake, another touches the leg and says that an elephant resembles a tree-trunk, and so on. So there is an underlying basis of truth to be found in *all* the entries in this anthology, just as each of the blind men were "right" within the scope of their experience.

Meeting the contributors to this book has been an extraordinarily enriching experience: Without exception, they all possessed great intellectual acuity, spiritual perceptiveness, and deep compassion. And despite their differences in viewpoint, each emanated a clearly felt underlying "presence" on the level of soul that was more prominent than any external difference in perspective.

The book is divided into eight sections:

Part I: Living with Soul demonstrates how "extraordinary ordinary" people grew spiritually as they were transformed from agnostic to direct knower, conformist to sacred individualist, by various "life or death" challenges.

Part II: The Soul Before Birth explores "prebirth experiences," in which the souls of yet-to-be-born children from "the Other Side" contact people in announcement dreams, visions, materializations, and in various other ways.

Part III: The Soul After Death introduces the emerging field of "after-death communications," where people report meeting the souls of deceased loved ones. You'll read some amazing accounts, some of which demonstrate that not only does the soul continue its existence after death, but our sense of humor apparently follows us as well!

Part IV: The Soul in the Near-Death Experience shares the personal stories of the world's two most recognized near-death returnees, Betty J. Eadie and Dannion Brinkley. This section also includes an interview with Dr. Raymond Moody, the pioneering researcher who coined the term the "near-death experience."

Part V: Experiencing the Soul contains the wisdom-teachings of three of the most revered spiritual personages on Earth today: His Holiness the Dalai Lama of Tibet; Sri Daya Mata, the foremost living disciple of Paramahansa Yogananda; and Sant Rajinder Singh, a master of meditation in the highly regarded spiritual tradition of Sant Mat.

Part VI: Preparing the Soul for a Healing Passage points to a way of being in the world that helps us to first accept, and then prepare, for death, and simultaneously to live more fully in the moment.

Part VII: The Soul at the Moment of Death enlarges our understanding of what happens at the moment of death, and gives an overview of the wisdom-traditions and techniques that help us prepare physically, emotionally, cognitively, and spiritually for the transition we call death.

Part VIII: Science and the Soul—The Evidence presents scientific research on consciousness and paranormal experiences and offers various theoretical frameworks drawn from the fields of quantum physics, transpersonal psychology, the philosophy of science, and other disciplines.

Appendix A—Resource Listings—Taking the Next Step. Each contributing author offers various ways to contact them—phone numbers, addresses, websites, and so on. In addition, some authors have listed those organizations that might help you take the "next step" in your journey of soul-discovery. Others have listed the charitable organization closest to their hearts.

***Appendix B—About* For A World We Choose Foundation.** This brief section provides an overview of the activities and projects of the nonprofit organization that created this charity anthology book and companion video series.

I invite you to read the book in any order you wish—with two possible exceptions. If you consider yourself a scientifically minded "doubting Thomas," it might be better to first read Part VIII, "Science and the Soul— The Evidence." If you are someone who is grieving the loss of a loved one, I suggest you start this book at the beginning.

To conclude, from the time of this book's inception—when my soul was seeded in the Light—to this very moment as I write these words, I have intermittently experienced a benevolent and powerful presence in and around me that has shown me that, in truth, "we are not the doers." My prayer *for myself* is that I am never allowed to forget this, for such knowledge keeps one humble and receptive to the Divine. My heartfelt prayer *for you,* dear reader, is that this book inspires you to deepen your experience of soul, and that the same Power that enables me to write these words give you the courage to take the next step—whatever that may be for you.

In love and service,
Eliot Jay Rosen, LISW, ACSW

ACKNOWLEDGMENTS

All of the profits from this book are being donated to two nonprofit charities: For A World We Choose Foundation and the Hay Foundation, the charitable organization created by Louise L. Hay. Thank you, Louise, for selecting this book as the Hay House "Charity Book of the Year for 1998," as well as everybody at Hay House for their "beyond the call" high standards of excellence and loving attention.

I also wish to thank each and every distinguished contributor in this anthology who donated their time and wisdom to this book; the people in the process of dying who, as their last gifts to us, shared their messages of inspiration and hope; the generous support of the Institute of Noetic Sciences (in memory of Dr. Willis Harman); Elda Hartley of the Hartley Film Foundation; the Lassen Foundation, the Swedenborg Foundation, the Science of Spirituality, the Self-Realization Fellowship, Transformational Research, Inc.; the Board of Directors of For A World We Choose Foundation (in fond memory of Shelby Parker, the unofficial "grandmother of the human potential movement"); and the Bodhi Tree bookstore in Los Angeles.

On a personal note, I wish to thank my entire extended family, especially my mother, Roselle Rosen; Catherine and Michael Rakoff; Andrew Vidich; Laurie K. Schwartz; Dr. Jack Trop; Glenda Lockard; Dr. Mark and Princy Perrault; Margaret and Brian Lambert; Alan Myers; the memory of Sant Darshan Singh, from whom I received invaluable meditation instruction and spiritual guidance; and Sant Rajinder Singh, who continues to freely share the experience of the soul with sincere seekers of truth.

GENERAL INTRODUCTION

The Nature of the Soul—
From Believing to Knowing

The Nature of the Soul

In an English translation of a book published in India in 1894, the renowned mystic saint, Soami Shiv Dayal Singh—who spent a full 17 years in seclusion in almost continuous meditation—describes the "Original Region" from which the soul emanates as being "formless," "nameless," "unending," "fathomless," "without beginning," "spaceless," "quality-less" and "indescribable." He further remarks, "There is no symbol here from which an idea could be given as to what it is like."

In the same way that the "Original Region—the Home of the Soul" is impossible to describe but can only be experienced, describing the soul *itself* is also an impossible task. At best, we can only hint at the *attributes* of the soul using inferences, concepts, and metaphors, although it seems that we humans have an insatiable need to describe our soul experiences to others. This book is filled with such testimonies, and only begins to illustrate the diverse ways people experience their souls before birth, during life, and after death.

But is it possible to define the soul? Most people who believe in the existence of the soul agree that the soul is not a physical "something." The soul is usually conceptualized as a nonphysical, spiritual essence that mysteriously and paradoxically exists *in* physical creation, yet is itself *beyond* the time/space constraints of physical creation. Views on the nature of the soul can be reduced to three major schools of thought.

One view is that the soul is a formless essence—consciousness itself— which is much the same as God's essence. To use an analogy, the soul is like a drop of seawater that will ultimately merge back into its Source—God, the ocean of All-Consciousness.

A second view is that the soul has a permanent and indestructible form that, even though it is "created in God's image," is not in its primal essence the same *as* God. In this view, the soul, when it returns to God, experiences a separate, dual relationship, as would a servant to his or her master. On its homecoming, the soul is permitted to be in the presence of God for eternity.

The third view combines aspects of both views: Although the soul in its pristine, essential nature ultimately has no form, in its *progress* on its spiritual journey back to its Creator, the soul is covered by physical, astral, and causal layers of form—until its final dissolution into the Formless. The soul's homecoming consists of the progressive peeling off of these subtler layers of material form that have attached itself to its formless essence.

Resorting again to analogy, this would be like the soul wearing several protective layers of clothing, and while wearing this apparel, identifying itself *as* the clothes it is wearing. Over time, however, the soul begins to shed each layer, one by one, as warmer weather approaches.

In the wintertime, at the beginning of the soul's evolution, the soul wears a heavy "physical-matter" overcoat so that it can function in the physical plane of existence. In the fall, the soul only needs an "astral-matter" vest so that it can function on the astral plane of existence. In the spring, it wears only a thin "causal-matter" shirt so that it can function on the causal plane of existence. And in the summer, the soul removes even this last thin shirt worn in the causal plane so that the warm rays of the light of God shine *directly* on the soul for the first time since it left its Original Home in the Beginningless Beginning—*before* the Creator created the Creation. The soul now knows that it is not the physical, astral, and causal clothing it has been wearing all this time.

According to this third view, this last stage in the soul's journey is not unlike the scene in the movie *The Invisible Man,* when "Mr. Invisible" unwraps the white surgical bandages that give his body the *appearance* of form. With the bandages removed, he is formless and invisible, yet still present. That's as far as analogy can take us in describing the nature of the soul.

It is said by many spiritual traditions that all human beings consciously experience their souls at least once in their earthly lives—even if this one time is but a fleeting moment at the time of biological death. However, throughout recorded history, there have been people who claim to have the continuous, conscious experience of the transcendent nature of their soul *every* moment of life, even while engaging in everyday activities such as sipping a hot cup of homemade soup. To what degree we pursue this ultimate experience of soul is something that each of us chooses, consciously or unconsciously—by our thoughts, words, and deeds—every moment of our lives.

From Belief to Knowing

Perhaps a common starting point in our inquiry is to agree that the *direct* experience of the soul is the only way to truly *know* the soul. Roger Bacon (1214–1292), the great English scientist, philosopher, and member of the Order of St. Francis, clarified the distinction between the direct experience of the soul and analytical reasoning when he said:

> *There are two modes of knowing: through argument, and experience. Argument brings conclusions and compels us to concede them, but does not cause certainty nor remove doubts in order that the mind may remain at rest in truth, unless this is provided by experience. The very basis of non-belief in soul comes down to non-experience of soul.[1]*

In the winter of his life, the great "scientist of the psyche," Dr. Carl Jung, suffered a heart attack in which he experienced what today has been coined a "near-death experience." In the few minutes that he was clinically dead, before his physician administered the potent heart stimulant that brought him back to his body, Jung found himself:

> *...high up in space. Far below I saw the globe of earth bathed in a glorious blue light. Ahead of me I saw a shining temple and was drawn towards it. As I approached, a strange thing happened. I had the certainty I was about to enter an illuminated room and*

meet all those people to whom I was beloved in reality. There I would understand at last the meaning of my life.[2]

The experience of transcending his physical body had a profound and enduring effect on the life and work of this trail-blazing scientist/psychiatrist. Again, from his autobiography, Dr. Jung wrote:

What happens after death is so unspeakably glorious that our imaginations and our feelings do not suffice to form even an approximate conception of it.[3]

The aftereffects of this transforming event forever broadened Jung's view of human nature and the universe. For him, the sheer force of this metaphysical experience expanded the frontier of human possibilities to include "the soul" as well as the psyche.

At least for Dr. Jung himself, the reality of life after death was no longer dependent on mere belief or traditional religious conviction. His understanding was now firmly grounded in *direct experience.* This inner knowing, based on direct revelation, is sometimes called "contemplative knowing." Afterwards, in his efforts to share this experience with others, Jung clearly recognized the age-old philosophical dilemma—that the impact and truth-value of *one* person's inner experience cannot fully be imparted to *others.* For in the very process of sharing inner experience, the firsthand immediacy of the experience is lost. The inherent difficulty lies in the fact that the direct experiencer's inner knowing becomes *someone else's mere belief,* which all too often devolves into unfortunate misunderstandings and meaningless debate.

Though contemplative knowing cannot be *proven* in the strict scientific sense—at least at this time in history—this doesn't make "the life of the spirit" any less real, meaningful, or effective as a way of being in the world. Nobel Peace Prize recipient Mother Teresa was once asked why she didn't use her worldwide recognition to actively support political causes she believed in. She replied, "I find the power of prayer much more powerful." Her firsthand spiritual experience of the power of prayer informed her way of being in the world.

The question then arises, in reading this book, how do you *really* know that the accounts shared by the contributors are authentic? The answer to this question represents—in miniature form—a basic challenge we face all throughout life: By what criteria do we choose our sources of information—and how do we know what we know?

Speaking for myself, I realized that it all came down to some type of faith—faith in God, faith in the findings of science, faith in a chosen spiritual tradition, faith in the inherent goodness of human nature, and faith in life itself. So, too, with this book—some measure of faith is necessary in order to decide for yourself its meaning and truth-value. In asking you to approach this book with this experimental faith, all I can say, dear reader, is that in interviewing each of the contributors, this writer used all of the faculties at his disposal—the discriminative faculties of head, the felt-sense of the heart, the intuitions of the soul—and then took "a leap of faith" based on the unmistakable, palpable genuineness and integrity that I recognized in each of these individuals. I hope that you also recognize these qualities in them, and throughout this book.

— Eliot Jay Rosen

PART I

Living with Soul

INTRODUCTION

Some people live with such courage, verve, and endearing panache that we say they live "with soul." These individuals may have never had a conscious experience of their soul in the transcendental, spiritual sense, yet their lives are imbued with an intangible but unmistakable soul quality.

It is not uncommon that these soul-filled individuals die in an unusual way, or at a young age. Their earthly lives are extinguished—as the saying goes—"like candles in the wind." It's almost as if they arrive on the stage of the play of life, make their cameo appearance, and exit stage right—not even waiting to read the reviews in the morning paper. Yet their words and deeds are indelibly etched in our memories and inspire us onward when the sandstorms of life threaten to blow us off our feet.

The contributors to *Part I: Living with Soul* embody the spirit of Gautama Buddha when he said:

> *Let me not pray to be sheltered from dangers,*
> *but to be fearless in facing them.*
> *Let me not beg for the stilling of pain,*
> *but for the heart to conquer it.*
> *Let me not look to allies in life's battlefield,*
> *but to my own strength.*
> *Let me not crave in anxious fear to be saved,*
> *but hope for patience to win my freedom.*

Disco Harry's Last Dance. *Harry, pictured with his granddaughter, loved to dance—wheelchair in tow—up to the very last moment of his life.*

CHAPTER ONE

Experiences of My Soul in Life and Death

ELISABETH KÜBLER-ROSS, M.D.

Dr. Elisabeth Kübler-Ross is a medical doctor, psychiatrist, and a world-renowned expert in thanatology (the scientific discipline specifically studying death and dying). Her pioneering research in thanatology can be found in dozens of books and articles, including the classics *On Death and Dying* and *On Life after Death*. The world owes a great debt to Dr. Kübler-Ross for her pioneering and courageous work. More than any other individual in the modern era, she has laid the foundation for the flourishing hospice movement—the newest social institution that is taking death "out of the closet" and back into the heart of life.

This chapter is based on an excerpt from a film interview that took place in Kübler-Ross's beautiful home in the Arizona desert.

> *"Death is simply a shedding of the physical body like the butterfly shedding its cocoon. It is a transition to a higher state of consciousness where you continue to perceive, to understand, to laugh, and to be able to grow."*
> — Dr. Elisabeth Kübler-Ross

The best teacher I ever had, in all my 68 years of living, was an uneducated black cleaning lady in the Chicago hospital where I was working. She taught me, Dr. Elisabeth K.-Ross, the world-renowned death and dying specialist, more about death and dying than anyone else in my entire life. She didn't talk from theories—stages of dying and all that stuff—she talked from *knowing,* from her soul.

There was something special about this woman, but I couldn't figure it out at first. After she would clean one of my dying patient's rooms, I noticed that afterwards the patient was often in a place of great peace. I had no idea what she [the cleaning lady] was doing in there, but I was anxious to find out. So one day I cornered her and said, "What in the world are you doing with my dying patients?" She became very defensive and said, "I'm not doing *anything,* I *only* clean their rooms." I tried to convey to her that my question was not meant to be critical; I just wanted to find out what she did when she was in the room with them. Well, she denied everything and walked away from me—too afraid to tell me anything for fear that she might lose her job. You must remember, this occurred over 30 years ago, when it was even *more* intimidating for a white psychiatrist to confront a black cleaning woman by asking her, "What in the world are you doing with my dying patients?"

After sort of "snooping around" each other for a few weeks—checking each other out—this incredible woman had the courage to grab hold of my white lab coat and lead me into a private area in the back of the nursing station. Out of the blue sky, she began to tell me how hard it was growing up in the slums of Chicago; how she became the mother of several sick, starving children; how they had so little money at times that they lived on maggot-infested grits and oatmeal just to survive. She told me about the time her three-year-old child got weaker and sicker in the middle of a terribly cold winter of Chicago. This poor, desperate woman took this sick child in her arms and brought him to be treated at a local hospital. She was refused treatment because she still owed the hospital five dollars from a previous visit. Knowing that the county hospital could not legally refuse to treat her little boy, she carried her child in her arms and walked all the way from 69th Street to the Cook County Hospital—a long, long walk, especially in the bitter cold. After arriving, she waited another three hours in the emergency room, but her little boy did not receive treatment. The child died in her arms before her name was called.

In listening to all this, there came a point where I couldn't contain myself any longer—as you might have guessed—I'm *not* a very patient person. I said, *"Why* are you telling me all these gruesome horror stories?" And with a great peace in her voice, she said, "Dr. Ross, death is an old, old acquaintance of mine. I'm not afraid of death anymore. And sometimes, when I clean a patient's room who is very close to dying, and that person looks afraid or lonely, I cannot help myself from walking over to them, *touching* them, *being* with them, and talking to them about how death is not so terrible."

This woman had met death hundreds of times. She knew death as an old friend and was totally unafraid. I said to myself, *"That's* the woman I need to teach me and be my assistant." She had a way of being with people that I had no idea *even existed!* Much to the dismay and resistance of my academic colleagues, I hired this wonderful black cleaning lady to be my assistant.

Life After Death and the Meaning of Life

For people who don't believe there is life after death, they have a surprise coming for them when they make their transition at the time of death. I know firsthand what it's like not to believe—I myself used to be a wishy-washy Protestant, a scientific skeptic who thought belief in life after death was just a form of psychological denial.

There are millions of people who *talk* about the wonders of heaven, but *deep down* they don't *really* believe a word of it. When these people have some pain in their chest, their spiritual beliefs go right out the window! They become petrified and say, "Help, I'm having a coronary!" Hopefully, they'll one day *know,* and not just *believe*—and then they'll be really able to practice what they preach.

If we can do this, we will be able to spread love through the whole world. Love is *always* stronger than hate. The positive is *always* stronger than the negative. For me, it's nice to know that even though the world is in terrible shape with all the fighting, politics, and negativity going on, *nothing* is stronger than love.

In our work with dying people over the last 30 years, we interviewed over 20,000 near-death experiencers. These people came from almost every walk of life, race, religion, and culture. Upon their return to Earth, we found that almost everyone now felt that the most important thing in life was *love*—both giving *and* receiving—and serving others.

As far as *love* goes, it is said, "Love thy neighbor *and thy self.*" Nowadays, people forget about the *"thy self"* part. That's what I'm still learning how to do in my life—love myself.

As far as *service* goes, it can take the form of a million things. To do service, you *don't* have to be a doctor working in the slums for free, or become a social worker. Your position in life and *what* you do doesn't matter as much as *how* you do what you do.

Fear at the Moment of Death

Many people are afraid of the *moment* of death. They see all those television programs where people choke to death or people suffocate, so it is not surprising that they are petrified of the moment of death. Most people who are dying benefit from having another human being with them who is *not* afraid of death and who does *not* take off quick as a bunny. I say to people who care for dying people, "If you really love that person and want to help them, *be with them when their end comes close.* Sit with them—you don't even have to talk. You don't have to do anything but really be there with them."

And when the time of death comes, don't expect a terrible gurgling sound or a gasping for breath or a horrible scream. Most of the people I've been with—and I've been there many, many times—there's just a very quiet cessation of life. Very rarely do you have to calm someone down. You just sit with them, hold or stroke their hand a little bit, and totally be with them. If you're there, and they whisper that they need something or want to share some last words with you, then you'll be able to help them.

Sometimes family members and friends are very amazed at the peace, serenity, and calm in the room when somebody makes their transition at the time of death. It can be a very beautiful experience. Sometimes they talk to an invisible person, saying the name of a deceased father or grandfather who has come for them. This can be a very consoling experience for family members.

The Spiritual Side of Life

Depending on how we have lived here on Earth, after death we go to different vibrational levels of reality. When people make their transition at the time of death or in a near-death experience, people travel to the Other Side through what they describe as a tunnel or a gate, a bridge, a meadow—what they report seems to be culturally determined. In my own near-death experiences—being a Swiss hillbilly—I went through what looked like a gorgeous Swiss mountain pass with beautiful wildflowers all around.

After making this crossing, a Light appears in the distance like a bright star. You head toward that Light. For me, this was a very exciting moment—one of the highlights of my whole life. I hastened toward that Light and went smack into the center of it. I literally melted into it, like falling into a water-bath of love. Suddenly, I became aware that this was Home, that we are part of that Light, that this is where we come from. I didn't have any other desire than to stay in the love of that Light, but it wasn't my time to make my transition so I had to come back.

From this experience, I realized that all beings are connected. We are all children of one parent, our Creator. In that Presence, we have knowledge of the agreements we made before coming into physical life. This includes understanding why a child had to die at such a young age, why we picked our mate or our parents—everything. We learn that the reasons we're with the people that are closest to us may not always be because of compatibility or love. It is sometimes because the personality characteristics of the people we are with specifically help us learn the lessons we need to learn. In life, we may have had to associate with a "schnook," but we needed that schnook to learn patience and tolerance and unconditional love.

So in the Light, the puzzles of life become clear. After I die and go back into the Light, I will find out more about why my house was burned down by arsonists. Everything I owned disappeared overnight. My lifelong collections were destroyed—a library of over 4,000 books, and a collection of thousands of rare sewing thimbles from all over the world that I wanted to give my daughter on her return from her honeymoon the same day of the fire. All my prized material possessions are now gone, but I'm living perfectly well without them. So I think God knew what He was doing when he allowed the arson fire to happen. The fire has given me a new beginning in that I am now totally unencumbered by material possessions. I never felt such freedom in my almost 70 years on this earth. So good can come from tough experiences. The windstorms of life are blessings for our growth.

So if we learn all of life's lessons, then we don't have to return to Earth. But if we haven't learned very important lessons such as unconditional love, tolerance, and patience, then we cannot return to God with "dirty hands." You cannot be a Hitler and kill millions of people and expect to be allowed to return to God and not have to come back.

As far as Hitler goes, in my fantasy I imagine the soul that was Hitler, in order to redeem himself, has to return to Planet Earth as a physician who discovers a cure for AIDS. In this way, he would help millions of people on every continent and give them a chance to survive. That would be a way to redeem himself for the part he played in killing and torturing so many millions of people. However, with all that Hitler did, God is love-personified and will give even the soul that was Hitler other opportunities to learn his lessons.

The Early Years

I've always wondered why throughout my life I've thought so often about Hitler and what he represents. Then it dawned on me that the seeds of my lifework really started in Poland when I was doing relief work in a concentration camp soon after World War II ended. At the time, I was just a wide-eyed teenager who had come from Switzerland to serve in whatever way I could. My mouth dropped when I saw, firsthand, the horrors of what man can do to his fellow man. I saw trainloads of baby shoes from 280,000 murdered children. I smelled the gas chambers. I saw mountains of corpses. I saw these things with my own eyes and smelled these things with my own nose. This is very different from reading about it in a book, just as there is a big difference between reading about near-death and out-of-body experiences and actually having them.

When I was working at that concentration camp, one day a young Jewish girl was watching me when I uttered to myself, "What kind of men and women could have done this to innocent children?" This young girl heard me say this and looked at me and said, *"You* would be capable of doing this, too." I said to her, *"Me?* You *must* be kidding, I'm *not* a Hitler!" She said, "Just watch your life, and you'll understand that in every human being there is both the potential to be a Hitler and be a Mother Teresa." At the time, she didn't actually say the name Mother Teresa, but another comparably saintly person who was well known in Europe at the time.

Soon afterwards, I left Poland with plans to return to my native Switzerland. As I hitchhiked through Germany, for several days I sometimes didn't have even a piece of bread to eat. In my extreme hunger, it dawned on me that if a child would have happened to walk by me holding a piece of bread in her hands, I was so hungry that I knew I would steal this piece of bread from this child. A light went on in my head. *That* is what this girl meant when she said there was "a Hitler in all of us"—that under certain circumstances, a mean part of us can come out. This was one of the greatest lessons of my life. I didn't fully realize it at the time, but the goal of my life was profoundly molded by this experience—to help produce, in the next generation, more Mother Teresas and fewer Hitlers.

I eventually made it back to Switzerland, but not before collapsing in a forest from typhoid fever and having to recuperate in a hospital. When I returned to Switzerland, against my father's wishes, I studied medicine, moved to the United States, and married a guy from Brooklyn, New York. I spent the next 30 years working with dying patients.

The Search for Life-After-Death Evidence

Whenever there have been times in my research when I needed assistance in solving a particular question, I asked my spooks—what I call my spirit guides—for guidance. Within five days, I get an answer in some form, although I don't have any psychic gifts such as being clairvoyant or hearing messages directly.

Everyone has at least one guardian angel. Some people have dozens and dozens. When I'm in some trouble, I have at least 44 guardian angels that help and protect me. These beings are referred to by various names in different religions and cultures, but the terminology doesn't matter.

There came a point when I asked my spirit guides to help me gather evidence on life after death. Shortly afterwards, I met a man who told me an incredible experience. He was driving on the highway when he saw a woman in her 30s lying on the side of the road. She had been injured by a hit-and-run driver and had been left lying on the roadside curb for hours. One car after another drove by. Nobody stopped to help her except this one guy, whom I call "the Good Samaritan," who stopped his car and went over to the woman. Supporting her in his arms, he asked her, "Is there anything I can do for you?" She looked at him and said, "No, there is nothing else anybody else can do for me now." She then lost consciousness, but this Good Samaritan stayed with this woman and did not leave her. Then after about ten minutes, she opened her eyes and said, "Maybe *there is* one thing that *someday* you can do for me. When you can, please go to the Indian reservation where my mother lives and give her a message. Tell my mother that I am okay. I am not only okay, I am *very happy* right now because I am *already* with my Dad." The young woman gave him her mother's name and told him what Indian reservation she lived on and then died in the arms of this total stranger.

This Good Samaritan was so excited that he had been at the right place at the right time that he immediately drove 700 miles out of his way to the Indian reservation! When he told her mother the news, she did not seem terribly distraught in hearing about the death of her daughter. In fact, the mother apologized to him for not being more upset about the news of her daughter's death. She said, "You understand, the message that my daughter gave that she was *already* with her Dad, she could not have known that my husband died an hour *before* the car accident of my daughter, 700 miles apart."

When I heard this story, I thanked my guides for the gift of this wonderful true account that shows that *there is* a reality to the realm of existence that people go to after death.

My Own Experience of Cosmic Consciousness

I'd like to share some of my own mystical experiences that have helped me *know* rather than only *believe* in the existence of realms beyond this Earth. I want to make it very clear that in my earlier years, I had *no* belief or comprehension of higher consciousness. I never really meditated in my life except that I've been told that when I am with dying patients, I am so totally focused and tuned in, that in a way this can be considered a form of meditation. If that's the case, then I've meditated thousands of hours in my life.

One of my first mystical experiences occurred during a research project where I had out-of-body experiences at the Monroe Institute, an experientially based laboratory for consciousness research located in Virginia. I was accompanied and observed by six skeptical scientists from the prestigious Menninger Foundation. It was during one of my out-of-body attempts that I was told to "slow down" by the laboratory chief. He felt that I was going too fast in my initial attempt to leave my body. On my second attempt to have an out-of-body experience, I was determined to circumvent the interference of this man. Using a self-hypnosis technique, I told myself that I would leave my body faster than the speed of light, and go further than any human being had ever gone in an out-of-body experience. The moment I gave myself this self-induction, I left my body with incredible speed. I don't remember a thing that happened when I was out of my body. The only memory I had when I returned to my physical body were the words *shanti nilaya.* Only months later did I find out the meaning and significance of these two words, which I'll tell you about a little later.

After I returned to my body, as I said, I had no conscious memory of the out-of-body experience whatsoever. All I knew was that after the experience, I was healed of an almost complete bowel obstruction as well as a very painful slipped disc that had formerly made it impossible for me to even pick up a book from the floor. When I returned from the experience, however, I was literally able to lift a 100-pound sugar bag without any discomfort or pain. My bowel obstruction was also completely healed. I was also told by many people at the Monroe Institute that I looked radiant—20 years younger. The scientists from the Menninger Foundation tried all their fancy psychological techniques to press me for information as to what had happened to me in this experience, but they couldn't elicit anything from me. I couldn't remember a thing.

I spent that night alone in a remote forest cabin in the Blue Ridge Mountains. Soon, an ominous, eerie feeling came over me, an awareness that I had "gone too far" in my out-of-body experience, and that I now had to accept the consequences. I had a vague, inner foreboding that something very impactful was going to happen in that cabin. Then "it" happened—the most painful experience of my life. I literally had to experience what it felt like to die a thousand times over: Over the next few hours, I experienced the deaths of each of the over 1,000 patients I had attended to up to that time. My body doubled up in excruciating physical pain. I could hardly breathe. As this was happening, I had total knowledge and awareness that I was out of the reach of the help of any human being. During those agonizing hours, I had only three momentary reprieves to catch my breath.

During the first reprieve, I begged for a shoulder to lean on. I literally expected a man's left shoulder to miraculously appear so I could put my head on it to help me bear the agony. In the same instant I asked for the shoulder to lean on, a firm but compassionate voice of a spirit guide simply stated, "It shall not be given." The pain resumed unabated until what felt like an endless amount of time later.

In the next brief reprieve, I begged for a hand to hold. I again expected a hand to somehow show up on the right side of my bed so I could grab on to it and better endure the agony. The same voice spoke again and said, "It shall not be given."

The third and the last time I was able to catch my breath, I contemplated asking for but a fingertip. But very much in character, I immediately thought, "No, if I can't get even a single hand to hold on to support me through this, I don't want to settle for just a fingertip!" Imbedded in this "no" was my acceptance that I had both the strength and the courage to endure this agony—we are never given more than we can bear.

At this point, something in me surrendered. I realized that I needed to stop being such a warrior, such a rebel—fighting all the time—and move to a place of positive surrender. Then the simple word *yes* emerged in my mind, symbolizing my humble submission. At the moment that yes came into my awareness, the incredible agony stopped, and a miraculous rebirth experience began. First, a very fast vibratory pulsation of my abdominal wall spread throughout my entire body. Then this pulsating spread to each and every molecule that my eyes beheld. In front of me appeared an incredibly beautiful lotus flower amidst a nonphysical Light. I entered into the Light through the open lotus flower—the whole world still vibrating at an incredible rate. However, the moment I merged into the unconditional love of this Light, all vibration stopped. A deep silence came over me as I fell into a deep trancelike sleep for about an hour and a half. I woke up just before dawn. When I awoke, I somehow just knew that I was supposed to walk down the hill, and "it" would occur—at the exact moment when the sun would rise over the horizon. I put on my robe and sandals and walked down the hill. As I walked, I experienced such ecstasy. I was in total love and awe with every leaf, every cloud, every blade of grass, every living creature. Everything was alive. I felt the pulsation of the pebbles on the path. My feet literally hovered *above the pebbles* without touching them, conveying to them, "I cannot step on you, I cannot hurt you." As I reached the bottom of the hill, I became aware that I had not touched the ground of the path as I walked. It was absolutely beyond words to describe the love I experienced in me and in everything around me.

It took me several days to completely come back down to normal, physical existence—to be able to do my daily work of cooking meals for my family, doing laundry and washing dishes.

The first time I shared this mystical experience with other people was at a conference on transpersonal psychology a few months later. Afterwards I was told by my fellow speakers and participants that what I experienced was called "cosmic consciousness." I later went to the library and found a book with the same title, *Cosmic Consciousness,* so that I could learn on an intellectual level about the state I had experienced firsthand. I was also told by an orange-robed Buddhist monk that the words *shanti nilaya* meant "the final home of peace." I believe that this will be the Final Home where all of us will return when we have learned all our earthly lessons.

This experience touched my life in ways that are very difficult to put into words. It seems that I had to go through "dying a thousand deaths" to be able to understand what death, and life after death, was about. Looking back, undergoing the agony of this experience was well worth it. Afterwards, I went through another type of agony—I had to bear the harsh criticism of society, particularly the media—that tried to shred me to pieces when I began to teach publicly about the reality of life after death.

Meeting One of My Spirit Guides

A short while later, I was invited to a spiritual group and was inwardly informed that this would be the day that Dr. Elisabeth K.-Ross would meet with one of her own spirit guides in person. I would not have believed this miracle if it wasn't also witnessed by 75 other people with their own eyes. That night I saw what most of you will only experience at the moment of death. One of my spirit guides, a large figure about 7' 10" tall, appeared right in front of me, identified himself as "Salem," and started to talk to me. A few moments later, he not only touched my sandals but stroked my hair and held my hand. Salem told us that night that humans are loved by God beyond our comprehension, and that we will feel how blessed we are when we learn compassion instead of judgment, empathy instead of pity, and realize that this life in the physical body is a very small part of our total existence. Planet Earth is the place where we go through trials, tests, and tribulations. When we have passed all these tests, we are allowed "to graduate" and eventually return back Home where we all came from.

My Last Commitment Before I Die

I don't believe I'm only going to be here on Earth much longer. In the remaining time I have here, my main job is to learn how to relax; have good thoughts; take care of myself; and not work, work, work until I drop dead. Those are the last lessons I have to learn.

I've known for a long time that I made three commitments upon entering this life. The first was the work in death and dying. Then, out of the blue sky, about 20-plus years ago, I was told by my spirit guides that I have to tell the world that death *does not* exist—that *there is* life after death! When I was first told this, I said, "You must be kidding. Death does not exist? Do you know what my nickname is?—the 'death and dying lady.' Now you want me to tell people that death does not exist? Give the job to a minister!"

They said, "No, we can't give it to a minister." I said, "Why not?" They said that the person chosen to give this message to the world has to be a woman, someone with professional credentials, and someone who is also a scientist—a whole long list of why it had to be me! So I finally gave in. I said, "Fine, I will teach people that death does not exist, *but you better help me!*" And I have to say, they *did* help me because in almost no time I received all the help I needed. So I shared this message with thousands of people, thousands of times. Now I'm finished with that commitment, and others are continuing this aspect of the work.

My third commitment—the only thing I have not learned yet—is how to love unconditionally—how to accept and love myself, how to live in joy and *just be.* I think this is the right environment for me to learn these final lessons in my new location in the Arizona desert. I love to feed the coyotes and birds and other wild animals that come right up to my house.

I am not afraid of death—in fact, *I can't wait!* The moment I die, I know my guides will be there for me, and I'm going...whoosh...*straight into the Light!* I will be welcomed with open arms. I have lots of helpers on the

Other Side, and we'll have a ball! I've told my children that when I die, to release balloons in the sky to celebrate that I graduated. For me, death is a graduation.

I was promised that this will be my last life on Earth. I *will not* volunteer or choose to come back to Earth. I've had *enough* this time around. If they try to send me down to volunteer again, I'll say, "No, thanks." I know that Buddha came back to Earth out of compassion, but I'm not going to be a Bodhisattva Buddha and come back. *Look at my belly, it's not big enough to be a Buddha belly!* No, out of compassion, I came back *this* time to tell people about death and dying and life after death. I've done my share here, and I can continue to do a lot of good work on the Other Side, too. I made the commitments, stuck to them, and fulfilled the work, except for the last one—to learn how to love myself more.

A Native American Elder once described his own inner struggles in this manner: "Inside of me there are two dogs. One of the dogs is mean and evil. The other dog is good. The mean dog fights the good dog all the time." When asked which dog wins, he reflected for a moment and replied, "The one I feed the most."

CHAPTER TWO

Cultivating Your Soul's Unique Path— Daring to Be "Spiritually Incorrect"

JOSEPH SHARP

Joseph Sharp is a writer, lecturer, and longtime AIDS survivor. He is the author of the internationally acclaimed book, *Living Our Dying*. The following essay was adapted for this anthology from Joseph's forthcoming work, *Sacred Individuality*.

"I've come to respect the voice of the dissenter and maverick when it comes to spiritual matters. The avenues of seeking that interest me today are not about trying to locate or discern a spiritual cooperative or single tradition that I can best fit within. To the contrary, I want to know how to more fully cultivate my soul's individuality. How is my soul trying to express itself through the unique particulars of my humanity—a humanity that is sometimes ecstatic and joyful, but just as often touched by sadness, anger, or despair?"

— Joseph Sharp

Let me begin with a story. . .

"I want to speak to the chaplain alone." Jim lifted the opaque oxygen mask away from his mouth as he whispered the words. Each breath was a gripping rattle, as if trying to pull life itself out of thinning air. We all knew that Jim wouldn't live through the weekend; his mother had arrived earlier in the day, and friends were beginning to gather. This man in his mid-40s would be the second person to die on my unit within two weeks.

Jim looked to his mom. "Alone," he repeated. Then he looked to me and winked.

I was the chaplain for the Infectious Disease Unit at Parkland Memorial Hospital in Dallas, Texas. A teaching hospital for the university's medical school, Parkland also serves as Dallas County's welfare hospital. Since the hospital had no official religious affiliation, its intern chaplaincy program was considered "interfaith"—meaning everything and no thing. Our patients ran the gamut—from Fundamentalist Christian to Buddhist, from Voodoo to New Age, to no religion whatsoever.

"Well, Rev," Jim said after the others had left the room. He called me "Rev" sometimes as a joke. He knew I wasn't ordained. He knew that, as far as my internship at the hospital was concerned, I had no agenda or affiliation with any particular religion. During the last few days, we'd discussed religious affiliation thoroughly. Jim had been a full-time choir director at a large suburban church before he became ill with AIDS.

Jim looked me directly in the eyes. "I just want you to know if I could do it all over again, I'd be more outrageous. You know, give 'em more hell. Be more myself and less what everybody said I'm supposed to be. That's all. Just wanted you to know that."

Jim brushed a bony finger toward the oxygen mask, and I helped him lift the plastic cup back, snug and fit to his face. I could see the smile from beneath the mask. His eyes twinkled now, so vibrant and alive within his dying body.

"More myself," he repeated softly. "More myself."

It is said that as the Buddha lay upon his deathbed, he directed his student monks to abandon each of the precepts and doctrinal rules he'd taught them over the years. What was most vital, he whispered, was to "Be a light unto yourself." According to legend, these were the Buddha's last words. *Be a light unto yourself.* It is the same wisdom Jesus taught when admonishing his students not to look for the Sacred "Lo here! or Lo there! for, behold, the kingdom of God is within you."

I believe this wisdom of seeking "within" or being a "light unto yourself" is not only advising us of where to seek, but also of *how* to seek. This perennial wisdom is directing us to acknowledge, honor, and even cultivate an authentic uniqueness—what we might call a sacred individuality—that is innate, particular, and "within" each of us. It is what I believe my patient Jim was teaching me when he said, "I just want you to know if I could do it all over again, I'd be more outrageous. You know, give 'em more hell. Be more myself and less what everybody said I'm supposed to be."

Regardless of religious affiliation, race, gender, or sexual orientation, this wisdom is one of the most common refrains I've heard while working with those who are terminally ill. Sometimes it is said with a wry smile of larger understanding, almost as if privy to a vast cosmic joke. Sometimes it is said with deep regret and bitterness. Either way, the teaching, the message from the bigger picture at life's end, seems to be the same: "If I could do it all over again, I'd not be as concerned about what other people thought. Instead, I'd do more of the things that I really enjoyed. I'd take more risks, be more unique. More myself."

A profound yet simple wisdom, this practice is about cultivating a depth of individuality that is authentic to your own unique expression. It is about being true to yourself, and how that trueness is a spiritual practice we can invite into our daily lives and our own religious traditions. Often, in our attempt to maintain a sense of "spiritual correctness," we can forget this teaching. We try to be a light unto our *idealism* of spiritual perfection, a spiritually correct posture of peacefulness and equanimity, devoid of one's particular and unique outrageousness.

The Within Teaching

"It is God's nature to be without a nature."[1] So said the 13th-century Dominican monk, Meister Eckhart. By the end of his life, the Vatican had charged him with heresy. Today, Meister Eckhart is considered by scholars and seekers alike to be one of the greatest mystics within the whole of Christian tradition, yet during his own time and life, he continually kept his church and religion astir because of his often blunt, spiritually incorrect pronouncements. We see this time and time again, regardless of religious tradition: The individualistic imagination of the brilliant soul usually annoys the rather dull hallowed halls of The Established Way. From Jesus, who was branded a heretic and troublemaker for his teachings that went against official Jewish law, to this century's J. Krishnamurti, who irritated thousands of Theosophical followers by dissolving and renouncing the spiritual hierarchy that had organized around him, the history of our world's religions is filled with saints, adepts, and seekers who were ridiculed as spiritually heretical for their time. As long as I can remember, the unspoken rule was: If your personality doesn't fit the basic model of your spiritual or cultural tradition, your path is clear. Change your personality.

For years I thought the game of life, socially as well as spiritually, was to figure out the way, the style, the pattern of someone else who knew—say, an enlightened person—and follow his or her way. For me, like most of us, the Way to the Sacred seemed to lie elsewhere, outside of my own inner kingdom, light, self, and experience. Of course it wasn't only the great spiritual sages who knew the big secret. The great artists knew, the great writers, and even some great statesmen such as Gandhi or Martin Luther King. In my mind, they were all privy to a special knowledge that made them almost infallible gods. If my experience differed from what any of these enlightened ones said, well, I must be wrong. Again, this was what I thought the journey of life was about: finding someone else who knew and following his or her rules, seeing life through his or her eyes.

But as the story of my dying patient with AIDS reminds us, the message from that bigger perspective at life's end seems to be what the great teachers have said all along: Seek within. The territory for appropriate spiritual exploration is that which is found "within" our moment-to-moment experience of life itself—infinite, spacious, and unrestrictive.

And still another radical possibility: Could it be that these teachings are not advice of merely *where* to look, but of *how* to look, of how to begin seeking one's own individually authentic way within a larger culture of spiritual tradition? I believe this is so. I believe the great spiritual teachers are asking us to acknowledge and honor an authentic sense of our own one-of-a-kind individuality that is likewise "within" each of us. In other words, there is no spiritually correct costume to wear, only an injunction to try to be as honest, as true to yourself, as possible. This is not about outer appearance, but inner awareness.

From this understanding, the "Within Teaching" advises us to listen to and learn from who we truly are within ourselves. It directs you to pay attention to your innermost desires, feelings, thoughts, impulses, passions, peculiarities, idiosyncrasies, yearnings, and so forth. It asks you to honor and cultivate those qualities and characteristics that make you unique unto yourself.

The Within Teaching asks: What are your own particular enthusiasms in life? What are the kinds of things that make you enthusiastic? Where does your own deep passion reside? Or, to put it in the terms of popular spirituality, what's your bliss?

Certainly, most institutionalized religions don't commonly encourage seekers to "follow their bliss." Usually, we're encouraged to follow the spiritually correct, well-traveled-by road of propriety and doctrinal conformity. For example, in my own childhood, I don't recall a single one of my Sunday School teachers mentioning the concept of Biblical myths— mythology was something the Greek pagans worshiped; and they all died horribly painful deaths because of it. As far as I remember, none of my Sunday School teachers ever mentioned anything that did not toe the literalist line, and none made room for sincere questioning, for mystery, or for authentic enthusiasm to arise. (I've since heard of differing experiences, particularly from a few of my Catholic friends, who tell of that occasional wild nun or outrageous Jesuit. Still, these were always the exceptional teachers, not the rule.) As far as my middle-class Protestant spiritual teachers were concerned, a good child was a quiet child. What a missed opportunity for so many of us.

Thankfully, as noisy adults we can recognize our innate calling to what truly fascinates, excites, and enthuses us. We can decide to follow our bliss. But this is not easy. We've been conditioned not to think in that direction, not to question, not to get "too excited"—enthusiasm and bliss aren't dignified, are not considered "adult" behavior. As I said earlier, one of the primary refrains I've heard while working with terminally ill patients is something like: "If I could do it all over again, I'd be more outrageous, and do more of the things I enjoy." A few years ago, there was a widely circulated poem by an elderly woman who summarized her life's lesson by saying that if she could do it all over, she would eat more chocolate, take more chances, and wear purple more often. Unfortunately, it often takes a life-threatening illness or event for us to begin reconsidering our cultural bias against authentic enthusiasm and bliss in the first place. Wouldn't we feel supported if our society and its institutions encouraged us to seek out our bliss? If one's inner passions and desires were respected and even nurtured as integral elements with the soul's greater maturation? Imagine how art-filled, richly diverse, and spiritually potent our experience would become.

As a culture, we've a long way to go. But as the Taoists are fond of saying, *The journey of a thousands miles begins with a single footstep.* Following your own enthusiasm, passion, and bliss is one of the best ways I've found to begin exploring the individualized path of your soul's particular calling.

Following Your Enthusiasm

The novelist and poet Natalie Goldberg tells a story about her Buddhist teacher, Katagiri Roshi, who first encouraged her to see her particular calling—creative writing—as a spiritual practice itself. Katagiri said, "Make writing your practice. If you commit to it, writing will take you as deep as Zen."[2] There is a plethora of books available now on how different kinds of creative acts and artistry can be consciously used in our spiritual deepening. That which gives us enthusiasm in life, from gardening or decorating a house, to writing poetry or journaling, to raising children or playing a sport like basketball or golf, or exploring the woods in search of a certain species of beetle or butterfly—all of these, as long as they bring you personal enthusiasm, can be integrated into a larger way of seeking the Sacred in everyday life.

A writer friend of mine, Marcia Tyson Kolb, explains how her "work with the earth" has deepened her own spirituality and become a potent form of practice and worship. She calls the time spent in her garden "direct communion." For her, the intimate dependence of her garden and land to life's cycles, seasons, and unsuspected events (such as a hurricane) have made her more keenly aware of the interconnectedness of all things, and of her own intimate part within that larger whole. "Having spent most of my childhood in traditional Christian religions and then studying Buddhism with various teachers," Marcia said, "I'd usually experienced 'spirituality' as something you do with a teacher, you know, like a priest or a Roshi. Whether I knew it or not, subliminally I'd gotten this message that spirituality was something you did *with* and even *through* a teacher, through another person outside of you. But the garden undermines all that.

"In the garden, I get a sense of direct communion. I see hundreds of plants come to flower, mature, and go to seed, dropping their seed-children everywhere, and then all these precious mother-plants die; but by next Spring, the children-seeds are shooting up sprouts out of the ground. When I watch this whole process, and feel myself as part of it—I'm in the garden throughout the year, caring for the whole thing—I get this immediate teaching. Yes, the best way to describe it is like a 'direct communion' of the ongoing qualities of life, death, and rebirth. It's not a teaching in words or concepts. It's there. It's real. I'd always heard teachers talk about reincarnation or life's eternal nature, but when I'm out in the garden I really feel it, this continuity, this ongoing life. In the garden, I just stand out there in wordless wonder and watch God happening all the time. Just direct communion. I might never have experienced that directness, if I hadn't loved gardening so much. So much that I'd let it become my spiritual teacher, too."

I know that for myself, writing has become one of the primary practices within my own larger spiritual odyssey. Often, I write what I need to learn. And it seems I catch many of the sublime lies I tell myself about life and God much quicker when I try to write about them. This was the case with my first book, *Living Our Dying*. I would write something about conscious dying— about what I thought I believed, about how a particular event taught me some spiritual lesson—and then I'd read it again a few days later. By rereading it and rewriting it again and again, I came to realize just how dishonest or shallow my original interpretations were; or, at the least, that I didn't really believe what I was saying. I may have *wanted* to believe it because a revered spiritual teacher said it was so, but I didn't really believe it myself. For me, the deep joy and enthusiasm I feel from writing serves to excite me enough so that it can cut through my own spiritual self-deceptions.

One's enthusiasm can be used as a powerful sword of spiritual truth. A path that includes this intensity of joy or enthusiasm is much harder for us to deceive because we have to—*need to*—do this; it is our passion. If a seeker uses her own soul-level enthusiasms to consciously and intentionally travel deeper along her particular path, she will find the determination to not settle for the mere appearance of spiritual propriety. She will demand authentic spiritual growth and muster the spiritual courage to be honest about her own failings. That is why our true enthusiasm is great grist for the spiritual mill—because it is the kind of grist that is ultimately too big for the conceptual mind to trick. Our enthusiasm penetrates to the bone, cutting deep.

The Within Teaching reminds us that the authentic way to the Sacred doesn't really exist "out there" in one perfect model of spiritual propriety and appearance. Instead it is to be found "in here," within our own very imperfect and passionate experience of everyday life. As Jon Kabat-Zinn says, "You are on a path whether you like it or not—namely, the path that is your life."[3]

A Favorite Outrageous Example

Thomas Jefferson is said to, more than any other historical figure, embody the "spirit" of America. Just to scratch the surface of his paradoxical and complicated life, we see the bright light of a Renaissance man: keen intellect, philosopher, architect, designer, statesman, husband and father, amateur horticulturist and archaeologist, writer, musician, Epicurean, and wine connoisseur. Most of us would assume that Jefferson was a Christian, and no doubt he considered himself one. But his powerful inner calling toward individualism reflected greatly upon his particular practice of Christian spirituality.

Jefferson struggled all his life to make sense of the teachings of Jesus as they appeared in the New Testament. His ultimate solution was very true to his own spirit of profound individualism. Audaciously cutting, rearranging, and pasting selections from the four gospels into one, Thomas Jefferson edited his own version of them into his own book of scriptures. In his way of seeing, he had extracted what he called the "diamonds" of authentic Christian teachings from the corrupted text of the official church.

Like it or not, Thomas Jefferson's individualized spiritual path included editing the gospels of the New Testament into a much shorter, less confusing scripture of his own—a personalized scripture that spoke intimately to his own mind and heart, and provided him with what he felt to be a more authentic vision of Christian life and teaching. Ultimately, Jefferson could not separate his soul's rich calling and enthusiasm toward intellect, individualism, and (in a manner, at least textually) architecture from his religious life.

Dare to Be Spiritually Incorrect

If I were restricted to only one message, one thought to ponder, it would be this: Let's give ourselves a wide range, a grand permission to fully experience all of this human life, the grit as well as the grace. Let's try not to get caught in the illusion of spiritual correctness or incorrectness. Let's be wary of the censoring mind that says, "Don't feel this, it's spiritually incorrect." Instead, let's go deeper into those feelings and see where it takes us. Feel where it takes us. We each have a unique soul within us that calls out for creative expression through our individual human lives. Let's try softening ourselves to this innate sacred individuality so we can hear its call, feel its pull back toward a larger experience of life, compassion, and grace. If what Meister Eckhart said is true—that it is God's nature to be without nature— then we must also consider that the road to God is without a generalized nature as well. That's a wide road—a road extending far beyond what we think we see now, far beyond any preconceived ideas of spiritual correctness we could possibly imagine.

Again, the history of our world's religious traditions is replete with saints, mystics, and visionaries who were ridiculed as spiritually incorrect, if not outright heretical for their own time. So be forewarned, to cultivate a depth of intimacy with your own "sacred individuality" may, at times, put you at odds with the idealism of popularized spiritual correctness.

The good news is, you are not alone in this great endeavor. And, historically, you're in some pretty good company.

"Direct your eye right inward, and you'll find a thousand regions in your mind yet undiscovered. Travel them and be expert in home-cosmography."
— Thoreau, from *Walden*

CHAPTER THREE

Attitudinal Healing—
The Essence of Our Being Is Love

GERALD ("JERRY") JAMPOLSKY, M.D.,
AND DIANE CIRINCIONE, Pн.D.

Husband-and-wife team **Gerald Jampolsky** and **Diane Cirincione** are transformational speakers, and the co-authors of *Change Your Mind, Change Your Life.* Jerry is founding director of the first Center for Attitudinal Healing (there are over 100 affiliated centers worldwide) and author of the bestseller *Love Is Letting Go of Fear.* Diane is a clinical psychologist. This chapter is excerpted from a film interview that took place in Kailua, Hawaii.

*"Health and healing ultimately has nothing to do
with the body. Real health is inner peace."*
— Dr. Diane Cirincione

"Love is letting go of fear."
— Dr. Gerald Jampolsky

Jerry: When I was a consulting physician at the University of California Hospital, I happened to be present when a little eight-year-old child asked her doctor, "What's it like to die?" The doctor didn't answer her question and just changed the subject. This event made a deep impression on me. I began to wonder how kids with life-threatening illnesses get these types of questions answered. The next day, inner guidance came through to create a free-of-charge center that would help young children who were facing death. Since the opening of our first center in 1975, over 100 Centers for Attitudinal Healing have been created worldwide.

Diane: Throughout the years, we've been inspired by many people—young and old—who, despite the disease and pain in their bodies, are filled with love, a sense of joy, a resiliency, a simplicity, that has *nothing* to do with the body. We'd like to share some stories of these real people whom we've had the honor of meeting.

Jerry: One of the principles we honor is that anyone, regardless of age, can teach us about life. A 3-year-old can teach as much as a 93-year-old. Children are wise souls that happen to live in little bodies. They come to us to teach us another way of looking at life, death, and the spirit. The first child who died at our Center was an 11-year-old named Greg Harrison. He was so close to death that his medications were discontinued. One of the little kids in our support group said, "Hey, Greg, what's it like to know that you're probably gonna be dead in two weeks?" Greg responded very calmly, "Well, I think when you die, you discard your body, which was never really you in the first place, and then you are in heaven with other souls, and sometimes you come back and act as a guardian angel." There's no question that in my meditations, Greg continues to be a guardian angel.

I remember Carney, a ten-year-old child with sickle-cell anemia. I asked him one day, "What's it like to be your age and to come so close to death so many times?" He said, "I think God has a library. In this library there are these books, but the books are really children. Some have very short due dates and some have longer due dates. And God lends these books out to parents. I am not afraid of dying, because I know that I'm always in God's heart all the time. I never really left."

Carney concluded this remarkable reply by saying that even though he knew he was sick, he inwardly felt he still had more work to do down here.

Carney wanted to become a pediatrician. The last we heard, Carney is now a premed student.

So, people whose lives are threatened by illness—whether they are small children, teenagers, adults, or our elders—provide us with the incredible gift of looking at life and death differently. When we first opened the Center, we only offered individual and group support to young children who were very ill. But we soon felt the need to work with a wider range of people. We found that the healthy brothers and sisters of their sick siblings also had a lot of problems dealing with illness and death. Later, we included adolescents who had life-threatening illnesses. Then we expanded our work to include parents. And when AIDS came on the scene, we began the work with AIDS patients. We also began to offer to serve people with non-catastrophic illnesses who wanted to incorporate the principles of attitudinal healing in their lives.

Diane: In working with all these different groups of individuals, we've found that health and healing ultimately has nothing to do with the body. Real health is inner peace. Real healing is the letting go of fear. The essence of giving and receiving are the same. As we learn to help *others,* we begin to help *ourselves.* Many of these principles are found in the book *A Course in Miracles.*[1]

We found that the goal is not to "fix people up" or get people to just live longer. An individual can be in the last hours and days of their life, their body can be completely racked and helpless, and yet, he or she can be in a place of complete inner peace. If we've been able to embrace ourselves, and those around us, through forgiveness, we see that as being completely healed and whole.

Jerry: Most of my life I was an atheist. I thought our only identity was a body—when you died, that was the end of life. So death was very scary for me. But then I came to understand the first principle of attitudinal healing—that the essence of our being is love. What we really are is an everlasting spirit. When we really know in our hearts we're really not these bodies, that they're just temporary vehicles, then the finality of death begins to shift. You really see that death is just a transition to a formless state.

Diane: I remember when I was about three years old, looking down at my hand and rubbing my three fingers together. I said to myself, "This is a trick. Somebody stuffed me inside this skin." I knew I was more than this body. Throughout the years, this memory has given me great solace. There truly is no death. These bodies come and go. Life is a transformation of form, energy, and consciousness. So death has always been a comfortable place for me to be with.

Jerry: When someone leaves this earth through death's door, we often feel that a person is "lost" or we've "lost them." I'll never forget a mother who shared a story with us about her daughter. She said, "People always say to me that they're so sorry that my daughter is lost, but my daughter *is not* lost. When something is lost, you don't know where it is, but my daughter continuously lives within my heart, within my existence. I feel her presence in my life. So even though she's physically gone, she's not lost; she's not in some abyss somewhere."

Diane and I still feel the presence of many people who we knew who are no longer still here in physical form. Minds can communicate with each other—you don't need bodies to do this. It can be a very joyful and learning experience to experience that there isn't really any separation. The separation that we feel is that we miss the physical form. The reality is that spirit and love are interconnected and never go away. It's a timeless love, an eternal love. What is really true, what never changes, is the essence of God's love that we're all part of.

I remember our dear friend, Ted, who battled AIDS for a very long time. We became very close as part of a support group. Ted was one of my great teachers, especially close to the end of his life. He once related to me that he was having an ongoing argument with someone. It seemed that whenever they were together they always clashed. One day Ted said to me, "You know, one of these days I'm going to really give him a piece of my mind." Then he stopped for a moment and said, "Oh my God, I just realized after all these years of battling with him, I *have already* given him my *"peace of mind."* And from that moment on, he realized that this ongoing conflict was costing him the greatest price of all—his peace of mind. He was then able to release it all and just let go.

On another occasion, I asked Ted what he felt was the purpose of life. He told us, "We come here to share the experience of learning about letting go of our judgments of each other." Even after his death, Ted is still a very powerful teacher for me and so many others.

Another time, I asked a 14-year-old who was dying what he felt was the purpose of life. He said, "Well, as long as you're breathing, your purpose is to give love to people. A lot of people come in the hospital and they're scared. Our job is to give them love. Lots of times the doctors are scared to tell you the truth. Our job is to give them love. God says that doctors need love and forgiveness, too." It can be that simple.

I remember Don, a volunteer at our Center who had AIDS. He shared this story about his friend who had been killed in an automobile crash one week before. Don told us that this friend had never really confronted death, and that this friend, like many of us, thought he was going to live forever. Then Don said to us, "You know, given the choice, I would not have chosen to have AIDS. But if I *had* the choice of being the person I was years ago— *without* AIDS—or being the transformed person I am today—*with* AIDS— I have no doubt that I would choose to have AIDS to be who I am today."

There was a young woman named Jennifer, with nonfunctioning kidneys, who spent most of her teenage years on dialysis. Before she died, she told us what she would do if she knew she only had seven more days to live. She said, "Other people around me say that they would spend these last seven days with family and friends. Of course, it would be easy for me to enjoy being with the people I love for those last days. But if I had only seven days left to live my life, I would spend my time thinking of every person that I had an unhealed relationship with. And anyone who had a grievance against me, I'd ask that person for forgiveness, and I would offer forgiveness to them in return. I would do this either by letter or phone call or just in my own mind. Before we leave this life, our purpose is to heal all of our unhealed relationships. This is why the universal spirit gives us each other—to find a way to heal among each other and within ourselves. I could just lie here in my bed and accomplish all of this."

This beautiful young woman knew that healing can take place within our own minds and hearts and doesn't necessitate the physical presence of another person. It doesn't take having your father or your mother come to you, finally see it *your* way and say, "Oh yes, it's okay, *now* we can forgive each other." It doesn't take that at all. Jennifer had spent her whole life helping others in the hospitals she lived in. She died in her 20th year. Her mother told us that her final words in this life were, "I would rather have lived my life as a sick person helping others than having lived it as a healthy person living only for myself."

A lot of times we hold on to guilt in our lives without ever realizing how much it affects us. I remember visiting an 82-year-old woman who was having uncontrolled angina attacks. Her angina medication wasn't working. I felt intuitively guided to ask her if she was holding on to any self-condemnation. She shared with me something that she'd never before told anyone—she *still* felt guilty for stealing a candy bar from a store when she was six years old. As if this was the greatest sin in the world, this 82-year-old woman had been holding on to unforgiving, guilty thoughts toward herself for 76 years! As she continued the process of self-forgiveness, her medications finally began working.

When it comes to forgiving ourselves, we are so often the "King or Queen of the Procrastinator's Club." So, self-condemnation causes us so much difficulty. Forgiving others is really a way of forgiving ourselves. Holding on to grievances through unforgiveness reinforces the illusion that we're separate from each other.

In our own spiritual path, we're recognizing more and more that when we really know we're connected with God and each other, there really isn't any more separation between us. One is truly at peace when one knows that. A lot of our work here on Earth involves letting go of our identification with the body. We learn to be kinder to others and more tender toward ourselves. Even in our last days here on Earth, it's not too late to deepen our love and forgiveness for others and ourselves.

My own 98-year-old mother is a good example of "it's never too late." She was probably the most fear-filled person I've ever known. In her last years, my mother lived at the Jewish Home for the Aged. Throughout her life, she was very much a guilt-ridden person who projected her guilt on others. She was usually very upset with us and everyone else "about something." As but one example, she used to blame all of us for not visiting her *long* enough. Eventually, no one wanted to visit her anymore.

So she was in a terrible state. And we *were also* in a terrible state, because we wanted her to be pleasant and happy and a nice little old lady in her last years. We finally realized that if we really wanted to have peace of mind for ourselves, our job was not to change her and want her to be a certain way, but to love her and accept her as she was, even if this included her decision to be miserable—if that is what she wanted.

After we did this, we felt a lot more peace, and as time went on, a tremendous shift in her personality took place. She became very gentle and very loving to everyone around her. She began to talk about things that I never thought she'd talk about—even reincarnation! This was at 98 years of age, coming from someone who hadn't before believed in any of this stuff all her life! She began having visions and dreams of seeing my father on the other side of a fence, reaching out for her.

I was very blessed to be able to be there when she died peacefully in her sleep at four in the morning. It was a very beautiful time for me. And although I thought I was complete with my mother—thought that I'd said all my good-byes, I remember about two days later, I was calling my answering service and no one answered. After the phone rang about ten times, all of a sudden I realized that I *hadn't* called my answering service— I'd called my mother's phone—which hadn't been disconnected yet. I burst into tears simply because I missed her. So although I *thought* I had said good-bye, I was reminded once again that attitudinal healing is an ongoing, continuous process that offers us an opportunity for profound spiritual transformation to take place in our lives and the lives of others.

"My cancer has metastasized to the bones. The doctors have said it's incurable—which says 'death' to me. The weird thing about knowing I am sick is that I know in the heart of me there is wellness. And that's the paradox—in the midst of my illness, I am getting well. And that even death cannot take away."
— Rev. Colin Campbell, Episcopal priest,
from the video *Experiencing the Soul*

CHAPTER FOUR

From Psyche to Soul—
The Healing Power of Archetypes

MARION WOODMAN

Marion Woodman is an internationally acclaimed Jungian analyst who has pioneered the exploration of the unconscious using the power of dreams, metaphor, and the balancing of feminine and masculine archetypes to bridge inner and outer worlds. She is the author of *Leaving My Father's House, Addiction to Perfection, The Pregnant Virgin,* and the co-author of *Dancing in the Flames,* from which this excerpt is drawn.

"Soul is eternal; its language is metaphor, which belongs in this moment and in the timeless, spaceless moment."
— Marion Woodman

I have never doubted the existence of soul. I have never doubted that part of me that soared into music, art, and literature, and responded in bodily delight. Nor have I doubted my shimmering response to beauty—the sun rising in a pink pool out of Georgian Bay, chickadees chatting as they lunch on peanuts, the majesty of thunder in mountains.

Most of all, I have come to know soul through dreams. As a Jungian analyst, I have sat for many hours opposite people who are well positioned in the material world, but within whom something will not be still. As they speak confidently, I see the twitching of their feet or hands. I see the desperation in their eyes, I hear their souls crying, "See me. Hear me. Love me."

And I watch their dream life unfolding. I see a reality living its own truth within them, trying its best to communicate with their conscious ego, whether they listen or not. If they do take time each day to listen to their soul story, they gradually find wholeness. Inner and outer partner each other. If they fail to honor soul, it eventually roars out in physical or psychic symptoms.

Dreams speak the language of the soul. Soul is eternal; its language is metaphor, which belongs in this moment and in the timeless, spaceless moment. The imagery of our dreams comes out of our own bones and muscles; it, therefore, gives us a picture of our present body-soul condition. That imagery carries an emotional charge that can activate the whole Being—thinking, feeling, intuition, sensation—the totality of who we are. If the image is honored—meditated upon, danced, painted, put into music or words—it comes into conscious life with healing power—that is, power that brings wholeness. It is the bridge between the temporal and eternal worlds. The image carries a charge that can ignite our whole Being into life more abundant.

The power of metaphor was brought home to me in a situation from my own life. In 1968, I was in a car accident that left one side of my head and face badly damaged. A brilliant plastic surgeon, to whom I am eternally grateful, cut through my scalp, and with his delicate instruments went under my skin and pulled my broken bones back into place. Two weeks later, the swelling subsided, and I knew I still had an eye. Two years later, I had regained the feeling in my face, but one major symptom remained. Night and day there was a loud ringing in my ear and the sensation of a mosquito continually flying inside—a disorder known as tinnitus. I went to specialists in Canada and England, and they all told me they could do nothing. I would have to learn to live with it.

I was in analysis with Dr. Bennet in London at the time. The more intense the analysis became, the louder the bells rang and the faster the mosquito flew, until I thought I was going crazy. I had a dream in which someone and I were working on a machine that transforms one kind of energy into another kind (a metaphor machine). I became confused because I didn't know how to work the very complicated switches. But the other presence did. Then someone said, "How do you feel on the eve of becoming everything you have fought all your life against?"

The ringing was now so loud that I rushed out of bed and landed on the floor of the kitchen before I knew I was awake. I prayed to God to take away that ringing or let me die. Immediately, a vision of a mock-orange bush in full bloom appeared, with its delicate ivory-colored blossoms that perfume the month of June. I was so enthralled by the beauty of the bush that I was not at first aware of the perfume in my feet. But slowly, slowly, the perfume rose in my legs, and its sweetness moved into every cell of my body until the perfume and I were one. I became the metaphor. Gradually, unknowingly, I had come to a standing position, with my arms raised. When the vision faded, the ringing in my ear had ceased. It has never returned.

I had gone to the kitchen and was fed: My body was ensouled. This, of course, changed my life. The efficient, clock-and-calendar, always-in-control woman was no more. I realized that my empowerment was through concentration on an image, a gift from the unconscious. I realized that the fear and chaos in my rational mind could be stilled by the order of my unconscious. The archetypal image rising out of the depths of my body—the Dark Goddess permeating the orange blossom bush—could bring conscious and unconscious into harmony with each other and with the natural order. Then, I could be whole.

At the time, I did not care much about what had happened psychologically. I only knew that I had been visited by divine light, that I had experienced a love I never knew before, a love within matter that shattered the world as I had known it. Reason was silenced. I could only say, "Yes, thank you."

Later, when I read Jung, I began to understand what had happened psychologically. Tension, fatigue, and pain had taken me into a regression, metaphorically into the dark side of the mother, where death seemed the only way out. The emotion was so intense that the ego had to surrender. At that crossroads where conscious and unconscious meet, the dynamism of the instinct, "Let me die" (the infrared end of the spectrum) transcended the conflict and took me right out of the pain. The image, the orange blossom bush (the ultraviolet end), pouring perfume into every cell of my body, brought about a harmony, physically and psychically, that transcended any feeling I had ever experienced. Someone who knew how to work the switches created the metaphor of the blossoming bush and transformed the energy of the distraught consciousness into the harmonic energy embodied in the unconscious. The archetype of the dark mother, Death, was transformed into the archetype of the loving mother, Sophia, she whose light permeates matter.

Knowing that Someone is moving you, whether you understand it or not, is an awesome experience. That nonrational knowing, which is *being known,* is what brings the heights and depths together. That is where healing lies. Without ego interference, my soul perceived the light in matter. That was the dawn of becoming what I had fought against all my life. The sweetness of my body surrendered to her love. In *being known,* I knew myself as part of the one.

"Everyone, I suspect, has a relationship to a field or a family or an archetype. One feels oneself partnered by the archetype; it becomes a kind of inner beloved of the soul. And in one's meditation of life, one knows oneself to be the 'exotype' in time and space—an outward expression of an archetypal being who lives beyond time and space."

— Dr. Jean Houston

PART II

The Soul

Before

Birth

INTRODUCTION

B eliefs about "life *before* life" are as divergent as the many views on "life *after* death." These beliefs are supported by various forms of life-before-life experiences that come about as a result of "soul flights" to the Other Side; from the spontaneous recall of prebirth memories in hypnotic regression; as a by-product of near-death experiences; or by spiritual training, as in meditation and the shamanic arts.

There is, however, an *other* way that evidence for the existence of life-before-life is revealed to us: by the visitation of "soon-to-be-born souls" who seek *us* out in a variety of ways. This last category of life-before-life encounters are called *prebirth experiences (PBEs)*. The importance and meaning of prebirth experiences will be our focus in the following section, *The Soul Before Birth.*

CHAPTER FIVE

Meeting the Souls of Our Children Before Birth

SARAH HINZE AND BRENT HINZE, Ph.D.

Sarah and **Brent Hinze** are the parents of nine biological children and nine foster children. Pioneers in the emerging field of prebirth experiences, Sarah is the author of *Coming from the Light;* and Brent is a clinical psychologist, educator, and researcher. This chapter is based on a film interview that took place in Los Angeles, California.

"Listen to the whisperings of your inner spirit-self. Before birth, you were a royal child in the kingdom of heaven. There is a royal child within each soul, sometimes astray or misguided by earth trials, but the royal self is here for a purpose: to overcome, to fill a mission, to return Home in glory."
— Sarah Hinze

Sarah: We are the biological parents of nine children. In five of these nine births, I was blessed with the gift of meeting the unborn souls of five of our children before they were born into our family. These "life-before-life" encounters are called prebirth experiences. They most often happen to mothers, fathers, relatives, and sometimes even midwives involved in the birth. When these unborn souls are met, they bring with them some of the incredible radiance, love, and purity that exists in the premortal realm where they live. I'll share some of my personal experiences, and I'm sure that Brent will also offer some of his own insights.

In one of my pregnancies, I had a very sorrowful and traumatic miscarriage. I felt particularly bonded to this female soul, because even before I conceived, her loving presence had entered my dreams on several occasions. When she appeared, I saw her as a young woman with beautiful brown hair and brown eyes. I received the impression that she was fearful of coming to Earth, and this is probably why I lost her. Afterwards, I prayed with all my heart for another chance to bring this soul to Earth as her mother.

Shortly after offering up this prayer, I had a very moving vision that came in a dream. In this vision, I was in a hospital room where a nurse placed a newborn baby girl in my arms. At the moment the baby was placed in my arms, a voice said, "This is your daughter, Sarah Rebekah." The vision was so vivid that I remembered the intimate details of the room and what the baby looked like.

I awoke from this dream-vision with the realization that I had been granted another opportunity to bring Sarah Rebekah into the world. I conceived shortly thereafter, but within three months, pain and hemorrhaging threatened another miscarriage. I was so troubled that I might lose this child again that I fell to my bedroom floor in prayer that God would allow this soul to be born through me. During prayer, I lost awareness of my immediate surroundings and was transported to another dimension. I saw myself leaving an indescribably beautiful Celestial Home and traveling through starry space toward Earth, which looked uninviting, cold, and very far away. Then a "Being of Light" escort appeared by my side and said, "The Earth is indeed a great distance, but it is important that you go there."

The vision faded, and I again became aware of my physical surroundings—I was still face down on the floor. I then felt a very powerful and loving presence enter the bedroom. I stood up. I don't know how, but I knew this presence was Jesus Christ. I begged him to heal my body for the sake of this child. Jesus spoke to me through mental telepathy—mind to mind—and said, "I am the Great Physician. I will heal your body, and this child will come forth whole and well, for I have so decreed it."

As I moved to the bed to rest, I felt His healing power descend upon me. Within a few hours, the hemorrhaging totally stopped. I knew I had been healed and that everything would be all right.

A few months later, Brent and I were driving through heavy rain to the hospital to deliver our child. I closed my eyes and saw the same beautiful girl with brown hair and brown eyes that I had seen in my previous vision. She was saying her good-byes to other beings in a heavenly realm in preparation for her arrival on Earth.

I checked into the hospital and was wheeled to my room. During a period of the labor that was most difficult for me, I silently prayed. A male personage, dressed in white, appeared in spirit by my bed and said, "I have personally escorted your daughter to mortality." A few minutes later, our daughter was born.

After the birth, a nurse told me that the maternity floor was full, and they needed to move me into a different room in another part of the hospital. When I entered my new room, it was the same one in every detail that I had seen in the vision months before. And when the nurse brought our precious daughter, Sarah Rebekah, and placed her in my arms, this was also exactly as I had seen her in my previous vision.

Sarah Rebekah—we call her Becky now—was a very happy baby. She would make the most delightful cooing sounds, particularly upon awakening from her naps. In addition to our own biological children, at the time we had several foster children living with us. We used to comment among ourselves that Becky must be entertaining angels in her room. Little did we realize that this was indeed true.

One afternoon, I heard Becky's joyful cooing sounds as usual. This signaled that she was awake, and I went to see if she was okay. As I placed my hand on the doorknob of her room, I felt an unusual sensation, a feeling that I was entering "sacred ground." I walked into her room ever so slowly and sensed a holy male presence hovering above her crib. I could tell that Becky was telepathically communicating with this being by the way she was looking upward in the direction of the presence above her crib. Her face was radiant, and she was making babbling sounds and excitedly kicking her feet. I received an inner knowledge that this was the spirit of my unborn son—Becky's future brother. I heard with my spiritual ears, "Tell mother I need to come soon."

A few months later, I was again visited by this same spirit-soul who told me, "My name is Matthew. The time has arrived for my conception." I shared this message with my husband, Brent, and I became pregnant very soon afterwards.

Later on in the pregnancy, we were visited again by Matthew during our family prayer time. Laura, our ten-year-old daughter, told me, with wonderment on her face and tears in her eyes, that while we were all kneeling in prayer, she had opened her eyes and had seen a tall, blond-haired man dressed in white standing behind Daddy with his hands placed on his shoulders. She told me this man would be her brother, Matthew, and that she loved him very much, even more than she loved her own life. We were all very moved.

During the last part of the pregnancy, after a long, tiring day, I was deeply reflecting on the wonderful experiences we'd already had with our child-to-be, Matthew. While absorbed in these thoughts, Matthew appeared before me, not in his baby form but as a handsome, tall man with blond hair, broad shoulders, and olive skin. He looked radiant. Telepathically, he thanked me for the sacrifices I'd gone through during pregnancy to allow his spirit to come to Earth and be housed in a mortal body. After he delivered this message, he disappeared. I was very moved by this visitation and felt the powerful bond of our relationship. I was now even more eager to have him in my arms as our child. Within a few short weeks, he was born. Matthew is now 15 years old and is developing in appearance as his sister, Laura, and I beheld him in our visions.

Brent: Can you imagine how wonderful it's been being married to this woman for 27 years? I can tell you with 100 percent assurance—this lady tells the truth! She has indeed seen or felt the unmistakable presence of five of our children before they were born.

As a clinical psychologist, I have given over 30,000 counseling sessions in my career. I have been impressed by the power of prebirth and other spiritual experiences to transform people's lives. In my professional counseling work, profound emotional healings have taken place as a direct result of people getting more in touch with their spirit-selves.

In the West, this climate of spiritual openness hasn't always been around. When I was a graduate student over 20 years ago, I would have been tossed out of school if I'd insisted on doing a doctoral dissertation supporting the reality of spiritual phenomena. Back then, mainstream Western psychological theories on the nature of man did not include this spiritual component. Today, scientific research is gathering more and more evidence that increasingly points to our divine origins—that we are more than just biological beings, that we come from a premortal existence, and that our souls continue after physical death.

The scientific method drilled into me in graduate school still rules in mainstream scientific circles. It still holds that to prove something scientifically, only *certain* methods of conducting research are acceptable. There is nothing wrong with this, except that, unfortunately, what may be *true* and *real* may not be *readily testable* by present-day scientific methods of measurement. Spiritual experiences cannot be reproduced *upon command* in a laboratory, and reproducibility is one of the tenets of scientific method. Please understand that I am not anti-science. Science is a wonderful and useful tool if used wisely.

A case in point is a recent Gallup poll that found that over 20 million people in the United States reported having had a near-death experience at least once in their lifetime. This type of data—testimonial accounts not verified by controlled experiments—is generally not recognized as the strongest form of evidence in scientific circles. However, 20 million people are a lot of folks to discount! And if you think about it, in courtrooms around the world, the testimony of *only one* credible witness is enough to condemn a person to death. So I find it ironic that science has a tendency to prematurely dismiss *some* forms of evidence, which in itself is antithetical to the true spirit of openness that should be part of scientific inquiry.

Sarah: Thankfully, there *are* certain testimonial accounts that are harder to explain away. There's a wonderful account of a little three-year-old boy who almost drowned in a swimming pool—he was actually clinically dead and was later revived. When he came back to consciousness, he told his mother, "Mommy, I met my brother on the Other Side, and he was very sad." And his mother said, "Your brother? Honey, you know you don't have a brother." And the little boy said, "Yes, I do, Mommy. He was pulled from your tummy before he was born."

The mother had in fact aborted a male child before this boy was born. The little boy was never told by anyone about the abortion of his little brother. He only found out by meeting the soul of his brother on the Other Side. So when I'm asked my views on abortion, I share stories like these that help us appreciate the sanctity of life and the sacred responsibilities of parenthood.

When I look into the eyes of children, I see their divine origin. Children are not our possessions. We have only been granted a stewardship to raise them with love. We must honor their divine purpose by helping them bring forth their unique talents. As their parents, we help launch their missions on Earth.

Brent: Both Sarah and I feel that each human being is a royal child who comes from God's court on high and will return thereto. I would add a bit more on the dimension of marriage. Sarah, when I look at you, I see you not only as my wife and the mother of our children, but as a daughter of God. If all of us could see each other as royal children of God, there would be peace on Earth. I truly believe this is what God wants of us.

After a presentation a few years ago, a woman told us a beautiful account that was shared at a seminar given by Dr. Elisabeth Kübler-Ross. As the story goes, a young couple had a four-year-old daughter who kept asking them if she could be alone with her newborn baby brother. The parents were hesitant to grant their little girl's request because they knew about sibling rivalry and didn't want anything to happen to the newborn. But the little girl persisted over the next few days, so her parents decided to give her a chance to be alone with her baby brother for a few minutes. Her parents escorted her into the baby's room and left her alone with him. As a safety precaution, however, they listened in on the meeting with an intercom connected to the baby's room. For a few moments, all was quiet. Then they heard their daughter say to her baby brother, "Tell me about God. I'm forgetting."

After this story was shared in the seminar, Dr. Kübler-Ross told the participants, *"That,* my friends—the spiritual origin of man and where we come from—*that* is the next great area of exploration."

It is our hope and prayer that prebirth and other spiritual experiences bring us closer to our families, to our neighbors, to all of humanity, to all life on this planet, and to our divine Creator, God.

"The child is God's gift to the family. Each child is created in the special image and likeness of God for greater things—to love and to be loved."
— Mother Teresa, the late Nobel Peace Prize recipient

The Hinze Family—*Sarah and Brent Hinze and some members of their very large family. In the front row, on the left, is Becky, who saw the vision of the unborn soul of her brother, Matthew—who is pictured in the front row on the right.*

CHAPTER SIX

The Emerging Field of Prebirth Experiences
HAROLD WIDDISON, PH.D.

Harold Widdison, Ph.D., is a professor of medical sociology at Northern Arizona University. For the last 25 years, he has been a pioneer in the fields of thanatology, bereavement, near-death studies, and—more recently—prebirth experiences. He is the co-author of *The Eternal Journey,* and he is the author of *Listen to the Children: What Children Can Teach Us About Life and Death.* This chapter is based on an edited phone interview with the author.

*"Researching prebirth experiences has had a profound
personal effect on my wife and me in that we more fully
appreciate that our adopted daughter, who suffers from fetal
alcohol effect, and our mentally handicapped daughter—
are both very special children of the Divine. We now know
that their spirit-souls are untouched by these disabilities.
Both these girls have unique missions to fulfill and
special lessons to teach us on Earth."*
— Dr. Harold Widdison

By now, I've interviewed hundreds of people who report that they were contacted by unborn souls who later come to Earth as children. Before I share some of the fascinating ways these prebirth experiences occur, I'd like to give a brief overview of how prebirth experiences (PBEs) compare and contrast to near-death experiences (NDEs). I would also like to touch on some of the tremendously exciting implications of this research, which, to all indications, points to our divine origins as souls—that we indeed come from a premortal existence.

The scientific study of PBEs is presently where NDE research was about 20 years ago. Because of its newness as a scientific field of study, the number of PBE cases we've collected are not large enough to conclusively say that PBEs are a *universal* human experience. However, PBE researchers Sarah and Dr. Brent Hinze, myself, and others in the field share the working hypothesis that PBEs *are* in fact universal—and that this type of spiritual experience has been occurring in all cultures throughout human history. In addition to our research findings, resource quotations supporting this hypothesis can be found in both modern and ancient literature, as well as numerous religious texts drawn from diverse cultures. These literary and scriptural references contain descriptions similar to the accounts that we are collecting and analyzing today.

Let's begin our comparison of NDEs and PBEs. NDEs suggest the existence of a *post*-Earth life where we go to *after* physical life ends. The soul crosses over from the Earth realm to a nonmaterial realm.

In contrast, PBEs suggest the existence of a *pre*mortal realm where souls reside *before* they come down to Earth. In PBEs, the not-yet-born soul crosses over into this *Earth* realm from the realm of pre-Earth life and makes some form of contact with people living on Earth.

I do not believe that all of the varieties of PBEs have been chronicled as yet due to its newness as a field of study. Some of the ways in which people are contacted by the souls of the unborn may include any one or all of the following: 1) The unborn soul gives a message that the time for conception is nearing; 2) the unborn soul shares that he or she has a special mission to accomplish on Earth; 3) a radiation of love emanates from the unborn soul; 4) gratitude is expressed by the unborn soul for bringing him or her to Earth; 5) the unborn soul predicts a significant future event that affects the mission of the unborn soul and/or the family that the unborn soul will be born into; 6) the unborn soul expresses excitement or reluctance about entering Earth life; 7) a message of warning or protection is given by the unborn soul regarding an impending danger, especially if this danger may jeopardize the unborn soul's arrival on Earth. The most common examples of impending danger to the unborn soul are if a couple is contemplating an abortion or a mother is thinking about having a hysterectomy.

Who experiences PBEs? Based on an analysis of the case studies collected by PBE researchers Sarah and Brent Hinze, a little over one-half of PBEs occur *before* conception. A little less than half of PBEs occur *after* conception. Three-quarters of all PBEs are experienced by the parents of the preborn souls—whether they are the biological parents *or* the adoptive parents. Mothers are about five times more likely to have PBEs than fathers. The remaining one-fourth of the PBEs in this sample were experienced by siblings of the yet-to-be born souls, their grandparents-to-be, close friends of the family, or midwives connected to the birth.

There are several types of PBEs. Many PBEs come in the form of visions in a waking state, with the physical eyes open. PBErs [those experiencing PBEs] report that these unborn souls appear either as infants, children, or as fully grown young adults. What is especially intriguing about these visions is that years later, when the unborn souls are on Earth, their physical appearances do in fact match what they looked like in the previous PBE vision many years before. For instance, if a father sees a young man with large blue eyes, dark hair, and unique facial features in the PBE vision, that's exactly the way the person looks like after coming to Earth and maturing.

Dreams are another way that unborn souls come to PBErs. Some cultures call these "announcement dreams." Often the unborn soul will announce to a PBEr, "My name will be Michael. Thank you for bringing me to Earth as my mother." PBErs say that these visitations do not resemble ordinary dreams. Announcement dreams are extremely vivid, not unlike a vision when one is wide awake. Ordinary dreams are often hazy, unclear, and do not leave the lasting transformational impact of these PBE announcement dreams.

Another way in which these unborn souls come to us is through auditory messages. Their voices are heard either with the physical ears or telepathically.

Sometimes the PBE contact is made by a Being of Light from the premortal realm, and not directly from the souls-to-be-born themselves. The

Being of Light seems to function as a protective escort and speaks on behalf of the unborn soul.

Another fascinating type of PBE is when people living on Earth have flashback memories of their previous existence in a Celestial Realm. I have discovered that prebirth memories in some children are very much intact, especially when they are under three years of age. These memories fade when they get older, perhaps when parental and societal programming begins to crowd out these prebirth memories from conscious awareness.

At this point, I think it is important to say a few words about how PBE accounts are gathered. In interviewing people who have had PBEs, we collect data using a method called "grounded research." We let the data create and form the experimental hypothesis, instead of the other way around—making the data fit one's preexisting hypothesis. In this way, we do not unconsciously "lead the witness" by having a vested interest in proving a preexisting hypothesis.

Some critics say that even if our research *is* "grounded," the fact that our data is based on testimonial reports—accounts that cannot be reproduced in a laboratory—means that they are not scientific enough to prove anything. Their challenge is basically, "How can you *prove* that these people are telling the truth?" The way I reply to this is by way of analogy. I say, "Can you prove to me that you love your wife?" Someone might reply, *"Of course* I can prove that I love my wife, I bring her flowers every week, and once I risked my life to save her from falling off a bridge." However, these statements won't fly by the rules in which strict scientific research is conducted. These actions in themselves—bringing someone flowers and saving someone's life, do not, in themselves, demonstrate proof of someone's love. The person could have performed these actions for some ulterior motive, or by some unconsciously driven motive beyond their conscious awareness. I conclude by saying that although "love" is not amenable to scientific methodology, does this mean that love does not exist in the world simply because it isn't particularly provable on scientific terms? I think not.

Further, the PBErs that are interviewed are sane, normal people who have nothing to gain by making these stories up—not fame, not wealth, not prestige. Many of them are even *reluctant* to share their PBEs because they're afraid people will think they're crazy.

Another very significant point is that in these interviews, almost everyone who shares their PBE accounts at one point gets teary-eyed and becomes very moved by their emotions. Just the retelling of their PBEs evokes powerful memories that flood over them. If these experiences were fabrications, these people would all have to be great actors and actresses to pull off this kind of show. So as a Ph.D. medical sociologist who's been in the field for over 25 years, as someone who has spent thousands of hours interviewing and researching the spiritual experiences of my fellow humans, I say with deep conviction that I am absolutely convinced that these PBEs are authentic descriptions of actual events.

The information gleaned from PBEs not only gives us a picture of the inner workings of premortal existence, but also answers some of life's more perplexing questions, such as: From the perspective of the soul, what is the purpose of life on Earth? Why do these souls often choose, or why are they given, difficult conditions and situations in their sojourn on Earth?

Well, based on the accounts we've gathered so far, the unborn soul agrees to the major events in their Earth lives *before* they come down so that they can learn specific lessons from these preordained Earth experiences. This explains why some children are born in abusive families, and why some children die at an early age or are born with severe handicaps.

I'll share one account that gives a sense of how profoundly the premortal realm influences our Earth lives. The following account is an actual PBE drawn from my case files. A woman—let's call her Mary—was physically and sexually abused both as a child and later by her spouses. During a flashback PBE, Mary saw herself selecting the pain-filled experiences that she would undergo in this life. In this same flashback vision, an angelic being says to her, "Are you really sure you want this? These experiences will be very hard for you." Mary replies, "Yes, I elect to have these experiences. I will learn more from adversity than if I have an easier life. I want it and choose it." The angelic being then said, "These experiences will be difficult, but know that we will always be by your side."

Another example: It is common to see young children communicating with what are called "invisible friends." In one account, a baby-sitter of a young child named Billy observes him playing with and talking to one such friend. She walks over to him, kneels down beside him, and asks, "Billy, who are you playing with?" He looks up at the baby-sitter with a puzzled look on his face, then looks back at his invisible playmate, then back at her, and finally says, "My baby sister. She hasn't come yet, but she will, and her name is Sarah."

Now as it happens, not long after I was told this account, the baby-sitter told me that Billy's mother had a baby that she named Sarah. The pregnancy was a complete surprise—the mother was well over 40 years old. The baby-sitter paid a visit to the family after the new baby was born and asked the mother, "How did you come up with the name Sarah?" The mother replied, "I don't know. It wasn't a family name. It wasn't even a name I particularly liked. I just felt very strongly that should be her name." It was only then that the baby-sitter shared the experience she had with Billy. The mother was both overjoyed and overwhelmed to hear this.

The implications of PBEs are staggering. If the divinely inspired messages behind PBEs are really embraced by the world, then we will know that we are all children of God, and we will raise our children with more love and respect. As our children *are* the future, the whole world will become more like the Celestial Realms from which we came.

As I look forward to my professorial retirement at the university, it is my prayer that I will be allowed to devote the rest of my Earthlife to researching PBEs and helping to get out "the good news." I invite any of you to contact me if you have had prebirth or other spiritual experiences you'd like to share.

"Your favorite doctrine, Socrates—that knowledge is simply recollection—if true, also necessarily implies a previous time in which we have learned that which we now recollect. But this would be impossible unless our soul has been in some place before existing in the form of man; here then is another proof of the soul's immortality."

— Plato, in *Phaedo*

PART III

The Soul

After

Death

INTRODUCTION

Communications with the souls of the deceased have been reported for thousands of years. The British Society for Psychical Research, formed in the late 1800s, was the first scientific organization to begin the systematic study of these and other paranormal phenomena. The researchers of the British Society were comprised of the greatest minds of the day, some of whom were Nobel Prize laureates. Late in his life, Dr. Sigmund Freud himself became a member of the British Society, and was so impressed with the impeccable research methods and the extraordinary cases being investigated that he once stated, "If I had my life to live over again, I would devote it to psychical research instead of psychoanalysis."

When some people think about communicating "with the dead," they often conjure up spooky images of seances held in darkened rooms. The use of human mediums to contact the dead has received quite a bit of criticism, not only due to deceptive practices performed by a minority of unscrupulous psychic mediums, but because, as a method of communication with deceased individuals, it is difficult to separate the true channeling of discarnate entities with the ever-present possibility that the medium is knowingly or unknowingly psychically reading the minds of the *participants,* and then feeding this information back to them.

This objection is being side-stepped by the emergence of two other forms of communication with deceased individuals. The first is the field of after-death communication (ADC), which is ably summarized in the following section by ADC pioneer Bill Guggenheim. He defines an ADC as contact with a deceased relative *without* the aid of a medium, where communications are made *directly* and *spontaneously* by the deceased individual and not by the earthbound human.

A second form of after-death communication is still in its preliminary stages of scientific validation and involves the receiving—and sometimes even the recording—of the voices and images of deceased individuals on electronic devices such as television and computer screens, telephones and telephone answering machines, radios, and other electronic instruments. This new field of ADC is called electronic voice recording, trans-instrumental communication, and various other names.

The following section, *The Soul After Death,* provides an overview of the field of after-death communications, including some very beautiful, intriguing, and unforgettable accounts.

CHAPTER SEVEN

The Varieties of After-Death Communications
BILL GUGGENHEIM

Bill Guggenheim is a pioneering researcher in the emerging field of after-death communication, internationally known transformational speaker, and the co-author of *Hello from Heaven*. This chapter is based on a film interview that took place in Tucson, Arizona.

"Whether the after-death communication happens only once,
or the person has ongoing contact with the deceased for the rest
of their lives, the person who is physically alive receives assurance
through after-death communications that their deceased loved
one is alive and well and cares about them."
— Bill Guggenheim

Throughout history, humanity's deepest questions have been, "Who am I?" "Where did I come from?" "Why am I here?" and "Where am I going?" Author Dr. Wayne Dyer expressed it beautifully when he said, "We are not human beings having a spiritual experience; we are spiritual beings having a human experience." Our human bodies are Earth-suit vehicles we use to express physical life while we are here on this Earth plane. After

Earthlife, our existence continues. Death is nothing more than our Earth suits ceasing to function. However, we *have* found through our research that even now—*before* death—it is possible to receive communications from deceased loved ones. These experiences are called after-death communications (ADCs). ADCs aren't new—they're as old as mankind, and have been reported in all cultures around the world.

I have given ADCs a precise definition: An ADC is when a person or persons have been contacted *directly* and *spontaneously* by someone they knew when they were alive, such as a deceased family member or friend. By "directly," I mean that the contact was made without the involvement of a psychic or medium or any other third party. By "spontaneously," I mean that the deceased person chooses the where, when, and how of the contact.

In describing ADC experiences, I prefer to use the word *deceased* rather than the word *dead* to refer to people who have died because *dead* has a feeling of finality to it that doesn't fit well with the reality that life continues after physical death. It's true that the *physical* body is dead, but the spiritual being who *occupied* that body is *not* dead. In reviewing thousands of ADC reports, I've found that deceased loved ones invariably give us the impression that they are more alive *now* than they were on Earth!

In 1988, Judy, my close friend and former wife, and I realized that no one had really studied ADCs in the United States or Canada in any formal way. In the seven years of research that followed, we interviewed people from almost every walk of life. We collected over 3,300 firsthand accounts that were drawn from over 2,000 people, from all 50 states in the United States, and from 10 Canadian provinces. Since then, we've easily come across another 5,000 ADC experiencers in the course of meeting the many people that attend our workshops. We've been deeply touched and personally transformed by the accounts that we've heard.

According to the most recent Gallup poll, over 22 million Americans have had near-death experiences (NDEs). Based on our estimates, ADCs are even more common than NDEs. But just as NDEs cannot be replicated in a laboratory, neither can ADCs. And so, while we can't produce these experiences in scientific settings, perhaps one day scientists will develop instruments to more scientifically study ADCs. At this point, however, it may be "proof enough" for oneself to have had this type of a spiritual experience, even though one might not be able to prove it to others. So while these accounts are admittedly subjective, ADC contactees are sometimes given specific information by the deceased person that they could not otherwise have known about. The specific information is later verified by credible witnesses. Skeptics and doubters are at a loss to explain how this is possible. The credibility of ADCs as being authentic is strengthened by these types of occurrences. We do not view them as merely grief-induced hallucinations, the delusions of people who are mentally ill, or the by-product of overactive imaginations. As we progressed in our research, Judy and I found several different categories of ADC phenomena, all of which have their own distinct characteristics.

Before I briefly describe each of these categories and share some actual accounts, I should say a few more general things about ADCs. First, in any ADC event, more than one phenomenon can be experienced, such as feeling the presence of a deceased loved one, hearing that deceased person's voice, *and* feeling the touch of the deceased loved one. It also seems that some people are more receptive to receiving ADCs than others. Some people may have experienced an ADC but assume it was just their imagination or wishful thinking, and dismiss the experience as being unreal. And there are those people who *don't even believe* in life after death who receive ADCs—quite to their own surprise. This happened in my case in 1977 when I heard the voice of my deceased father who told me to "go to the pool." When I got there, I found my 18-month-old boy, almost drowned. This experience changed my whole worldview.

Many people—bereaved parents, especially—desperately want to have some sort of ADC. They tell us, "Why haven't we heard from our daughter? Why haven't we heard from our son?" We believe that the deceased child may be *trying* to communicate with them, but for whatever reason, they "can't get through." In these cases, we especially recommend that people learn to meditate to help improve their receptivity to ADCs. This can be as simple as learning how to relax deeply enough so that the "spiritual senses" open up and increase the likelihood of having an ADC. Not only does meditation make us more spiritually receptive to ADCs, but people tell us that they've had ADCs *while* meditating.

When an ADC occurs, we sometimes suggest that people assume a comfortable position that helps them relax, take a few deep breaths, and then, with their mind's awareness, attune to the deceased family member or friend. In this receptive state, some people mentally ask the deceased person questions such as "Is there anything that you want us to do for you?" or "Do you want us to pass on a message to anyone else?"

In addition to helping us become more receptive to having ADCs, meditation can—with practice and over time—bring us more inner peace. True meditation gives us rest from the demands of the external world and brings us closer to our spiritual nature and the spiritual worlds of reality within us. Deep meditation creates a bridge between worlds that helps our loved ones make contact with us more easily. By learning some form of meditation, we can also become more loving and sensitive.

What follows are brief descriptions of the various types of ADCs that people have reported in our research thus far.

"Evidential" ADCs

An ADC is "evidential" when a person living on Earth is told something by the deceased loved one that they had no way of knowing about beforehand by any normal information-gathering methods. For instance, the information given by the deceased loved one may be the location of something of sentimental or monetary value, such as a family heirloom, jewelry, or a hidden will that nobody but the deceased person knew about. The person who is physically alive often doesn't even know about the very existence of these items, not to mention where they are located. The deceased loved one may give directions to a specific location and instruct the person what to do when the object is found. Often these items are hidden in the most unlikely of places, such as cookie jars in the attic or garbage bags with valuable items inside that are buried in the backyard. ADC experiencers often tell us that *just knowing* that their loved ones continue to exist is more important than the benefits they receive from the information conveyed and the valuables discovered.

I remember an unusual story in which a young boy's deceased grandfather was communicating with him over a period of time, telling him the details of his former life as a major league baseball player. The deceased grandfather was telling this young boy the names of his former baseball teammates, including their batting averages and other obscure statistics. This baffled the boy's parents until the information was later completely verified.

In a similar case, a young boy's deceased uncle—who was a master plumber in his Earth life—was telling him all about plumbing. The boy inexplicably began to talk to his parents about the names of the various kinds of antiquated plumbing tools that were in vogue decades ago. In researching this case, we ourselves phoned up hardware and plumbing supply stores to ask them if they recognized the names of these plumbing tools, but *even they* hadn't heard of them! It was only when we began calling the "oldtimers"—retired master plumbers who remembered using these tools as plumbers long ago, that we discovered the tools named and described by the boy were indeed used back in his uncle's time.

"Sensing a Presence"— Sentient ADCs

The most commonly reported ADC category is what people commonly describe as "feeling a presence." This is when a person senses and feels the presence of a particular deceased loved one. People typically report that they know immediately when the deceased loved one arrives, and when he or she leaves. Even after death, the deceased retain their uniquely recognizable feeling and energy pattern.

"Hearing a Voice"—Auditory ADCs

The majority of people who report they hear the voices of deceased loved ones experience this telepathically—inside their heads. Other people report that they hear these voices externally through their physical ears. In auditory ADCs, two-way communication is frequently reported.

People unfortunately dismiss these voices as imaginary, or, because they do not know that it is possible to communicate with deceased loved ones, they think or feel that they're "going crazy." The actual message delivered by the deceased loved is sometimes an urgent one—as in my own ADC when the voice of my deceased father told me to check our swimming pool. This not only saved my son's life, but as a nonbelieving agnostic at the time, eventually led to our research in the field of ADCs.

"Feeling a Touch"—Tactile ADCs

This touch may be a pat, a tap, a caress, or a kiss. Some say they feel an arm around their shoulder or waist, or even receive a hug. Touch ADCs usually occur between people who had a very close, intimate relationship, such as between a husband and wife or a parent and child.

"Smelling a Fragrance"—Olfactory ADCs

People report that they smell fragrances that are specifically associated with the one who has died. Whether it is the deceased person's aftershave lotion, a perfume that the individual often wore, the scent of their favorite flower, or the aroma of their favorite food, the particular smell is usually associated with that deceased person. When fragrance ADCs occur, very often two or more people are together at the same time and place. Often, one person will notice the smell first, and then the other person or persons will say, "Yes, I smell it, too." In our files, we have a case in which there were ten people who reported smelling a fragrance associated with the deceased loved one at the same time and place.

"Partial and Full Appearance"—Visual ADCs

It is a very moving and exciting experience for people to actually be able to see—with open eyes—the complete or partial form of the deceased loved one. In *complete* visual ADCs, the deceased loved one appears as solid and real, as would any other person who is physically alive. In a *partially* visual ADC, the visual form may appear less than solid, and one might see only the head and shoulders of the deceased, or see the person only from the waist up.

One very wonderful aspect of visual ADCs is that deceased loved ones appear healed and whole. Even if the deceased individuals had been blind, disfigured, paralyzed, or had some other disability when physically alive, in visual ADCs the normal faculties they might not have possessed during Earthlife are restored. They appear radiantly healthy and whole even if the manner of death was traumatic. It is very comforting and encouraging for people to have this experience if the deceased ones had suffered a difficult death or were severely disabled during Earthlife.

"Sleep-State" ADCs

This is a type of ADC in which a deceased loved one comes to us when we are sleeping. Sleep-state ADCs are not like ordinary dreams, which are usually fragmented, jumbled, symbolic, and often hazy in meaning. Sleep-state ADCs are qualitatively different in that they are usually crystal clear, not unlike a profound spiritual vision, and they have a distinct beginning, middle, and end. It is commonly believed in many spiritual traditions that in sleep, our spirit-souls leave our physical bodies and enter other dimensions of reality. When people report that they've had this type of ADC, they don't say, "I *think* this happened" or "I *wish* this happened" or "I *hope* this happened." They say, "I *know* this happened." In addition, in sleep-state ADCs, people not only say they've received a kiss, hug, or a specific message, they say they were also able to *give back* a hug or kiss or a message to their deceased loved one!

"Out-of-Body" ADCs

An out-of-body experience is when our souls—when fully alive on Earth—voluntarily or involuntarily separate from the physical body and travel to near and far places on Earth, as well as into higher dimensions of reality. In out-of-body ADCs, people report meeting deceased loved ones on "the Other Side." Out-of-body ADCs tend to be very dramatic, spectacular, and filled with love, for these inner dimensions are described as being filled with the most incredible colors, music, and scenery—truly beyond this world! Upon the return to their bodies, people say that the spiritual dimensions are much more alive and real than this physical plane.

"Physical Phenomena" ADCs

This is when people have unusual physical phenomena occur, such as the inexplicable turning on and off of electric lights, microwaves, radios, and TVs, and so on. These are not due to power failures. Typically, a light in one room is turned on, then another and another—one after the other—throughout the entire house. In the accounts we've gathered, we've noticed that deceased loved ones who left this world when they were in their teens tend to use physical phenomena as a way to let us know they're still around.

"Before the News Arrives" ADCs

In this very common form of ADC, a person is visited "in spirit" by someone who has just died, *before* the knowledge of the death is conveyed by conventional physical means, such as word of mouth, telephone, and so on. The physical body of the person who has just died may be thousands of miles away when this happens. What seems to be occurring is that the spirit-soul has come to say good-bye. Only afterwards does the person get the news that the recently deceased has just left their body. What makes these ADCs so convincing is that sometimes people write down the exact time that the visitation occurs, and only later do they discover that this was the exact time that the person died. This type of experience happens both when death is imminent and expected—as in a terminal illness—or in cases of traumatic events, such as car crashes, where the person was healthy up until the fatal incident occurred and death was not expected.

"Protection" ADCs

In these ADCs, the deceased loved one serves as a sort of "guardian angel" in that their messages serve to warn or protect the living from imminent danger or loss of life. As examples, people are saved from driving accidents by being told to slow down or stop the vehicle they're driving, shown passageways out of raging fires, informed that a physical attacker is approaching, or warned that they are about to be swindled. Protection ADCs can occur at a much later time—even 40 or 50 years after the death of the loved one. Generally speaking, though, when people are contacted many years afterwards, there is usually some important, specific message that is given at that time to help them through a difficult time in life.

"Deathbed" ADCs

It is a commonly observed phenomenon that very near the time of physical death, people in the process of dying are observed communicating with an unseen presence in the room. When the dying are asked about this—if they are strong enough to respond— they say that they are talking to the one who has come to "escort them to the Light" after they die. The spirit-soul they address is almost always a deceased relative or someone they loved and were close to during life.

What we have also found is that family members, hospice workers, nurses, social workers, and chaplains are also sometimes able to see and communicate with the spirits of these deceased loved ones, even though they may not know the identity of these beings at the time. Even a living relative at the bedside of the person who is dying may not know who the deceased presence is until they are identified later on, typically by way of an old photograph. These types of experiences particularly indicate that no one really ever dies alone.

"Multiple-Witness" ADCs

This is when two or more people—at the same time and place—share an ADC experience with the *same* deceased loved one. Sometimes it is only when these people "compare notes" that they find out that they indeed shared similar ADC experiences. In multiple-witness ADCs, smelling an aroma is most commonly reported. As an example, several people will simultaneously smell the scent of roses although there is no traceable external source of roses anywhere in the environment. The fact that more than one person at a time shares ADC experiences gives credibility to the view that ADCs are not just subjective hallucinations, wishful thinking, or fantasies made up in the mind of one individual.

"Suicide Intervention" ADCs

This category involves people who were planning to take their own lives, who, in many cases, already had well laid-out plans for carrying out their suicides—they had already written farewell letters, made funeral arrangements, had given away their belonging and pets, and so on. In *all* the cases we recorded, a deceased loved one intervened and dissuaded them from taking their own lives. They were told that committing suicide was not the way out of their problems. Because of the sheer transformative power of a suicide intervention ADC, these people were given another chance on Earth to work out the great emotional pain, fear, and confusion that led to their near-suicides.

An important message for those in the counseling profession who work with suicidal people is not to prematurely dismiss ADCs as psychopathological, as fabrications of the mind. For if these ADCs are invalidated as unreal by the therapist, this might cause clients to carry out their planned suicides.

Another extremely interesting aspect of suicide intervention ADCs is that people who are suicidal are often contacted by deceased loved ones who took their *own* lives by suicide. It seems that deceased loved ones who have taken their own lives by suicide have a special mission to dissuade others from taking their lives.

"Seeing and Communicating with the Soul at the Moment of Death" ADCs

People report that they see the full outline of the figure of the one who has just died emerge upwards from the physical body. Others do not see a recognizable form, but see something that resembles a wisp of smoke at the moment of death. This is sometimes accompanied by one-way or two-way communication where good-byes are shared with the person who has just died.

"Escorting Someone to the Light" ADCs

One of the most extraordinary forms of ADCs is when a living person known to someone who has just died has learned to enter into a transcendental state of consciousness, leave his or her body, and accompany the dying person to the Other Side. The living person who does this is typically told by a "Being of Light" on the Other Side, "You can't go any farther;

you must go back now." It is rare person who is able to perform this lovely form of service—to escort someone who has just died to the Light.

Grief and the Fear of Death Reduced by ADCs

In our modern culture, it is unfortunate that many people fear death to such a considerable degree. Psychologists know that to the extent that we fear death, we fear life, and, as such, we live less fully. In many cases, this is due to what people are taught about what happens after death, including the hell-and-brimstone notion of an eternal hell.

Others consider themselves agnostics concerning the existence of life after death, but death is a predominant fear for them, nevertheless. However, for people who have experienced ADCs, the existence of life after death becomes very real and comforting. ADC experiences time and again reduce or even eliminate people's fear of death.

We have also found that the intensity and duration of bereavement is reduced dramatically by ADCs. Whether the ADC happens only once, or the individuals have ongoing contact with the deceased for the rest of their lives, those who are physically alive receive assurance through ADCs that their deceased loved ones are alive and well and care about them. Over and over again, the gist of the messages received from deceased loved ones tell us that they are still alive and okay and that we should get on with our lives.

If you haven't yet had an ADC experience, the possibility is always available to you. Experiencing an ADC can be one of life's most meaningful and touching experiences. For me, the most joyous part of spending so many years researching ADCs is that we have helped so many more people realize that life is continuous. Earth life is just one phase of existence. Life is everlasting, and we are eternal beings.

"Death is no more than a passing from one room to another.
But there's a difference for me, you know.
Because in that other room, I'll be able to see."
— Helen Keller

CHAPTER EIGHT

Visitations of Our 15-Year-Old
Son After His Suicide

ANNE PURYEAR

Anne Puryear is a Gestalt therapist, minister, and author of *Stephen Lives—My Son, Stephen, His Life, Suicide, and Afterlife*. She co-directs, with her husband, psychologist Dr. Herbert Puryear, the Logos Center in Scottsdale, Arizona. The Logos Center is an interfaith church, holistic healing center, spiritual community, and metaphysical school. This chapter is based on a film interview that took place in Las Vegas, Nevada.

*"I truly believe that there will be a time when we'll be
able to pick up some phonelike instrument and perhaps
dial a number such as 1-800-HEAVEN and reach
loved ones who have died."*
— Anne Puryear

When my son Stephen was 15, he hanged himself from a tree across the street from where we lived. Stephen's suicide was the most difficult, traumatic time in my entire life. I remember during his memorial service, I was expecting that I would still be able to communicate with him from the Other Side after death and that it would be a simple thing to hear him speak. I found out that it wasn't so easy! Although there were times when I heard his voice or felt his presence, I was in so much emotional pain—being in the throes of grief—that some part of me was still skeptical and unable to trust that it was really happening.

Just a few weeks after he died, our daughter—Stephen's nine-year-old sister—saw him with her open eyes in the kitchen, dressed in the karate uniform he used to wear when he was alive. Stephen came to say good-bye to her—something I always wished would happen to me.

Finally, one night when I was meditating and inwardly praying for Stephen to be there with me, he placed his hand, one finger at a time, on my right shoulder. I immediately looked up and around me. I couldn't see him, but I felt him. For the first time since he had died, I slept peacefully that night.

Another time, I was sitting alone in my bedroom, and I heard Stephen's voice out loud from the corner of the room say, "Mom." There were other times when I found my own thoughts being moved to the side, and then I heard Stephen's voice speak *inside* my head. Although these types of things happened on a number of occasions, I still couldn't establish a communication with him that I totally trusted.

One evening, my daughter and I were sitting together in the living room. A little music box underneath the Christmas tree began playing "Silent Night" over and over again. No one had wound it up. My daughter said, "Stephen is here." I, too, felt his unmistakable presence. As Stephen began to speak inside my head, I wrote down what he told me. He said I would write books that he would dictate to me. He then said, "Mom, I know what a skeptic you are. In order to prove that this communication is not your imagination, someone will give you a piano, and it will be delivered before Christmas. Then you'll know that this is real."

The next day, I went to a medical program, and a couple came up to me and said, "We feel we need to give you money to buy a piano." The piano was delivered before Christmas, just as Stephen told us!

There have been times when Stephen had given me certain information that I had some doubts about. When this would happen, I'd often get a phone call from a friend who was also receiving ongoing communication from Stephen. She would repeat the same message that I had doubts about—that Stephen had told *her* to tell *me,* as added confirmation.

If for several days I'd been really busy and not receptive to Stephen's attempts to communicate with me, this same friend would call me up and say, "It's been four days since you've talked to Stephen. He needs to talk to you." And she'll be exactly "right on" every time.

For about four years after Stephen died, we conducted experimental research with paranormal electronic voice recordings. We were able to actually record Stephen's voice on an ordinary tape recorder. For reasons we do not yet understand, at this point in time we have very little control over whether paranormal voices show up on tape—sometimes there are voices on the tape and sometimes there are not. From the perspective of scientific exploration, one possible way to increase scientific validation of these phenomena would be to record people's voices *before* they pass away so that *after* they die, one could then scientifically analyze the paranormal voice recording with the predeath voiceprint.

New methods of electronic voice phenomena are now being developed using television sets. An ordinary TV is turned on, and the channel is set to a nonreceiving station. At this point, to the naked eye and ear, the television screen displays only the hissing of visual and auditory static. A video camera is then set up in front of the nonreceiving television and put in record mode for several hours. When the videotape is reviewed, sometimes the images of deceased family members inexplicably appear on the videotape.

With the popularity of home computers, there is an ever-increasing number of reports around the world of paranormal messages appearing on computer screens. For instance, a person will be doing word processing on their home computer. At a time when the person has his or her hands completely off the keyboard, a message will appear on the screen from someone who has died!

We also experimented with another exciting new area of research that was created by Dr. Raymond Moody, the psychiatrist-researcher who coined the term *near-death experience*. Dr. Moody modernized an old method of invoking visionary experiences of departed loved ones. What he calls a "psychomantium" is a specially designed, darkened room that has reflective mirrors set up at certain angles. At our Logos Center in Scottsdale, Arizona, we succeeded in creating a working pychomantium. While inside, one holds on to a personal object associated with the departed person and at the same time thinks of the deceased person while gazing into the mirror.

Since I really wanted to see Stephen again, I experimented with the psychomantium myself. One night as I looked in the mirror, a sphere of Light appeared in the darkened room and came outside of the mirror about 12 inches in diameter. Stephen appeared in three-quarters view, moving just as he did when he was alive. I tried it a second time, and the exact same thing happened. We then created a pilot psychomantium research experiment that we called *The Threshold Project.* In this study, we tracked the psychomantium experiences of 25 people for ten weeks. Seventy-three percent of these 25 people either saw, heard, or experienced someone who had died. Perhaps in the future, people will set up psychomantiums in their homes in order to contact loved ones who have passed away.

Research using computers, TVs, videos, tape recorders, and psychomantiums hold great promise to bring us closer to scientifically proving the continuity of life after death—that the soul *does* continue. Of course, through deep meditation, people from time immemorial have been receiving messages from departed loved ones *without* the aid of instrumental technology. The most common message from departed loved ones is, "We're not dead; we're more alive than you are."

So I truly believe that there will be a time when we'll be able to pick up some phonelike instrument and perhaps dial a number such as 1-800-HEAVEN and reach loved ones who have died. We will then know that our loved ones simply have changed form and that for the soul, there really is no death. This will be extremely comforting, healing, and wonderful, especially for those who are grieving.

"Edison and I are convinced that in the fields of psychic research will yet be discovered facts that will prove of greater significance to the thinking of the human race than all the inventions we have ever made in the field of electricity."

— Dr. Miller Hutchinson, Thomas Edison's assistant. At the time, they had been collaborating on an attempt to invent a device that could communicate with deceased persons.

CHAPTER NINE

We Are Citizens of a Multidimensional Universe

JEAN HOUSTON, Ph.D.

Jean Houston, Ph.D., is an internationally known philosopher, author, and seminar leader who has developed revolutionary new ways of unlocking the latent human capacities that exist in all individuals. Her books include *The Possible Human, The Search for the Beloved, A Mythic Life,* and *A Passion for the Possible.* This essay is based on a film interview that took place in Honolulu, Hawaii.

*"By 'essence,' I mean that part of our nature we recognize as
the god in hiding, the source quality or soul quality that
links us to our highest becoming, that transcends
time and space, life and death."*
— Dr. Jean Houston

As someone who has lived with many traditional cultures around the world, I have found that every one of these cultures supports the belief that life is continuous—that there is part of the self that simply does not die when it's the physical body's time to go.

I've worked with over 3,000 research subjects and over a million and a half seminar participants, exploring what might be called "depth probings of the human psyche." I've found that we've barely begun to tap the immense depths of who and what we are. We have many more parts, many more levels to us, than we can even imagine.

Modern science and consciousness research is coming together to paint a portrait of the universe that exceeds our wildest expectations. We are indeed citizens of an enormous universe—more complex than we ever dreamed. The New Physics speaks about how at the time of the Big Bang, the newly created universe did not only "bang" in three or four dimensions, it banged in many more. This means that there are not only many more dimensions in the universe, but there are many more dimensions *within* us that are possible to experience. The New Physics calls these other dimensions "hyperspace." It appears that we live in a huge, universal school of life that has no real ending. There seems to be a constant, continuous graduation and initiation into higher and deeper levels of reality and beingness.

There is a very great poem by Christopher Fry called *Sleep of Prisoners*. This poem contains within it immense seeds of discovery—not only for us now, living in present time and space—but also for our eventual passage to a much larger life *beyond* time and space. The poem reads [Jean recites from memory]:

> *The human heart can go to the lengths of God.*
> *Dark and cold we may be, but this is not winter now.*
> *The frozen misery of centuries, cracks, breaks, begins to move.*
> *The thunder is the thunder of the float*
> *Of the flow of the upstart Spring.*
> *Thank God our time is now*
> *When wrong comes up to meet us everywhere.*
> *Never to leave us 'til we take*
> *The longest stride of soul folk ever took.*
> *Affairs are now soul-sized.*
> *The enterprise is exploration into God.*
> *What are you waiting for?*
> *It takes many thousands of years to wake.*
> *But will you wake, for pity's sake?*

So the enterprise is exploration into God, and those who have begun this exploration into a deeper reality share many extraordinary experiences. I'll share a few of my own.

When I was 19 years old, I used to jump out of planes as a parachutist. On one occasion, my parachute didn't open right away, and I fell and fell. I tried my backup chute, and that didn't open either. Suddenly, the adrenaline leapt to my brain, and soon after I was transported into another state of consciousness where I experienced a life review as I continued my freefall to the earth. Every major event in my life passed before me, from the time I was a tiny child up to the present. I even saw future events that later came to pass, which in itself says a lot about reality and the universe of possibilities. Well, one of my parachutes *did* finally open, but the overall sense of this powerful experience was that all of life was available, glorious, and full—independent of whether I lived or died.

A few years later, I came down with typhoid fever in a tiny village in Crete where there were no doctors. When my temperature reached 107 degrees Fahrenheit, the light of my bedside hotel lamp faded away, and in my mind's eye, I found myself at the threshold of another dimension of reality. Some part of my body-mind system crossed into an enormously pleasant and delightful realm. There was art on the walls, lovely furniture, extraordinary music—I met marvelous beings. I thought, *My, what a wonderful place; this is the best place I've traveled so far.*

I was about to travel deeper into this otherworldly domain but said to myself, "Wait a minute, I'm very young, I'm not ready to leave the world. No, I don't think so, not yet." A being of the realm replied, "Okay, we'll see you some other time." Then, with a tremendous effort of psychological will, I pushed my consciousness back into my body and again found myself in the light of my hotel room. My fever broke upon my return.

Another fond memory was my grandmother's passing. For the last six years of her life, she had arteriosclerosis of the brain and nervous system. We took care of all her basic bodily functions—she was like a vegetable. However, to our amazement, an hour before she passed, this old lady suddenly woke up from the stupor that she had been in for six long years. Looking at the upper left-hand corner of the room, she began to address the invisible presence of her deceased husband, Prospero, who had been dead for many years.

Now, my grandfather, Prospero, had been a very fat man. He used to eat pizza by the stack! We used to say that he knew of his feet only by rumor—his double chin was so big!

My grandmother kept on speaking to the upper left-hand corner of the room. In beautiful, lyrical Italian, she said things like, "Hey, Prospero, que bella, how beautiful you look. Eh, you gotta your figure back."

She then began to address her daughter, who had died 40 years before; and she also spoke to her son, Paulo, who had died only three months before—whose death we didn't think she knew about because she was in a coma the whole time, and nobody could have possibly told her about his passing. So she continued to talk to these invisible presences, then she would listen for a while, then laugh and laugh, then talk again, and then listen, on and on.

My Aunt Gracie excitedly said to my grandmother in Sicilian, "Mama, Mama, do you recognize me?"

And grandmother replied strongly, "Hold it, Gracie! Can't you see they've come for me?"

Aunt Gracie said, "Hey, Mama, there's nobody there."

Grandmother replied, "Hey, Gracie, you can't see them because they haven't come for *you*, they've come for *me*."

Then Aunt Gracie said, "Mama, for the last six years you've been...*cumma legume*...like a vegetable."

"Ah, Gracie, to *you* I may have seemed like a vegetable, *but the places I've been!*"

So my grandmother had been on her inner travels, by golly. That's why I always say that when people are taking care of folks who have Alzheimer's disease, are in a coma, or are senile—do not think that because their surface mind doesn't focus in "normal ways" that their "depth mind" is not intact—traveling, experiencing, and preparing to enter a much larger universe beyond physical reality.

Here are a few stories about my father, who was a great comedian. He wrote many of the very famous comedy shows of early radio and television. My dad was a complete atheist throughout his life. He used to say, "When you're dead, your dead, and that's it."

Ten days after his death from leukemia, I was guiding a meditation with several hundred of my students. I asked them to imagine that they were going though successive doors of the mind—one door opening into another, into another, into another. At one point, I decided that I might as well do the meditation myself. I closed my eyes and found a particular door. This door was paisley colored on the bottom and made of glass on top. Suddenly, my father appeared behind that door in my meditation. Now, I'm not good at visual imagery. I'm an auditory thinker, a muscular thinker—like an athlete. I don't tend to see much with my eyes closed. However, *this time, there was my father,* grinning his typical happy grin. And for some reason, I asked him, "Dad, what should I call you?"

He said, "Call me Popsicle!" He laughed and immediately disappeared. Later that day, I phoned his wife and said, "I've had the darnedest experience." I told her about meeting Dad in meditation and that he had said, "Call me Popsicle."

Well, she began to laugh hysterically and said, "I just heard from the Forest Lawn Mortuary. They told me the cremations were so backed up that they were keeping him on ice" [Jean laughs]. My comedian father's line, "Call me Popsicle," was so much like him—playing on the words *Pop* and *Popsicle.* I admit it's a rather macabre story [laughs again].

About six months later, I had another after-death visionary experience with my father. It was a lucid dream in which I was asleep but consciously awake in my sleep. My dad again appeared and said, "Hiya, kid"—just like he always used to say to me. Still in my lucid dream, I said, "Dad, what are you doing here? You're supposed to be dead?"

He replied, "Eh, death's a relative term—besides, I got some time off for good behavior, so I'll tell you what I've been doing. I'm able to go all over the world, instantaneously. Nobody can see me—it's great. I can get in for free into these comedy clubs. Now kid, I've been checking out this club in Manchester. I want you to go to Manchester and check out this chicken act." Then he'd given the name of the comedy club in Manchester where he had seen this comedy act.

He continued, "Hey, kid, there's this other wild act with two ladies and an ostrich"—and he again gave the name of the club where this act was appearing. He went on to describe about a dozen or so of these comedy acts and clubs and then said, "Now look, I know that you're asleep, and you think I'm not really here, *but I really am.* Please try to remember the names of these clubs. This way, you can go to these places and can get all this comedy material together, create your own act, and can quit this scam you're into" [laughter].

Upon awakening, I was able to remember three of the names of the clubs he had described to me. I looked up the phone numbers, called and asked them about these comedy acts, and, by golly, *they were really there!* I still don't exactly know what to make of this experience, but it really happened!

A few weeks later, I was again guiding a meditation with my students down in Venezuela. This time I was taking them back to the time of the ancient Druids. In the guided meditation, I said things like, "Imagine that you are an ancient Druid at Stonehenge. You are wearing white robes. You possess the chalice of abundance. You have been given the sword of discrimination. There are many ravens flying overhead." I went on and on with this type of descriptive imagery.

After the meditation, a lady came over to me who couldn't stop laughing. She told me that someone who identified himself as my father appeared in her meditation dressed as one of the Druids. I asked her to describe him. She said, "Well, he was tall and bald and had a big grin on his face."

She continued. "Your father told me, 'Next time, tell my daughter not to send in so many stinking birds' " [laughter].

I couldn't figure all this out, so afterwards, I called his wife and told her the story. She again began to laugh hysterically. She told me that as a joke, one of the last things he had said just before he died was "In my next incarnation, I think I'll be an ancient Druid."

I had no way of knowing! So what do you make of it? *What you make of it is this:* The universe is extraordinarily vast and complex, and at the same time, it seems to have this seamless web of interconnectivity and kinship. We are indeed participants in a much larger life. Whether you believe in reincarnation or not, one thing I am convinced of is that life is an ongoing teaching-learning experience that continues after physical death. Those who feel that life comes to an end at death—life *does not* come to an end. Death is the closing of one door and the opening of another.

The ancient Aramaic word for death,
maw'ta, *when literally translated, means "not here, present elsewhere."*
The Persian word for death, intakaal, *when translated, means*
"to change, to move from."

PART IV

The Soul

in the

Near-Death

Experience

INTRODUCTION

According to the latest Gallup poll, over 22 million Americans have had a near-death experience. If you're one of these people, then this section, *The Soul in the Near-Death Experience,* will undoubtedly bring back memories of your own near-death journey. For those who have *not* had a near-death experience, this section will hopefully shed light on what it's like to have one—without having to go through the pain and the trouble of almost dying.

Nowadays, the subject of debate on the near-death experience is no longer whether people *have* near-death experiences, but what do they represent? Are they but fabrications of the mind—real only for those who are experiencing them? Or are near-death experiences actual journeys to other dimensions of reality, as the overwhelming majority of near-death experiencers claim after they return?

As someone who has had a near-death experience, and has also studied much of the near-death scientific literature, I believe that the weight of evidence points to the latter. I leave it for you to decide for yourself based on both the contents of Part IV and on Dr. Kenneth Ring's chapter, "Evidence Supporting the Spiritual Reality Behind Near-Death Experiences," which can be found in Part VIII, Science and the Soul—The Evidence.

CHAPTER TEN

Graduating to Another Reality

RAYMOND MOODY, M.D., Ph.D.

Dr. Raymond Moody coined the term *near-death experience,* which first appeared in his groundbreaking book, *Life After Life,* in 1976. Dr. Moody holds a doctorate in philosophy, and he is also a psychiatrist. This chapter is based on a film interview that took place in Chicago, Illinois.

"Personally, I can tell you in all openness and honesty,
I have absolutely no fear of death. From my near-death
research and my personal experiences, death is, in my judgment,
simply a transition into another kind of reality."
— Dr. Raymond Moody

When I was six years old, I had already built my own telescope and was gazing out into space. I started life with a very scientific perspective. I was totally and completely a "nonbeliever" in life after death. So, I can well understand how people of a skeptical bent of mind could listen to accounts of near-death experiences (NDEs) and say, "Oh, this life-after-death thing is just a dying person's wish fulfillment, or they're simply hallucinations." As a psychiatrist who has talked with over 10,000 people who have had NDEs, I can tell you that this experience does not conform in any way to what we know of as hallucinations, delusions, or wish-fulfilling fantasies. It's a totally different kind of human experience.

The issue of whether there is survival after death is something that each one of us has to make up our own minds about. In my own personal life, I'm perfectly satisfied that there's nothing to fear in death. At the same time, however, we always have to be respectful toward others who may still may be afraid of death, or who do not believe in life after death.

People who have had NDEs frequently tell us that when they leave their bodies, their spirits are able to travel to another part of the hospital—even to places thousands of miles away. And it turns out that the scenes they report—of knowing what relatives said and did far away from their hospital rooms where their bodies lay unconscious—are later verified as having transpired at that *very* time, *exactly* as they described it! I've personally had many patients—who were at the time believed to be dead—describe detailed conversations that they witnessed taking place among their relatives in an entirely different part of the world. Afterwards, we went to these relatives to verify these NDE accounts, and they would say, "Absolutely, this was exactly what was going on at that time."

In one case, a woman arrived at the hospital in an enclosed ambulance, was wheeled directly into the emergency room, and was put on the operating table. According to medical records, this patient was clinically dead for a few minutes. Shortly after she was resuscitated, she told her social worker that she'd had an NDE. In addition to describing the classic stages of an NDE, she happened to mention a curious detail: As her spirit left her body and floated upwards above the hospital, she saw an old shoe dangling from a cable on the hospital roof. After hearing this, the social worker immediately went up on the roof and retrieved the shoe exactly where the patient had said it would be! So these are just a few accounts that indicate that phenomena quite outside the ordinary range of conventional expectations occur during these NDEs.

Common Features of the Near-Death Experience and the Process of Death

Over the past few decades, we've really learned quite a bit about NDEs and the process of dying. And what we've learned is that death does not have to be a frightening experience for the people who go through it. As a matter of fact, some people who return from close calls with death tell us that it was one of the most wonderful experiences of their lives. They report that they felt a great peace during the experience, and that the presence of deceased loved ones were there to help them through to the Other Side.

From millions of NDE accounts, we now know that there is a definite progression of events that are reported time after time. Based on what these people tell us when they return, there is a state of consciousness one enters into at a certain point in the process that is actually very comfortable for the people who are going through it. Physicians, psychologists, and psychiatrists all over the world continue to study the patterns that unfold at the point of death. They are finding remarkable similarities in all the cultures they've looked at.

The patients who return from these experiences tell us that at the same moment their physician believes that they are dead, from their perspective, they report that they leave their physical bodies, drift upwards, and look back down and see their own physical bodies lying there on the bed, surrounded by medical personnel who are trying to resuscitate them.

Typically, at this point, they tell us that they're wondering what all the fuss is about. They're actually trying to tell the physicians, "Don't worry, I'm fine." From their perspective, they're completely vibrant and alive. As the NDE experience progresses, they may become aware of a passageway that they often describe as a tunnel. They go through this tunnel and come out on the other side into an incredibly brilliant, warm, and loving Light. They say that as they enter into this Light, it completely permeates them with feelings of love, acceptance, and peace.

They may be greeted at this point by relatives or friends who have already died who are there to meet them and help them through this transition. Also, they often describe an incredibly loving personal presence—a Being of Light. This being helps them review their lives and to see what they have learned in the process of living while on Earth.

In this life-review process, most people say on their return that learning how to love is the most important thing in life—that's what comes up time and again in the life review part of the NDE. Our spiritual progress in life is measured from the point of view of love.

The more than 10,000 near-death returnees whom I've talked to have come from every walk of life, every educational level, and from many cultures around the world. Out of all of these people, I've yet to see one single case of a person who was not met by understanding and love in this life-review process. This doesn't mean that we all haven't done things that we wish we hadn't, or that we didn't feel remorse if we were mean to someone. The Beings of Light that are involved in this life-review process fully realize that being human means that we make mistakes—we all do.

Another interesting point: NDErs who recover from their close calls with death tell us that as soon as they were out of their bodies and in this alternate space—this light realm—they felt no pain at all, even if they had terrible pain up to the point of death. And sometimes as they pass over, their last words refer to how completely peaceful they feel.

At the Moment of Death

NDErs are people who were clinically dead but returned from this *close call* with death to tell their accounts. However, I've also been at the bedside of many people who *did* go on to die. And one can sometimes observe that people on their deathbeds who *do* slip on over and die begin to describe similar experiences that NDErs tell us about.

As they are dying, people very close to death will typically look up and say, "Oh, there's Grandpa!" or whomever. They consistently report being met by spirits of relatives and friends who have already passed on.

Near the moment of death, people sometimes open up to some other kind of reality, say their "good-byes" to us, and move on in great peace. As they are dying, people will look up and say, "Oh, a Light, a beautiful Light!" This happened to my father when he died about a year and a half ago, and then to my mother as well when she died about a month ago. It was very comforting for me to be there with my mother as she died and to see this firsthand—quite remarkable!

There was another thing that was particularly wonderful about my mother's death. Throughout her life, she was never a very assertive person. She was always trying to make everybody else feel good and help *them* to do what *they* wanted to do. She was a wonderful hostess and always very sweet and kindly to others—but she had a hard time saying no. However, to my amazement and great joy, I noticed in her last few days on Earth that her personality was transformed into someone who now wasn't afraid to speak her opinion to the hospital staff, even refusing in a very strong way some of the treatments that the doctors wanted to perform on her. This transformation occurred only after she had slipped over to the Other Side in a close call with death. Something very profound must have happened to her on the Other Side to account for this change in her personality and behavior.

It is also said that in the dying process, it is important for relatives and friends to say good-bye—and it is—but we often say the word *good-bye* as if it's so final and terrible. Well, based on my experience, what I've come to say is, "Good-bye *for now,*" because I'm highly confident—as are most all of the people who have been through these NDEs—that we will meet up again with our deceased relatives and friends on the Other Side. So in this light, "good-bye" is only temporary.

I often think that it would be great if we could develop some sort of way to give people a near-death experience while they are still alive—without, of course, subjecting them to any sort of danger, discomfort, or anything like that—so that we can recapture some of the positive aftereffects that people have from their close calls with death. *[Editor's note: chapter 16, "Experiencing the Soul in Meditation," addresses this issue.]*

Death As Graduation to Another Reality

Personally, I can tell you in all openness and honesty, I have absolutely no fear of death. From my research and my personal experiences, death is, in my judgment, simply a transition into another kind of reality.

There's a wonderful metaphor that an old friend of mine used in order to describe death. This woman was one of the first people I met who had an NDE who passed on many years ago. After her NDE, she spoke about death as "a graduation." When her friends and relatives would die, she would say that they had "graduated." And from what I've experienced, I can accept this metaphor completely. The physical realm that we're in now, this is *only one* level of reality. But there are lots of *other* levels of reality. And death is a transition into some of these other very intriguing spaces.

People sometimes ask me about my own death: "Do I want to die alone or with other people around?" For me, when I contemplate my own death, I'm drawn to going through the process alone rather than having a big flock of people around me. This is probably because I've always been a very introspective type of person. Everybody is different, though.

I hope this doesn't sound flippant or bizarre or anything—it's a heartfelt thing with me; I really mean it. I'm looking forward to death as a great adventure—the trip of a lifetime. I have a very strong sense of this from the many thousands of people I've talked with who have had NDEs, and people who have gone on to die—that death is the "ultimate adventure." I remember one woman put it to me in these terms: "At a certain point when you are close to death, when you leave your body, you are not the spouse of your spouse, you're not the child of your parents, you are not the parent of your children. You are totally and completely yourself. It's really the trip of a lifetime!"

On the Lighter Side—
Dr. Moody's Stand-up Comedy Routine
[Dr. Moody is smiling and laughing throughout his delivery]

Some say that in an NDE, when you get through "the Tunnel," there are some pitfalls: Sometimes, you have to sit at a real estate dinner, and they try to sell you real estate. But all of the people I know who have been through that, say, "Don't buy"—that there are much better bargains *past* the Tunnel.

Also, don't let anybody trick you by saying that you have to pay a toll in the Tunnel, because it's not true. If somebody comes up to you in the Tunnel and asks for a toll, you tell them that you want to see the manager, because these guys are like squeegee people wanting to wash your car windows and get a tip. I understand that they get kind of stuck on the edge of the Tunnel there, and they're just trying to make a few dollars off you. But don't let them fool you. There's no need to pay a toll [big laugh]!

"Under the sod and under the trees, here lies the body of Solomon Peas,
The Peas are not here, there is only the pod—
the peas shelled out and went to God."
— found on a tombstone,
as quoted by Dr. Joan Borysenko

CHAPTER ELEVEN

What It's Like on the Other Side

BETTY J. EADIE

Betty J. Eadie is a near-death returnee, transformational speaker, mother of eight children, and the author of the internationally acclaimed bestsellers *Embraced by the Light* and *Awakening Heart—My Continuing Journey to Live.* Her account of her near-death experience has been heralded as one of the most complete and detailed accounts ever written. This chapter is based on an excerpt from a film interview that took place in Honolulu, Hawaii.

"None of this was really new to my spirit. It was a recalling of what I've always known—how we come up from Earth to heaven, how we select our parents, how we select our life situations, how we are here on Earth to learn to love."
— Betty J. Eadie

When I was four years old, I was attending a Native American boarding school where I caught double pneumonia and whooping cough. They took me to the hospital, and I heard the doctor say to the nurse,

"We've lost her." Now to a four-year old, this means you're *lost,* not dead. I was thinking, *Well, I'm right here, why are they thinking I'm lost?* I was out of my body, right above them, looking down. They thought I was dead. I saw them pull a sheet over my head. Then my spirit was cradled by an incredible Being of Light that had a long white beard. At the time, I thought that this person was my grandfather. For years afterwards, I looked for this grandfather figure to appear, but he never did.

Throughout my life, I drew comfort from the memory of that grandfatherly image that I had met as a four-year-old. Many years later, in my second NDE, I finally realized that this grandfatherly figure was actually a Being of Light that had been protecting and sustaining me all throughout the trials and the pain of my life. Back then, no one spoke about NDEs. This was *before* Raymond Moody wrote the book *Life After Life* in 1976, *before* he even coined the term *near-death experience.*

The next time I had an NDE was in 1973. It happened in the hospital after my hysterectomy when I hemorrhaged heavily throughout the surgery. The doctors thought I was fine and wheeled me into the hospital recovery room. Later that evening, around 9:30, I awoke and felt myself dying. There is a knowingness about dying that is very peculiar—I could feel parts of my body literally closing down. Then I felt this tremendous sinking sensation— as though every last drop of blood was draining from my body. Then there was a "pop," and my spirit rose above my body. I turned and looked down, and I could see myself lying there, just like I did when I was four years old. I came down for a closer look, because I was looking at my body in a different way, from a multidimensional point of view. As I viewed my body, my first thought was, *Oh my God, I'm dead, and there is no one here I can tell this to!* And then, as I looked to my left, three Celestial Beings appeared. They had soft brown robes on and golden bands around their waists. They said that they were my guardian angels, that they had been with me throughout all my time here on Earth, and throughout eternity.

Just then, I had the desire to go home to see my family. In spirit, I was able to do just that, simply by desiring it. I traveled there very swiftly. I could see my husband sitting in the chair reading the newspaper. My children were laughing, throwing pillows, and preparing to go to bed. I looked at the clock. It was a quarter to ten in the evening. I remember being very annoyed with my husband because he had promised me that he would put the children to bed at 8:30. When I later told him about the experience, I made a point to tell him, "You didn't put the kids in bed at 8:30 like you promised!" He replied, "Oh my gosh, this is never going to end—*you're like this even after death!*"

After this visit to my family at home, my spirit was drawn into a tunnel-like space. I saw a pinpoint of Light that grew brighter and brighter. I traveled toward this Light very swiftly. This Light was not like ordinary external light. There was a Being in the Light. Then I saw that there was Light emanating from this Being—He *was* the Light. As I came toward Him, I was traveling feet first. I rose up on my feet and then began to run toward Him, much like a child would run to a parent who has been absent for a long, long time. I remember saying to him, "I'm home, I'm home, I'm finally home—and I never want to leave You ever again." I even remember the tone in my voice as I said this, even though we were not actually speaking verbally. The communication was telepathic, heart to heart. There is no possible way to misunderstand in this form of communication.

So I was finally Home, and I never wanted to leave again. It was almost like I was chastising Him, knowing that somehow or other He was in on the fact that I had been away from this Heavenly Home during my Earth stay. But He just wrapped His arms around me and embraced me. I knew that He loved me with a love that was total and pure—an unconditional love that we will never have here on this Earth, as much as we might try. I knew with perfect clarity that this Being was Jesus Christ. I knew Him because I knew Him before I came to Earth. I knew Him just as I would know my mother or my father if they were there to meet me.

This whole experience was more than just dying. Almost all of the common elements associated with NDEs were there—the tunnel, the Light, guardian angels, heavenly music, prayers, cathedrals. . . . Jesus wanted me to remember what heaven was like. None of this was really new to my spirit. It was a *recalling* of what I've always known: how we come up from Earth to heaven, how we select our parents, how we select our life situations, how we are here on Earth to learn to love. You see, my spirit had always known that. I believe that on a deeper level, each and every person here on this Earth knows what this is about, but it seems that we need a reawakening of the spirit for us to remember.

With all that I went through in my NDEs, how do you prove to others that you've had a spiritual experience? You cannot. It's usually very personal. I don't try to prove what has happened to me. I truly feel I don't need to. I think that on some level, everyone's spirit knows, but only when they are ready to awaken. If they want to remain dormant and asleep, they will stay that way until it's their time to wake up.

I learned from my NDEs that there's never a time when you lose consciousness. There's a transformation, but you never lose consciousness. There's no such thing as death. I don't even like to use the word *death*, because they don't like that word on the Other Side either. Death does not really explain what happens to you. You go from one state of being into a more perfect state of being, your natural state.

Another thing: You're never alone, absolutely never alone. You even have a welcoming party to greet you on the Other Side. Also, a lot of people at death's door see loved ones who have passed on who are waiting for them even when they are on *this* side.

I've been at the bedside of many people who pass on to the Other Side. Sometimes, people who are very close to making this transformation near the time of death are held back by the grief of those who are still here on Earth. Their grief, and their holding on, makes it harder for departing ones to cross over. Now if I were dying, lying in bed, and my family was around me, I would forgive them for not understanding that it's time for me to go. I'd probably say to them, "I know you're in grief that I'm going, but I'm sorry, I have to go Home." And then I'd go. Because I've met far too many people who will linger here in pain, and hold on just for their loved ones' sake. Sometimes the person who is dying serves as sort of a teacher for the persons who are caring for them, but we must learn to let them go and not to fear death, because in reality there's nothing there to fear.

I am against doctor-assisted suicide, because before we come to this Earth, every one of us chooses the time of our death, even down to the last minute. We have also chosen the way that we will go, too. There are certain lessons to be learned down here, so I believe that we should let go naturally and not abort the process with doctor-assisted suicide. If possible, during the passing, it is very healing to be surrounded by a vibration of love. Although I believe that pain-control medicine can be helpful, being surrounded by loving people is probably the greatest pain reliever there is. Death is much like childbirth—if you can do it naturally—without painkillers—do it. If not, it is okay to use pain medications.

I feel that hospices are divinely inspired by God. So are the many people who work in them. I did volunteer work for a major cancer research center, and I can tell you that for those people who are holding on, it's painful—not only to the families who are remaining, but for those who are holding on to life. Talk about false hope! That's basically what it is. We are all born terminal. From the moment of birth, we are terminal. So when my patients, say, "Well, Betty, I'm terminal; the doctors say I only have so long to live," I say, "Well, I'm terminal, too. I could walk out this door and get hit by a car and die before you." So you're terminal, I'm terminal. Let's celebrate life right now in the moment.

"Whenever I close my eyes, I can see Light, white Light,
which I believe is coming from God. I trust that this Light
is part of the power of God, and I will experience this Light
even more fully after my death."
— Dr. Janina Starceswski, a physician and hospice patient
very close to physical death (from the video, *Experiencing the Soul*)

CHAPTER TWELVE

We Are All Great, Awesome, Powerful, Spiritual Beings

DANNION BRINKLEY

Dannion Brinkley is a near-death returnee, transformational speaker, and the author of the bestsellers *Saved by the Light* and *At Peace in the Light*. His first NDE was particularly extraordinary and deserves a brief introductory description.

While Dannion was "in the Light," he was shown future events that appeared in what he describes as "television screenlike boxes." Soon after he returned to physical life, he was able to remember 117 of these future scenes and shared them with pioneer near-death researcher Dr. Raymond Moody. In the last 22 years, 95 of the 117 foreseen events have taken place.

As a few examples, while on the Other Side, Dannion was shown a devastating explosion at a nuclear facility that took place in a desolate wintry forest. The word *wormwood* appeared on one of the boxlike screens in his NDE. At the time, Dannion had no idea what this meant. Later, he discovered that in the Russian language, the word for wormwood is *chernobyl*.

Another screen showed the seal of the presidency of the United States, accompanied by the initials, "R. R." There were also cartoon caricatures that portrayed an actor with a cowboy persona who was to become president of the United States At the time, Dannion thought "R. R." represented the initials of actor Robert Redford. However, in 1980, Ronald Reagan (R. R.)

became president. Ronald Reagan had indeed starred in several cowboy movies, and he was often portrayed by newspaper columnists as a Wild West cowboy.

Dannion has predicted many other major world events, including the fall of the Berlin Wall and the Mideast Gulf War. Dannion's prophetic visions are chronicled in detail in his first book, *Saved by the Light*. This chapter is based on an excerpt from a film interview that took place in Las Vegas, Nevada.

✳   ✳   ✳

*"Once we begin to really understand that we are not from Here,
we are from There, that we all chose to come Here and were chosen
to come Here, that we were somebody and something long before we
came Here, only then do we comprehend that we are not poor, pitiful,
stupid human beings. We are all great, awesome, powerful and
mighty spiritual beings! What then really becomes important
is realizing the true purpose of our lives."*
— Dannion Brinkley

In 1975, I was clinically dead for 28 minutes after lightning struck a power line that went through the telephone I was speaking on. Afterwards, I was *completely* paralyzed for six days, and *partially* paralyzed for seven months. It took me a full two years to learn to walk and feed myself. I lost more than 50 pounds. Fourteen years later, I had a second NDE when I collapsed and had emergency open-heart surgery.

As a result of my NDEs—and from the research that later came out—I have come to the following conclusion: *"Who we really are"* does not die! We not only do not die, but there is a systematic process by which we leave this world. NDEs and the process of dying are not what religious fundamentalists or authoritarian institutions say they are. The system of leaving this world is built on Love. And once we have experienced that Love, our lives are changed forever.

In my NDEs, I lifted out of my body and moved down a tunnel. I was met by loved ones and relatives and came into a place of bright, brilliant, beautiful Light. I experienced a 360-degree panoramic life review where I saw everything I had ever done—both the good and the bad. In this life review, I felt the direct and indirect results of all my interactions with everyone whom I had ever had contact with in my entire life. As it was happening, it was like watching another friend go through something you couldn't do anything about—I was experiencing it all from a unique empathic perspective.

To be honest, in my first 25 years on this Earth, I was mostly a jerk—I really didn't spend much time being very nice. As a result, in my first NDE, I felt all the pain, anguish, frustration, fear, and anxiety I had created for all those many people. But in my second NDE, later in my life—when the panoramic life review came—because I had changed my ways, I got a chance to meet everyone I'd ever helped, and to feel all the joy, love, and kindness we had shared.

Once we begin to *really* understand that we are *not* from *Here*, we are from *There*, that we all *chose* to come Here and were *chosen* to come Here, that we were somebody and something *long before* we came Here, *only then* do we comprehend that we are *not* poor, pitiful, stupid human beings. *We are all great, awesome, powerful, and mighty spiritual beings!* What really becomes important then is realizing the true purpose of our lives. I've found that acts of kindness, and loving and caring for each other, are the most important things in life. And it's not only the *big* things we do in our life that matter. It's where our hearts are. It's the *why* behind the things we do—our loving, good intentions—that helps make a better world Here and Hereafter.

A lot of times people tell me, "You make death sound so good." Well, I'm just being honest about the process I directly experienced. By understanding the NDE through direct experience, our understanding of life becomes clearer.

So love each other with *all* your heart, with *all* your mind, and with *all* your soul. Because once you begin to understand the process of dying, you better appreciate the value of living a life of love.

If you spend time with those who will be leaving this world soon, they may have anxiety, frustration, fear, and doubt about what's going to happen. Sit quietly with them and ask them to tell you anything they want about their lives. Be a good listener. Encourage the family to share precious moments of togetherness. Sit and talk together. Even talking about the fun times in life and laughing is okay—it doesn't have to be serious all the time just because someone is dying. If you are caretaking people who are dying, you should be spending as much quality time with them as possible, and not spending your time out in a hospital hallway, waiting for a doctor to tell you about the next medical procedure—we sometimes turn things over to scientists and doctors instead of trusting our own spiritual wisdom.

And after you've listened and listened, ask these individuals if they would be interested in hearing what you know about the Other Side. If they say yes, and you speak from your heart and soul, this will help them prepare for leaving. By having loving conversations and "sharings" among family and friends, those who are preparing to leave this world often find out they really did a better job here on Earth than they thought they did.

One of the most important things to remember is that because we are spiritual beings, no matter what we've done in our lives, what we've gone through, we did a lot of good work. Even though we all have regrets, pain, and suffering, we also have shared joy. If we try to count our blessings, we'll see that the distance we've traveled in life was well worth the difficulties.

A lot of times we do not recognize the value of what we have contributed to others. It is the wondrous *little* things we may have forgotten about that count for a lot. Because that was the divine part of us acting— the part of us that is spiritually connected to our divinity that flows through our veins. We should take time to remember the times we've helped someone and patted someone on the back. Because it was those times that, through us, *we* were the difference that God made.

Preparing for Death

There are many ways to prepare for death—meditation, relaxation, music, healing touch, aromatherapy—so many things. We don't have to just lie there just waiting for each day to pass. We can discover and feel the peace of our spiritual self *on this side!* If we do this, we can lessen fear and anxiety, and strengthen our understanding of ourselves as spiritual beings.

People sometimes ask me how I feel about suicide. After my NDEs, I've come to understand that suicide is not a way out. Even though we have the right to make our own decisions—as stupid as they may be, as smart as they may be—I say this: To take one single breath away from the deal we made before we came here to Earth is a mistake.

An example that shows the power of knowing that we are spiritual beings in our essence is a study of several years duration conducted by Dr. Bruce Greyson. This was a study with over 400 suicidal people in the early 1980s. Dr. Greyson found that people who attempted suicide and *didn't* have an NDE went on to attempt suicide at least three to six more times, in some cases until they succeeded in committing suicide. *But not one person who had some form of NDE ever attempted it again!* The reason for this is that the process by which you leave this world—and the system on the Other Side—informs us of our greatness. *We realize that we cannot die, that we are powerful, mighty, awesome spiritual beings!*

For those people who feel inclined, becoming a hospice volunteer can be extremely valuable. At this time, I've been a hospice volunteer for 17 years and have been with 153 hospice patients. By being with these people up to the very end of their lives, I've *gained* far more than I've given. It's a two-way street. Not only will serving people in the process of dying help them prepare for the inevitable, but one day someone from our own family may depend on us to help them. We will then be better able to give them support and help create a better quality of care.

Coming into this world and leaving this world is a natural process that completes the circle of life. I remember a grandmother who was dying at home. It was beautiful seeing her little granddaughter bring her soup and both of them just talking together very sweetly. Understanding the natural process of death can lessen our fear of death and bring families together. Without this true understanding of what death is, we are sometimes afraid.

Always remember, the Light is the Light. Its warm, soothing nature totally permeates us—we permeate It, and It permeates us. There are so many ways that we can prepare to meet this Light, ways that help us come to a place of recognition. Deep states of meditation and contemplation can be experienced through many different paths—Christian mysticism as well as Eastern practices.

So remember, the Light is the Light. We are all a part of this Light. And as we make the transition from *this* world to the *next*, we become more assured that we *are* Light, there *is* Light, and where there is Light, there is Love. The Light is the Light and will always be the Light.

I love you all very much.

"And after death, when most of you for the first time realize what life here is all about, you will begin to see that your life here is almost nothing but the sum total of every choice you have made during every moment of your life. Your thoughts, which you are responsible for, are as real as your deeds. You will begin to realize that every word and every deed affects your life and also touches thousands of lives."
— Dr. Elisabeth Kübler-Ross

PART V

Experiencing

the

Soul

INTRODUCTION

"The question of immortality is a...question of inner existence, a question which the individual must confront by looking into his own soul."
— Søren Kierkegaard, philosopher

We have arrived at an important turning point in this anthology. In the previous four parts—*Living with Soul, The Soul Before Birth, The Soul After Death,* and *The Soul in the Near-Death Experience*—the experiences of soul were largely "involuntary" in the sense that they were initiated either by medical emergencies, terminal illnesses, imminent death, or in spontaneous spiritual experiences that appear to be beyond the conscious control of the typical individual to produce "at will."

The next three sections, *Experiencing the Soul, Preparing the Soul for a Healing Passage,* and *The Soul at the Moment of Death*—point to ways we can deepen our soul experience and "voluntarily" contact the more transcendent aspects of our souls.

How is this accomplished? Some believe that "The Way" is through our own efforts—through a combination of meditation, contemplation, prayer, "right attitude," and cultivating a foundation of ethical living based on universal spiritual principles. Others believe that our individual efforts are surely necessary, but insufficient in themselves. They believe that the benevolent grace of the Creator and/or Creative Principle within and around us is essential—if not *more* important—in order to make inner progress on our soul's Homeward Journey.

The Role of a Spiritual Teacher

There are, however, other spiritual traditions that add an additional element to the interplay of individual effort and the saving grace of the Creator. This is the view that it is possible for a spiritually realized human being—a saint, guru, master of meditation, or whatever name one uses—who serves as a benevolent intermediary to escort the spiritual seeker's soul back to its Source—its original home in Godhead.

In this connection, it is fascinating that the original etymology of the Indo-European word *guru*, when literally translated, means "one who leads from darkness to light." Throughout history, millions of student-disciples have taken refuge in the protection and guidance of such spiritually advanced or fully realized human beings who have attained a direct experience of higher consciousness and offer to lift us "in and up" by the power of God they have contacted within themselves.

Unfortunately, in recent times, the spiritual teacher–student relationship has fallen into disrepute—especially in the modern society—due to the abuse of power on the part of deceptive, deluded, or incompetent individuals who have made a sacrilege of this most sacred trust. As a sad commentary to people's difficulty in recognizing a genuine spiritual teacher, the status of a teacher is all too often judged by the size of their audience and the number of books they've sold.

Many people have even forgotten that there is a spiritual goal to be actively strived for and attained during Earth life. The words of Sant Darshan Singh, mystic poet and meditation master, echo these concerns when he says: "Sainthood is *not* a myth created by human imagination, but life's highest possibility actualized from age to age by an infinitesimally small minority of individuals. The terms *God* and *Truth* acquire force and meaning for us only through the examples of lives like theirs."

True spiritual teachers will not elevate themselves above others, but teach that the soul-consciousness they experience on a moment-to-moment basis can equally be realized by us. We cannot determine the competence of a spiritual teacher by the display of miracles or the power to effect instantaneous physical healing, the intellectual brilliance or emotional appeal of their spiritual discourses, or by external appearances—the donning of holy robes or the adopting of austere lifestyles.

The most important criteria that should be used to judge competent spiritual teachers are the love and truth that they personify in their daily lives, and their ability to uplift and protect us *on the level of soul.* Only a true saint can give another soul a direct boost in the form of a transcendental spiritual experience. Only a true spiritual teacher can function as an inner guide on the planes of consciousness that lead back to our Creator. Only a true spiritual teacher will be able to come to us at the time of death to protect and guide us on the inner planes.

In the following section, *Experiencing the Soul,* you will meet human beings who have demonstrated a consistent ability to *directly* access various levels of soul-consciousness on a voluntary, "at-will" basis.

If you feel inclined, it is possible to meet these and other extraordinary human beings, since they live as our contemporaries on Earth at this present time. It is important to remember, however, that although we honor spiritual teachers for their spiritual attainments, true spiritual teachers will always say that the divinity they have realized within themselves is *equally in all of us!* (Please see Appendix A for contact information on the contributors in this section.)

CHAPTER THIRTEEN

Artist As Spiritual Explorer—
The Visionary Art of Alex Grey

ALEX GREY

The inspiration behind the widely acclaimed visionary art of **Alex Grey** is based on his own spiritual experiences. It is rare to find someone who, through his art, can capture a sense of interdimensionality that the soul experiences in nonphysical realms.

Alex's work has appeared in many prestigious art galleries and museum exhibitions around the world. He lives in New York City with his wife, Allyson Grey—also a visionary artist—and their spiritually precocious young daughter, Zena Lotus.

Alex is presently completing a book called *The Mission of Art,* which presents the view that the highest function of art is to inspire us to the Divine. I am extremely honored to have Alex Grey share his vision of art in this book, as well as a few of his paintings following this chapter. (The greatness of Alex's art can only be hinted at in the humble black and white, reduced-size reproductions in this book. Please see Appendix A in the contributors' section, under the listing "Alex Grey," for more information on his extraordinary art.)

This chapter is based on a phone interview with the artist.

"In the painting, Universal Mind Lattice, *which was
based on a mystical visionary experience, I was part of
one vast luminescent, transparent lattice system of love energy.
It was as if the veil of supposed 'reality' had been stripped from the material world to expose the bedrock reality, the scaffolding of spirit. I understood it as the intricate interconnectedness of the one and the many on a
level of awareness that was infinite and eternal. This was the
ethical ground of compassion, where all beings and things are
known to be part of us. I knew death need not be feared
because we would eventually return to the
profound bliss of this realm."*

— Alex Grey, from *Sacred Mirrors: The Visionary Art of Alex Grey*

Art can help us discover the sacredness in life. My mission as an artist is to display or express the condition of the soul in human life. Art reflects *both* sides of life—the light *and* the shadow side. For example, one of artist Andy Warhol's more famous works, entitled *Campbell Soup Can*—represents the existential emptiness of modern materialistic culture through a banal cultural icon.

I feel that art's *highest* purpose is to inspire spiritual awakening. This is what art accomplishes when it expresses what is sacred in a culture and expands our awareness and understanding of life. In my art, I attempt to unite the physicality of human existence, the archetypes of the mental/imaginal realm, and the ever-presence of the spirit.

Ever since I can remember, I've been fascinated by life's polarities, paradoxes, and mysteries—particularly as these find expression in pro- found transformational events such as birth; death; nursing a baby; falling in love; and our essential interconnectedness to nature, God, and each other. I approach these themes from a perspective that portrays reality as contin- uous and interpenetrating domains—encompassing the physical, bio- energetic, emotional, psychical, and the spiritual.

As an artist who spent several years in medical school studying and drawing human anatomy, the layering of these multiple realities in my paintings is built on a foundation of anatomical realism—of bone, nerves, blood vessels, and muscles.

I have also had my share of transpersonal, mystical experiences. It is always challenging to try to visually portray the Greater Reality of these transcendent events. This level of spiritual essence—*behind* all form—the artist can only strive to capture. Using any number of vehicles of expression—music, theater, painting—and by using archetypal symbols that resonate on a universal level, art can evoke the complete range of possible life experiences, including the boundless nature of our souls.

When I was in my 20s, I was drawn to "performance art" as a way of expression and a way to make sense of what life was about. To give you an example, one "performance" involved an actual pilgrimage to the earth's North Magnetic Pole. The work is called *Polar Wandering*.

As you probably know, Earth's magnetic lines of force converge at the North and the South magnetic poles, creating a large and powerful magnetic field. However, what some people *do not* know is that this magnetic field is continually shifting. This effect is known as "polar wandering." Every few years geo-magnetic maps must be redrawn to adjust for the polar wandering effect. It struck me as ironic that something we rely on to get our bearings was continually in flux. As the expression goes, "The only thing permanent is change."

To locate and travel to exact magnetic north, I first had to get the permission of the Canadian government because the area is under their jurisdiction. All the while I was there, I felt weird and disoriented in this frozen Arctic tundra. First of all, the sun never set—it just went around in the sky. Also, the earth's magnetic field was so powerful that the needle of my compass spun around all the time. So with my camera rolling, in negative 30-degree temperature one day—or was it night?—it all looked and felt the same—I took off all my clothes and ran in a circle in a performance art, moving meditation on the geo-electromagnetic forces at the earth's Magnetic North. The experience induced an altered state of consciousness, a merging of identity with the vast planetary magnetic field.

As an artist and human being who seems to be drawn to these kind of spiritual frontiers, this was the first of many nonordinary states of awareness that have transformed my art and experience of life as an artist, husband, father, son, human being, and soul.

So we find ourselves in a strange polarity at the close of the 20th century. We've witnessed the wholesale murder of millions of people. We've suffered terribly from the destruction of nature. We've completely lost or desecrated precious traditional cultures around the world. Atrocities cumulatively equal to the horrors of Hitler and the Holocaust, Pol Pot and the Killing Fields, are still going on around the world as you are reading these words. This shadow side that we collectively bear has profoundly affected everyone—*including* artists, so it is understandable how a dark, nihilistic representation of reality has infected much of contemporary art.

But as with all polarities in life, from this darkness has emerged Light. The seeds of a global, nondenominational, experientially based spirituality has been sown as we enter the next millennium. More people are directly experiencing the core perennial truths spoken about by the mystics and saints throughout history.

Now more than ever, there is a unique opportunity for artists to study the archetypes and sacred art forms of the world's great wisdom traditions. Along with that study, the artist needs to integrate the darkness of our personal and collective shadow with the Light of transcendence, revealing a new vision of World Spirit. Art can enrich and inspire us by pointing to universal truths that give our lives joy and meaning.

On the following pages, a few of my works are included in black and white. The originals were painted in full color, mostly in oils, and were often quite large in size. I do hope that you have an opportunity to experience these and other works in full color in an art gallery or in the book *Sacred Mirrors*.

"A spirit and a vision are not, as the modern philosophy supposes, a cloudy vapour, or a nothing: they are organized and minutely articulated beyond all that the mortal and perishing nature can produce."
— William Blake, artist and poet (1757–1827)

*[**Editor's note:** Alex Grey gives a description and interpretation of six of his paintings, reprinted on the pages that follow.]*

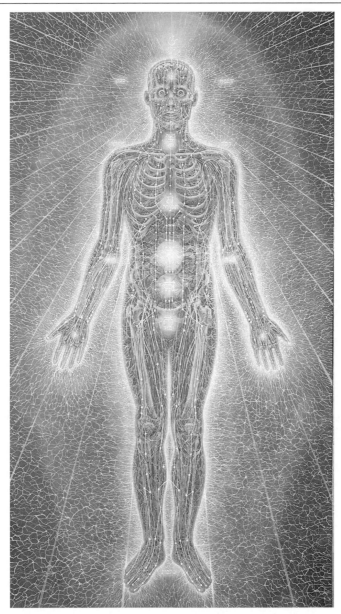

PSYCHIC ENERGY SYSTEM

Psychic Energy System is an x-ray view of the physical body that interweaves the non-physical psychospiritual energy systems. The metaphysical aspect of the human being includes the golden white light of the acupuncture meridians and points, the astral and etheric auras surrounding the body, and the seven chakras located on the central axis of the body. The chakras mediate the energies of the egg-shaped astral and other higher "bodies" with the etheric energy layer closely surrounding and interpenetrating the physical body. The chakras present a model hierarchy of the evolution of consciousness and its development, because they bridge the material and spiritual realms.

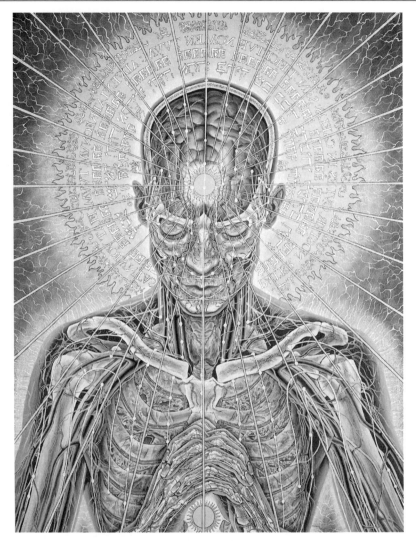

PRAYING

Praying is a portrait that reveals a sun in both the heart and mind. From the inner Light in the center of the brain, a halo emanates and surrounds the head. This center in the human body is sometimes called the "single" or "third" eye. Jesus Christ spoke about this center when he said, "If thine eye be single, thy whole body shall be full of Light."

In the halo is inscribed the signs of contemplation from six different paths: the symbols of Yin and Yang from Taoism; a description of the magnitude of Brahman from Hinduism; the watchword of the Jewish faith, "Hear of Israel, the Lord our God, the Lord is One"; the Tibetan Buddhist mantra, "Om Mani Padme Hum"—a prayer for the unfolding of the mind of enlightenment; Christ's words of the "Lord's Prayer" in Latin; and a description of Allah along with the Islamic prayer, "There is no God but God, and Mohammed is his messenger." I have attempted to present the spiritual core of light that transcends, unites, and manifests in the various religious paths.

THEOLOGUE

Theologue: During deep meditation, I entered a state where all energy systems in my body were completely aligned and flowing; it was in this state that I envisioned *Theologue*— the union of human and divine consciousness weaving in the fabric of space and time in which the Self and Its surroundings are embedded. I was wearing a Mindfold (a lightweight, inexpensively produced, sight and sound deprivation unit that combines a blindfold with earplugs), which allowed me to stare into total darkness. I peered into an infinite regress of electric perspective grids that radiated from my brain/mind and led to the horizon. A mystic fire engulfed me. Across the horizon, all I could see were perspective lines going into deep space. I was seeing both the perceptual grid of my mind on which space and time are woven, and the Universal Mind that was both the source and weaving loom. At this moment, faintly, a mountain range appeared. Transparent, but present, the mountains formed a vast and beautiful panorama and then disappeared back into the grid.

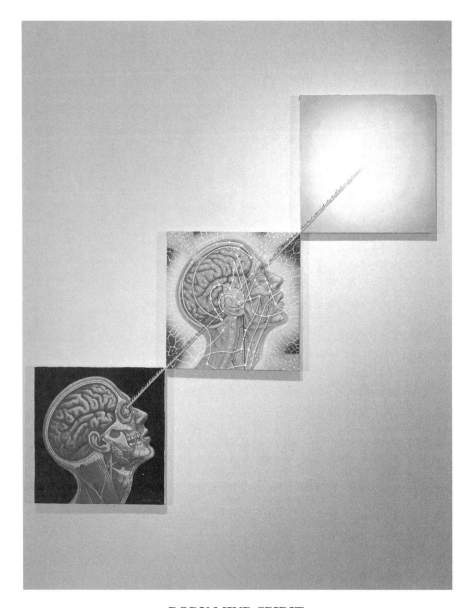

BODY MIND SPIRIT

Body Mind Spirit is a simple three-step painting that visually evokes the hierarchy of ascending dimensions of reality. The bright Light of spirit shoots its flames through the subtle energy of the mind, penetrating into, and animating, the dense physicality of the body.

PACKING SLIP:
Amazon Marketplace Item: Experiencing the Soul: Before Birth, During
Life, After
Death [Paperback] by...
Listing ID: 0604H060268
SKU:
Quantity: 1

Purchased on: 22-Jun-2005
Shipped by: lkcrowell@hotmail.com
Shipping address:

Ship to: Sandra K. Steffensmeier
Address Line 1: 115 Grassnut Court
Address Line 2:
City: Roswell
State/Province/Region: GA
Zip/Postal Code: 30076
Country: United States

Buyer Name: Matthew S. Boles

BIRTH

Birth: From a functional perspective, birth is the opposite of death in that at the time of birth, the soul *enters* the physical world through the vehicle of the biological body. At the time of death, the soul *exits* the physical world and vacates this biological body. From the perspective of the soul's experience, however, birth and death both share a sacred interdimensional quality. In this painting, I depict the birth process, wherein a tremendous flow of energy goes through the mother. In the throes of childbirth, the mother emits a scream that echoes from her own birth, to her own death, portrayed as silhouettes to either side of her head. The child will remain connected to the mother via a subtle heart cord, even as the umbilicus is severed.

DYING

Dying: I had a vision of dying in which a tunnel of eyes opened above me. The ecto-plasmic wisp of my consciousness was excruded through the crown of my head toward the Clear Light.

CHAPTER FOURTEEN

Levels of Consciousness— From Deep Sleep to Enlightenment
HIS HOLINESS THE DALAI LAMA OF TIBET

His Holiness, the 14th Dalai Lama, **Tenzin Gyatso,** is the spiritual and temporal leader of Tibet. He was born in a small village in Northeastern Tibet to a peasant family. In the Tibetan tradition, before the present Dalai Lama dies, he either gives hints as to where he will be reborn, or his future whereabouts in his next incarnation are discovered by advanced lamas in deep meditation, who then seek out the new Dalai Lama. When they find him, they test the young boy's memory of his previous incarnation to authenticate that he is the true successor, the next Dalai Lama. At the age of two, the (current) 14th Dalai Lama passed these tests and was recognized as the reincarnation of his predecessor, the 13th Dalai Lama.

The Tibetan people consider the Dalai Lama to be an incarnation of *Avalokitesvara*, the Bodhisattva of Compassion. A *Bodhisattva* is one who is on a path to enlightenment, who chooses—out of compassion—to incarnate on Earth to love, serve, and impart spiritual instruction.

In 1950, at the age of 15, His Holiness was called upon to assume full political power as the head of state of the country of Tibet. At the time, the invasion of Tibet by China had already begun. Despite several years of peaceful negotiations, Chinese aggression continued to increase, and the Dalai Lama, along with over 87,000 Tibetans, were forced to flee to India, where they were given political asylum. Since then, millions of Tibetans have died, and Tibetan culture and the beautiful land of Tibet is being systematically destroyed.

His Holiness received the Nobel Peace Prize in 1989 for his peaceful efforts to end the atrocities being perpetrated upon the Tibetan people. To this day, he continues to work to regain human rights and political freedom for the people of Tibet.

Tibetans refer to the Dalai Lama as "Kundun," which means "The Presence." There was certainly an extraordinary presence in the room during our private interview. Although His Holiness is not fluent in English, and it is more difficult to answer questions in his non-native tongue, for our benefit he chose to answer questions in English. Along with his simple but profound words emanated a palpable, spiritual force. This interview took place in Los Angeles, California, on June 5, 1997.

"The perfection of enlightenment is Buddhahood. Buddhas are reincarnated solely to help others, since they themselves have already achieved the highest of all levels. They are not reincarnated through any active volition of their own; such an active mental process has no place in nirvana. They are reincarnated, rather, as a result of this same innate wish to help others that allowed them to achieve Buddhahood."
— The 14th Dalai Lama of Tibet

All human beings experience different levels and states of consciousness—although they may not even be able to precisely remember experiencing these different levels in ordinary waking consciousness. This fact brings up many questions: What are these different levels of consciousness that are always working within our body? What is consciousness itself? How do we begin to recognize and identify these different states of consciousness? What training do we need to attain more awakened levels of consciousness?

First, what are some of these different levels or states of consciousness? One level of consciousness is what Buddhists refer to as enlightenment—

the fully functioning, awakened state. In this state, one experiences the luminosity of the Clear Light and the essence of mind. Even though a human being may not actively experience this, or have a conscious memory of this awakened state, this does not mean that the essence of mind and the Clear Light do not exist.

There is another state of consciousness that is called deep sleep. In deep sleep, consciousness is there, but there is no dreaming.

Then there is the dream state. This is when one dreams while sleeping. Other examples of different states of consciousness are when someone faints, when someone is in a coma, and the dissolution of ordinary waking consciousness of someone in the process of dying.

And then there are so many different levels of consciousness that can develop in meditation. Mystical experiences *do* occur in meditation, but are rather difficult to experience without special training through a spiritual teacher.

There are so many methods and spiritual traditions with which to experience these inner experiences. As far as original Buddhism is concerned, the methods to explore these deeper inner experiences emphasize the importance and intrinsic value of recognizing the Clear Light and the essence of the mind.

Frankly speaking, even if someone is motivated to meditate just out of curiosity, one can sit in meditation and have experiences of an inner world where one can have visions of the future, as well as remember the long-ago past. There are certain inner "appearances" of light and sound that can develop over time if you close your eyes in meditation in a dark room. Different lights may appear, but these different lights *are not* the Clear Light or Pure Luminosity that is described in Buddhist Tantric teachings. Only through real training over several years is it possible to increase one's awareness and reach enlightenment. It is impossible to realize this Clear Light before death unless one trains for several years.

I think it is quite interesting to investigate and probe into these inner appearances, these inner worlds. The exploration of these phenomena of mind extends our experience and attitudes beyond just external things. Experiencing the various states of consciousness and activities of the mind give us an indication that there are indeed certain mysterious, mystical levels we can experience. A lot of people do not know this and have not explored this, so, on that basis, it is good to experience these things.

Buddhism is one of the spiritual traditions that believes in the continuation of mind after physical death and the theory of rebirth over many lifetimes. Although there are some differences among various traditions, Buddhism believes that rebirth is essentially self-created—rebirth is caused by the propelling forces of the continuation of mind under the influence of ignorance. Under the influence of ignorance, birth and death are out of control and come again and again. As long as the grosser levels of body and mind are still there, physical rebirth takes place. When gross impressions are gone and only the subtle body and subtle mind remain, we can no longer make a distinction between life, death, or birth in the ordinary sense. At this point, physical rebirth ends, but the subtle body and subtle mind remain until reaching nirvana. Nirvana, or enlightenment, means no more birth under influence of ignorance. So that's the Buddhist concept [big laugh]!

"Thine own consciousness, shining, void, and inseparable from the Great Body of Radiance, hath no birth, nor death, and is the Immutable Boundless Light."
— Padmasambhava, in *The Tibetan Book of the Dead*

CHAPTER FIFTEEN

The Soul's Need for God
SRI DAYA MATA

Sri Daya Mata is the foremost living disciple of Paramahansa Yogananda. Since 1955, Daya Mata—whose name means "mother of compassion"—has served as the spiritual leader and president of Self-Realization Fellowship, the international, nonprofit, nondenominational religious organization founded by Yogananda in 1920. Born and raised in a Christian home in Salt Lake City, Utah, Daya Mata embraced the monastic life under the guidance of Yogananda in 1931 when she was only 17 years of age. She is the author of two books: *Finding the Joy Within You* and *Only Love.*

On October 9, 1997, I was granted a rare two-hour film interview with Sri Daya Mata. I will never forget the unmistakable fragrance of Divine love that emanated from this great soul. Her humility, joy, and powerful presence were extraordinary. I didn't need to sleep for two days afterwards.

This chapter presents excerpts from the film interview, together with additional thoughts that Sri Daya Mata later shared with me.

> *"What a vast world of love and joy is within the soul!*
> *We don't have to acquire it; it is already ours."*
> — Sri Daya Mata

When I was about eight years old, growing up in my hometown of Salt Lake City, I discovered that if I sat very still, with my eyes closed, suddenly a beautiful light would form in the middle of my forehead. It fascinated me and always gave me a great sense of peace and calmness. I thought, *What is this light that I see?* Only later, after I met Paramahansa Yogananda at the age of 17, did I understand that what I was beholding was the light of the spiritual eye—the "single eye" [Matthew 6:22] of divine perception through which one can see into the higher realms of God's creation, into the supernal light and beauty beyond this material plane. That is the light that some people perceive when they leave the body at the time of physical death.

"My child, this is death. Are you ready for it?"

In his book *Autobiography of a Yogi,* Paramahansa Yogananda gives a detailed description of the subtle realm of light and energy to which the soul goes after death. When you glimpse that finer world, you will find what he says to be absolutely true. It is far more beautiful, more glorious, than this world. Having had that experience myself, I know that death is not something to be afraid of, for it is indeed the portal to a higher plane of existence.

Once many years ago, I was suddenly stricken ill. The night before, I had been meditating for six or seven hours, and all that day I was in a state of great bliss because of that long and deep meditation. It persisted throughout the medical crisis I went through. After being taken to the hospital, I was rushed into emergency surgery. Although I was given a general anesthetic, I remained acutely aware of the doctors and everything that was going on in the operating room. Intuitively, I felt that I'd been misdiagnosed. My condition was actually much more serious than the doctors thought. When they began operating, I heard one of them say, "Uh-oh," and knew he had discovered the mistake. It was at this moment that the whole room lit up with that beautifully peaceful, radiant light of the spiritual eye. Gradually it expanded until it seemed to fill all space. At the same time came the great, comforting sound of the *Aum,* or Amen, spoken of in the scriptures as "the sound of many waters" [Revelation 1:15]—the cosmic vibration that creates and sustains all things. That blessed sound of the *Aum* just poured over my being.

Then I heard the sweet, loving voice of the Divine Mother: "My child, this is death. Are you ready for it?" Without hesitation, I replied, "Oh yes, Mother. I see ahead, and it is so beautiful in that other world, so full of joy. And I look back over this world—it is so gross, so material, so full of pain and sickness and disease and darkness. Let me go on." Again She spoke so sweetly: "But if I ask you to stay for Me?" I said, "Divine Mother, my life is Yours. Whatever You wish." Then She just soothed my soul—that is the only way I can describe it. "All right, my child. Now sleep." And I lost consciousness.

After the operation, the doctor came to see me. "Well, young lady," he said, "you gave us a fright. We didn't think you would live. When you're feeling better, I'd like to talk to you." Later, he asked me, "What is your belief?" "Why do you ask?" I said. He replied, "Do you know, throughout that entire operation you kept repeating again and again, with such deep feeling, 'My God, my God, dear God.' We doctors were deeply moved by it." One doesn't like to speak of such sacred experiences, except that they serve as an inspiration and a reminder that death need not be feared.

Of course, it is not necessary to die, or come close to death, in order to perceive the inner light or hear the cosmic sound or to feel the great comforting peace that they bestow. You can have that divine experience at any time. But it doesn't come just by wishing for it. There is a stillness of the mind and body that is needed. That stillness is cultivated in meditation.

"The Peace Which Passeth All Understanding"

We spend so many hours of every day indulging in material things when, in fact, we are not material beings. We are spiritual beings. You and I are in these physical bodies now, but these outer forms are not us. Each of us is an immortal soul, an indestructible spark of Spirit, dwelling temporarily in the body. Through meditation we begin to realize this—to find out what we really are.

Meditation is a deeper form of communion than ordinary prayer. Often when people pray, they concentrate on externals. They ask God to fulfill some need—a new car, a job—or to help them with some problem or to bless others. Meditation, rightly practiced, means to withdraw all of our attention from the world, in order to immerse ourselves in the Divine Presence. The energy and awareness that are usually directed outward, to physical activities and sensory perceptions, are redirected within. The body becomes still, the breath slows down, and the mind becomes interiorized to such an extent that everything else—thoughts, emotions, and sensations—recedes into the background. We enter into a state of great peace—the peace "which passeth all understanding," as the scripture says. That peace is the first sign of God's presence.

"Where Am I Going with My Life?"

Whether we are conscious of it or not, we all have a deep need to know God. People seek escape in physical pleasures, in sensual pleasures, but there's always something missing in their lives, always some emptiness. They can fall desperately in love, and after a few years they say, "What's wrong?" Look at all the divorces today; look at all the tragedies. That void can never be filled by another person. In the ultimate sense, God is the love, the complete satisfaction and fulfillment, that every human being is seeking.

Once a very wealthy and well-known person came to me, and she said, "I'm so unhappy; I'm so tormented. I need to know more about your teaching and what you believe." I started to talk with her about God, and she turned on me: "Don't you ever mention that name to me!" she exclaimed. So I didn't use it anymore. I spoke instead about the importance of her making certain changes in her life. One day I asked her, "Would you like to meditate with me?" She said she would, so we meditated for a while and then afterwards quietly walked outside in the evening air. "Do you know what I was inwardly saying?" she confided. "I was saying, 'I want to love You, God. I want to know You, God.'" And from that day, she changed; she was a different person.

We have to start our spiritual search somewhere. Usually it starts when we reach the point where we have had so many disappointments, so much pain and heartache, that we say, "I can't take any more." Then we begin to ask ourselves: "What is my life all about? Where am I going with my life?"

The Experience of Spiritual Ecstasy

There are so many pressures in this world. We all need to find some time to meditate, to be alone with God and feel His peace—even if only for a short period each day. After communing with God, we can return to our busy lives in the world and contribute in a more constructive, joyous way.

In deep meditation, we discover a spiritual nourishment that nothing material can give us—an inexpressible peace and well-being, a profound awareness of the Divine in everything. We realize that there is an unbroken link between ourselves and the One who is sustaining us every moment. These are just words. But when you meditate, you see this, you feel it. Not in imagination, but through direct perception. Then you begin to understand, "This is what I truly am. I am peace. I am joy. My nature is love, compassion, unselfishness."

In the highest state of God-communion—the state of *samadhi,* or what the Christians call spiritual ecstasy—a whole new world opens up to you. You suddenly see that you are not this little being, cramped in this physical body. You are something far greater than that. Your consciousness expands beyond the body, beyond this temporal realm. You behold a world of great joy—such intoxicating bliss, such overwhelming love of God. And you say, "Oh, my God, if only people knew what You are! If just once they knew the joy! You are the Love that is expressed through all human forms of love. Why can't they know?" And He replies, "I could give them that experience in an instant. But they must want it. I gave them free will; I am not going to force them. They must make the effort to change the direction of their lives."

So you see, yearning for God is the first step toward communion with Him. In time, you become conscious of that blissful presence of God—not only while you are meditating, but throughout all your activities as well.

The Role of an Enlightened Teacher

One can speak about God and try to explain what it is like to experience His presence. But it is only intellectual unless it leads beyond words to actual experience. I can tell you what a jackfruit tastes like. I can tell you how it looks, what it feels like, that it's sweet. But you won't know the taste. Yet if I take one little piece of that jackfruit and put it to your lips, you will say, "Ah, now I understand!" You have perceived it directly, and that's the difference.

Through the centuries, saints and sages of all the great religious traditions have described their experiences of God. But merely hearing such accounts will not enable us to know Him. We have to learn how to experience what they have experienced. In any field of endeavor, it is helpful to have the guidance of someone who is a master in that field. Similarly, in our spiritual quest, we need a qualified guide—one who can light the path before us and lead us in our soul's journey back to God, because he himself has trod that path and knows the way.

In my youth, I used to think, *Everybody talks about God, but doesn't anyone love Him? Why do I always hear that He's going to punish us? Why do I always fear that He's judging us, that He's off in the distance? Why can't I know Him if I'm part of Him?*

These questions remained unanswered in my heart until years later, when I first met Paramahansa Yogananda. As I stood at the back of the crowded auditorium where he was speaking in Salt Lake City, I became absolutely transfixed. I thought, *This man loves God as I have always longed to love Him. He knows God.* And from that moment I vowed: *Him I shall follow.*

When I came to live in the *ashram,* the monastic community that he had founded in Los Angeles, I saw firsthand: Here is one who not only talks about the life Divine—he lives it. That impressed me deeply. I had always been a "doubting Thomas." All my life I'd had to prove things for myself. I didn't accept blindly whatever anyone told me. But Paramahansa Yogananda didn't expect his students to just accept what he said. Through the science of meditation that he taught, and the example of his Godly life, he showed us how we ourselves could come to know our soul's oneness with God.

The role of a true guru, a God-illumined master, is to lead other souls to the same enlightened consciousness that he himself has realized. There are many who call themselves gurus, but that doesn't mean they really are. A person cannot choose to be a guru. It is a very serious responsibility, not to be taken lightly. The guru is one who is ordained by God to help and guide the disciple all along the way—through life and death, through many lifetimes if necessary—until that soul attains its own liberation.

I always feel a little concerned when someone regards himself as a great teacher. The truly great never think of their own eminence. Paramahansaji had such a beautiful humility. That inspired me, because I believe that the spiritual path is a path of humility. Every saint I have ever met or read about has expressed that Divine quality. There are some people who tell you how humble they are. When they say it, that *in itself* is an egotistical expression; it's not humility. My own observation is that a true spiritual teacher will always turn your mind away from himself and toward God.

From age to age, God's great enlightened ones come on Earth to awaken our hearts more fully to the reality of His presence and His love. The influence of these Divine teachers does not die with their physical passing. Their spiritual help and blessings are ever with those who dwell on their words and their lives, and who strive to live by their teachings.

Living the Life Divine

"Know ye not. . .that the Spirit of God dwelleth in you?" [I Corinthians 3:16] Indeed it does; we are part of Him! We think that *we* are beating these hearts, that *we* are taking in this oxygen, that *we* are running these bodies. No, it is *God* who is doing all of this. When that understanding comes, it makes you humble. It makes you realize, "Lord, You are the Doer, not I. I am nothing—and yet I am everything, because I am made in Your image. You created me. You gave me the power to think, You gave me the power to reason, You gave me the power to love. I could not do any good in this world except that You have given me that blessing."

How do we realize this? It's a gradual process of evolution that we have to go through. Some will resist it, some will mock it, and some will make an effort to change. But eventually every soul will embark on that Divine journey.

Begin where you are. Whatever your spiritual practice is, practice that. But be sincere about it and be concentrated. That is vital. And follow the universal principles that are stressed in the scriptures of both East and West. Let your mind dwell on: "What can I do for others? How can I be honest, truthful, straightforward? How can I be kind? How can I be generous and unselfish?" These are principles that lead us Godward.

It is important that we break down sectarian barriers and get down to the real spiritual teachings of the Great Ones. That's different from all of the outer rituals and symbols. These have their place, but there is a deeper search for God that we must undertake. When we leave this world, the Lord isn't going to say, "Now, you Christians, you go over here; you Hindus, you go over there; and you Buddhists, get in this line." He's going to say, "How did you behave? What did you do with your life?" That's what will be of importance to Him.

Let's practice what Christ taught, what Buddha taught, what Krishna taught—love for God and for God in every being. We need to spread the universality of God's love, of God's light—by our own example, by how we live our lives. Yes, there is darkness in this world. There's a great tug-of-war going on—between good and evil, darkness and light. But the light will prevail. God will never permit His world, which He created, to be over-taken by evil. His goodness and love are a greater force. That Divine Love is the most powerful force in the universe.

Shortly before Paramahansa Yogananda left his body, he spoke these words to me, which I will never forget: *"Be absorbed night and day in the love of God,"* he said, *"and give that love to all."*

"Find friendship with your true Self, the soul, in the sanctum of daily meditation; and after deep communion with God in the bower of peace, give divine friendship and goodwill to all."
— Paramahansa Yogananda

Sri Daya Mata in deep, Divine communion.

CHAPTER SIXTEEN

Experiencing the Soul in Meditation
SANT RAJINDER SINGH

Sant Rajinder Singh is an internationally recognized spiritual teacher and master of meditation who offers free meditation seminars and spiritual guidance for people who wish to experience their souls while maintaining a balanced life in the world. He is head of the Science of Spirituality, a non-profit, nondenominational organization dedicated to creating human unity through the cultivation of inner and outer peace.

The method of meditation taught by Sant Rajinder Singh has been endorsed by civic, educational, religious, and spiritual leaders worldwide; and he has received numerous awards, tributes, and honorary welcomes for his benevolent work. His publications have been translated into 50 languages, and he is president of the 16th International Human Unity Conference. I have personally had the honor of meeting Sant Rajinder Singh several times, and cannot adequately express in words the powerful spiritual presence that can be felt in his company. Sant Rajinder Singh resides in Naperville, Illinois; and Delhi, India. This chapter is excerpted from his book, *Inner and Outer Peace Through Meditation.*

*"We do not have to wait for physical death or an accident
causing a near-death experience to travel into the realms within.
Through a scientific method of meditation, we can learn how to come
and go at will through this inner door. All those who have had near-
death experiences describe a world of Light. We must remember that
these people are just entering the threshold of the spiritual world,
and then they are sent back to their bodies to continue in life.
But those who meditate can cross beyond the threshold and
explore more of those inner regions. The Light which people
describe in their near-death experiences is merely the
beginning. As one makes further explorations, one
finds regions of Light even brighter and more ethereal."*

— Sant Rajinder Singh

Some people have near-death experiences as a result of an accident.
There are other people who have an experience of the worlds beyond in
the period before they die. It gives them a sense of peace to know that there
is an afterlife. More and more investigations into this phenomenon have
been taking place. These out-of-body experiences might be new to the scientific community, but we find references to them in the lives of great saints
and mystics who talk about the sojourn into the beyond, their flights into
spiritual regions where there is nothing but bliss, love, and beauty.

Those who make a comparative study will find that accounts of these
experiences of life after death have been described in various scriptures and
traditions of different religions. The founders of some of the world's religions and faiths have spoken of their journeys into the beyond. We find references to life beyond and to the great Light beyond. In the Bible we read
of the entrance into the beyond:

*Enter ye in at the strait gate...Because strait is the gate, and narrow
is the way, which leadeth unto life, and few there be that find it.*
[Matthew 7:13-14]

The Gayatri, the 10th mantra of the 16th sutra in the 3rd mandala of the
Rig Veda, says:

Uttering the sacred symbol "Aum,"
Rise above the three regions,
And turn thy attention to the All-Absorbing Sun within.
Accepting its influence, be thou absorbed in the Sun,
And it shall in its own likeness make thee All-luminous.

Guru Nanak in the Jap Ji wrote:

Sach Khand, or the Realm of Truth,
Is the seat of the Formless One,
Here He creates all creation, rejoicing in creating.
Here are many regions, heavenly systems and universes,
To count which were to count the countless.
Here, out of the Formless,
The heavenly plateaus and all else come into form,
All destined to move according to His Will.
He who is blessed with this vision,
Rejoices in its contemplation.
But, O' Nanak, such is its beauty that to try to describe it is
to Attempt the impossible.
[Jap Ji, Stanza XXXVII]

Previously, any study or discussion of the afterlife in mainstream society was limited to the domain of religion. No mention of it was made in schools, in the media, or even in hospitals. If people had any experiences, they kept quiet for fear of being labeled "mentally ill" or as having hallucinations. But once doctors and scientists began finding cases of near-death experiences and documenting them, they found that it was happening to such an overwhelming number of people that they could not dismiss the evidence any longer. Personality assessments revealed that the people having these experiences were normal, reliable individuals. The investigations by the doctors showed startling similarities that crossed the boundaries of nationality, religion, and social backgrounds.

People who came from different religions and from different countries, who had never heard of near-death experiences, were describing the same incidents. Today, these experiences have been given considerable attention by the media and have become a popular topic of conversation within medical circles. This has opened up our thinking to new dimensions that occur concurrently with our own physical world.

Can We See Inner Light Without a Near-Death Experience?

With this increased interest in near-death experiences comes another study. People are beginning to wonder whether it is possible to reach these realms beyond *without* having near-death experiences. If these worlds of Light are occurring simultaneously and people are continually entering them through near-fatal accidents, then why can't we enter them at other times?

This question may be new to modern scientists, but it is not new to many in the East, to New Age thinkers, or to those who study yoga and meditation. In fact, having experiences of the beyond is one of the main purposes of meditation. Meditation provides an easy method to rise above the body easily and naturally. Students of this science have been able to have contact with the inner Light. This Light is not there only for those who pass through the gates of death at the end of their lives. It is awaiting each one of us to discover during life as well.

Just as inner Light is one of the main features of a near-death experience, it is also referred to repeatedly by those who rise above the body through meditation. Mystics and saints of various religions provide us with numerous references to the inner Light. Descriptions of divine Light and of heavenly realms are given in the Bible. Christ has said, "If thine eye be single, thy whole body shall be full of Light." [Matthew 6:22]

Sant Kirpal Singh (1894–1974), a great saint and master of meditation, also refers to this inner Light and Sound:

> The (spiritual) aspirant sees the real Light within him, whereas normally the inner eye is covered by a thick veil of darkness. He then realizes that the tradition of the lighted candle found in churches and temples is to remind him of the divine Light of Heaven within. This Light grows to the radiance of several suns put together as he advances on the way. He understands that the unceasing internal Sound he contacts within is the Divine Link called "Word"

by Christ, "Kalma" and Nida-I-Asmani" in the Koran, "Nad" in the Vedas, "Udgit" in the Upanishads, "Sraosha" by the Zoroastrians, and "Naam" and "Shabd" by the saints and masters.

It was in the 15th century in India that great saints such as Kabir Sahib and Guru Nanak began teaching the practice of meditation as a science. They taught that the art of rising above the body to experience the beyond is a science that could be practiced by anyone, irrespective of one's religious background. Thus, they taught this method to both Hindus and Muslims alike. Their tradition has been carried on, and, since that time, the practice of meditation has been given out as a method that can be followed by people of all religions and nationalities and from all walks of life. Through this method, we can enter these spiritual regions and find peace, happiness, and bliss.

In this technique, one can see the inner Light naturally, without having to have a near-death experience. It is a process that can be performed daily in the comfort of one's own home. Many regularly see the Light within. Absorption in the Light helps them transcend the physical body and begin to explore the beyond. Through meditation, one can travel into the beyond and enjoy the same bliss and love as described by those who had near-death experiences.

All those who have had near-death experiences describe a world of Light. We must remember that these people are just entering the threshold of the spiritual world, and then they are sent back to their bodies to continue in life. But those who meditate can cross beyond the threshold and explore more of those inner regions. The Light that people describe in their near-death experiences are merely the beginning. As one makes further explorations, one finds regions of Light even brighter and more ethereal. Here in this world, we could never imagine a light brighter than the sun. Those who have come back from clinical death describe a Light still more brilliant that does not hurt the eyes. Similarly, there are regions of Light yet brighter than those described by people who have had near-death experiences.

Inner Regions

Explorers of the inner realms, such as the great saint Kabir and Soami Ji Maharaj, have described a series of inner regions of varying Lights. They also speak of inner celestial Music. As this Light and Sound current flowed out from God, it created different planes. There is the purely spiritual region of Sach Khand. Then there is the supracausal plane that contains a predominance of spirit and a thin veil of illusion. Then there is a region in which there are equal parts spirit and matter known as the causal plane. The astral plane contains more matter than the causal plane. And the physical plane on which we live is predominantly matter and less of spirit. Thus, the density of matter increased as the current flowed farther from God.

Most religions teach that we have a soul within us that survives the death of the physical body. When the body dies, the soul departs. We also recognize that the soul is of an ethereal substance and not made of the matter of which our physical body is made. Those who have had near-death experiences describe themselves as having a body of Light, and seeing other people made of Light. This is why the people in the physical world cannot see them as they hover above their hospital beds watching the doctors trying to revive them.

Scientists have begun to question whether this body of Light that rises above the world is the soul. Whether they wish to call it the soul or not is immaterial, so to speak. The fact is that this body is of spiritual substance. Mystics and saints speak of the soul as being of the same spiritual essence as God. The current of Light and Sound flowing from God is also of that essence. The mechanics of the meditation process is that of connecting the soul within us with the current of Light and Sound as a method of traveling out of the physical body. When we can bring our attention or soul to the point where it can connect with the current of Light and Sound, it will merge in it and then travel along with it to the higher spiritual realms.

Until this recent explosion of interest in near-death experiences, few had any recognition of themselves as soul. We have identified so heavily with our body and mind that we have forgotten our true essence. Soul is of the same essence as God. God is all love, joy, and peace; and our true nature is also love, joy and peace. If we can re-identify ourselves with our soul, we will be able to experience this divine Light and love within us. We will also recognize our immortality. Death of the body will no longer hold any fear for us, for we will see during our lifetime what lies beyond.

Visiting Inner Regions Through Meditation

Saints and mystics who have realized these truths have been sharing this knowledge with humanity. They teach us the method by which we can come into contact with the Light within us. That method is known as meditation on the Current of Light and Sound. The same Divine stream that flows out from God also returns to Him. It is like a royal highway back to the Lord. The entry point to that highway lies within each one of us. Saints are able to connect our soul with that highway so we can begin the journey back to our Creator.

The connection point is between and behind the two eyebrows, called the sixth chakra or the tenth door. The great saints stress the importance of concentrating on this chakra because they know our life span is short. We have only 60, 70, or 100 years to realize God. The saints exhort us to begin our concentration at the highest point in order for us to reach our goal faster. By contacting the inner stream of Light and Sound in meditation, we can travel on the Divine Current back to God.

First, we voyage into the astral plane, and we experience a region of beauty, bliss, and Light that surpasses any enjoyment in this physical world. We experience a delight and a happiness that fills our whole being.

As we continue our journey, we enter the causal plane. The bliss and intoxication becomes greater and greater as we pass through each successively higher region. When we transcend the causal plane, we reach the supracausal plane and realize we are soul. On the supracausal plane, the soul cries out, "Sohang" or "I am That." Ultimately, we reach the purely spiritual region of Sach Khand, where all veils of illusion and matter are shed; and we are pure soul, pure Light, pure consciousness. It is here that we merge back in our Lord. The drop of water becomes one with the Ocean of bliss.

This experience of merging back in God is not one of annihilation where we lose our identity. Rather it is one in which we become all-consciousness. We gain all the Light, all the love, all the knowledge, all the bliss that is God.

Our soul cannot enter spiritual realms until it becomes free from all impurities. This is a simple law. If our mind is tainted with negative thoughts, we cannot sit still for meditation. Unless we meditate with full, unswerving concentration, we will not be able to withdraw our soul to the point where we can travel on the Light and Sound into higher realms. This is the reason why mystics and saints throughout the ages have stressed the importance of leading an ethical life. Developing the noble virtues restores us to the original state of the soul when it was one with God. That state is pure spirit, pure love, pure consciousness.

We all must face physical death, but those who can rise above the physical body know that there is no death. It is merely the shedding of the physical body for a lighter, more ethereal body. It is like removing an outer coat and wearing a thinner jacket underneath. With the knowledge of what lies after this life, we also become a source of strength and comfort to those around us. We can speak with assurance when we share with others the knowledge that death is but a change from one form of existence to another.

Transformation Through the Inner Journey

As we meditate and come in contact with the source of all love within, we begin to radiate that love to others. We have read about the incredible transformation that people who have had near-death experiences have experienced. Their brief contact with the Being of Light, and their review of their lives, makes them realize instantaneously what is important. They realize that they cannot take anything with them from this physical world. The only thing that goes with them is the soul, and the record of their thoughts, words, and deeds. They see how important it is to be loving and helpful to others in this world. That is what counts in the other world. They find that the little things in life that created stress and tension do not seem to be important when they acknowledge that this physical world is not reality, but an illusion; and when they understand that their real self is not the body, but the soul. Thus, they mend their ways when they return to life. They see that there is a great purpose to life, and that purpose is to be able to realize our true selves and realize God. They see the value of loving relationships with others and of being of service to humanity in this world. They start caring for other people, trying to bring joy into the lives of their fellow human beings.

We undergo this same transformation in meditation. Love begins to radiate from us to all humanity. As we come into continuous contact with the Light and love within, that divinity begins to spread out from us to all those whom we meet.

We begin loving all those around us, and others derive great peace and solace from our presence. We become gentle and loving to all creation, including the animals and lower species of life. Just as we would never think of injuring anyone in our family, similarly, we become nonviolent and loving to all in the grand family of God. We become the abode of all ethical virtues.

If each of us learned the art of meditation, this world would be filled with people who are peaceful and kind. There would be an end to wars and conflicts. We would each attain inner peace and happiness and help radiate it to all those around us. We would not only have peace within, but we would also have peace without.

We are but drops of the same fountain of divine beauty;
We are but waves on the great river of love.

We are diverse blossoms in the Garden of the Lord,
Who have gathered in the same valley of Light.

We who dwell on this earth belong to one humanity;
There is but one God, and we are His children.

— from the poem, "The Cry of the Soul," as found in
Love at Every Step—My Concept of Poetry, by Sant Darshan Singh

PART VI

Preparing

the Soul for

a Healing

Passage

INTRODUCTION

Why Prepare for Death?

The actual moment of irreversible biological death takes less than one second. However, great philosophers and the spiritually wise have always said that *preparing* ourselves for this universal human experience *takes a lifetime.* For some people, the idea that one *can* prepare for death—or would even *wish* to—might appear to be a rather peculiar notion. Most people don't even like to *think* about death, much less *prepare* for it. Our personality-selves' psychological defense system maintains a facade of illusory security that shields us from conscious awareness of death in the unknown future.

There is, however, tremendous value and practical wisdom in opening oneself up to life in a way that transforms the more challenging aspects of the process of death into an opportunity for profound inner healing. Moving toward the acceptance of one's death is one of the strongest catalysts for spiritual growth and inner transformation available to us.

Since most of us do not as yet know when or how we will die, the wisest life plan is to *begin now* to cultivate the lifestyle patterns, mental attitudes, and specific skills that will serve us in our hour of need—*before* the body and mind suffer any diminution of their powers, and *before* any distracting and debilitating physical symptoms make it extremely difficult to stay present and conscious throughout the process of death.

In traveling this lifelong journey of preparation for death, we do not morbidly seek or hurry along death's arrival as an end in itself. Readying ourselves for death is not an escapist dress rehearsal for real life. Nor is it a wishful psychological ploy in which we keep on telling ourselves how wonderful our post-mortem existence will be in "Camp Afterlife." From working with hundreds of people in the process of dying as a hospice social worker, I can tell you that death for most people is a difficult and challenging experience. But death *can* be enriching and beautiful—despite the pain and suffering that often accompanies it—*if* we have prepared physically, emotionally, cognitively, and spiritually.

The Fear of Death

In dealing with the issue of death, there is a great paradox: To be able to live fully, we must somehow come to terms with death, especially our fear of it. Our most primary fear of death is rooted in the body's survival instinct. As far as a protective mechanism to increase our chances of dying *later* rather than *sooner,* it's a definite asset to respond appropriately to loud noises and have other physiologically based protective instincts intact. However, from the perspective of our eventual awakening to aspects of ourselves that *transcend* our biological inheritance, the fear of death, when analyzed, is *not only* built into our nervous system's fight-or-flight programming—to a large degree, our fear of death is *acquired* through parental and societal "learned" programming. This acquired fear is composed of a constellation of internalized core beliefs that—more often than not—do not support the free expression of life or help us accept the inevitability of our physical mortality. Our beliefs about death—conscious or unconscious— are part of our "inner script" that profoundly influences the way we subjectively experience our lives as well as our thoughts, words, and deeds *throughout* our time on Earth. Until our issues on death are thoroughly examined and worked out, they'll surely still be with us when death comes knocking at our *own* door!

What *do* people fear most about death? The most common fears include concern about not being able to bear the accompanying physical pain; fear of the "unknown"; fear of ceasing to exist after death; fear associated with being separated from loved ones; and a fear of hell, usually of the eternal fire-and-brimstone variety, instilled in many of us by early religious training.

The magnitude of our discomfort surrounding death exists in direct proportion to how much we've been affected by at least three main factors: 1) the extent to which we've been exposed and imprinted by modern society's negative views on death; 2) misinformation on the physiological, psychological, and spiritual processes that occur during the dying process; and 3) ignorance of the scientific evidence and inspiring testimony that supports a redefinition of death as a transition to another reality—and not the end of life.

Where is the way out from this literal "dead end" that the fear of death locks us into? Some would answer that the "way out" is the "way in"—that we can literally "dis-cover" something within us whose existence is independent of the physical brain, body, and limited personality. This "something" is the direct experience of our souls. Wisdom-teachings from time immemorial counsel us to "go within" to discover the riches of the soul— what Socrates refers to in the dictum, "Know thyself." As long as we identify ourselves as *being* our bodies—and not *having* bodies—our "fate is sealed" in the sense that this very fear of death will become a self-fulfilling prophecy.

As a result of my home visits as a hospice social worker, it has been my observation that those people in the process of dying who merely *believe* in life after death are more "at peace" compared to those who *do not*. However, I find that even the "believers" retain much of their fear of dying because *mere belief* in life after death does not necessarily make the actual process of death any easier or less painful.

In contrast, words fail to convey the qualitative difference in demeanor—most notably the absence of fear—in those who have had some *direct* experience of their spiritual nature—of their souls. These people *know*—and not merely *believe*—there is life after death. This knowingness fundamentally transforms their whole experience of life *and* death. These people know, in the words of poet laureate Rabindranath Tagore, that "death is not the extinguishing of the light; it is only the putting out the lamp because the dawn has come."

When Freed from the Fear of Death

"There is no death, Only a change of worlds."
— Chief Seattle

If we finally know—from direct experience—that the Circle of Life is *not* broken at the time of our physical dissolution, then we become liberated from the subliminal fear that has insidiously been robbing us of our life-energy all our lives.

Freed now from the fear of death, we will increasingly experience the transcendent, eternal love of the soul and God—a Love that never dies.

Freed now from the fear of death, we will see beyond and through the perception-blinding prison of the shadowy past.

Freed now from the fear of death, we will discover an unlimited source of mercy within us—we will be able to truly forgive ourselves and others.

Freed from the fear of death, we will now have the courage not only to die, but to really live for the first time.

CHAPTER SEVENTEEN

The Final Frontier:
From Outer Space to Inner Space

EDGAR D. MITCHELL, PH.D.

Edgar D. Mitchell, Ph.D., was the sixth person to walk on the moon during the historic Apollo 14 mission. Dr. Mitchell holds a doctorate from the Massachusetts Institute of Technology, was a test pilot for many experimental aircraft, and founded the prestigious Institute of Noetic Sciences. His groundbreaking latest book is *The Way of the Explorer.*

As a fascinating aside, while aboard Apollo 14, astronaut Mitchell conducted an "unofficial" experiment (not planned by NASA) in which he successfully communicated telepathically with several earthbound humans. This chapter is based on a film interview that took place in Chicago, Illinois.

"The consciousness of man has an 'extended nature' that enables him to surpass the ordinary bounds of space and time—suggesting that there is a more ephemeral informational aspect to the material world."
— Dr. Edgar D. Mitchell

The life I've lived has been one of an explorer. I've been a test pilot, a warrior in the Navy, and an astronaut. Behind all these roles was my interest in exploring unknown realms—that's what excites me the most.

Very early in my career as a pilot in war, I came face-to-face with death. I've watched several of my friends die, and I myself have been close to death upon many occasions. As a result, I found it necessary to look death right in the face and confront it. As I get older, both the thinking and the feeling side of me are now in agreement that death is in some way a transition to a mode of existence that is just as normal as the existence we experience in the physical body and physical universe. Similar to the Tibetan view, I believe that some essence of our life experience can be transferred to a new being after death.

As an astronaut, I've experienced the universe outside of this little domain we call Planet Earth. When we enter the larger domain of outer space, we can transition from being just an earthly human to being a citizen of the universe. My experience in space helped me understand that the material universe is simply a larger analog, a larger model, of our physical body.

During life, we can experience a bliss, a sense of being at one with everything in the universe—individually and collectively—and merging into a larger sense of self that encompasses all that is. If I were to further attempt to explain what this sense of greater self is, I would say that the self I feel I am in this physical body is just a small part of the self that exists—that which we call "deity."

In this greater universe, the inner experience of self expands into a sense of the magnificent, the joyful, completely unified and whole. It's a sense of self that is perceived on a grander, more magnificent scale. As a result of all these experiences, I am not afraid of death, although I'm not expectantly waiting in line in the sense of wanting to leave this world before it's my time!

Facing death has also fueled my interest in scientific research into the nature of reality. Evidence is building for what might be called a "quantum holographic model" of the universe. I have been directly involved in validating and further understanding this scientific model by conducting laboratory experiments using very sophisticated devices such as Magnetic Imaging Resonance Machines (MRIs). I discuss this research in my book *The Way of the Explorer.*

In the many roles I've played in my life, in the many things I've done, the common thread I had to transcend was the invisible boundary of fear within me. When I felt this fear, I felt shrunken, condensed, and bound. It was only when I broke the boundary of this fear that I suddenly found that there was nothing to it—this fear was a result of my own thinking. When I broke the boundary of this fear and looked back at it, it was like seeing a shadow disappear. I fully believe that our fear of death works precisely in the same way.

Some people fear the pain of death, but one thing is certain: Any pain we experience here is a very body-oriented experience. As we transfer from the physicality of this body, the pain goes with it.

Whatever our career, lifestyle, and way of life has been up to at this point, we can still learn to become explorers. Eventually, we *all* have to explore the realms beyond at the time of death. And those who have had a glimpse into these realms assure us it is a wonderful adventure. It is a place of both excitement and peace, although we really don't quite grasp or understand this fully when we are in our normal state of consciousness.

I know that when I went into space, despite the risks and the unknown aspects of the exploration, I had a faith, I had a trust, I had an excitement connected to discovering this unknown. Although I hadn't done it before, *in the very act of doing it,* my natural apprehension was overridden by the sheer excitement of discovery. I recognized that I was being freed from the pull—and even the confinement—of being on Earth. I was able to experience the freedom of "freefall"—free of gravity—an experience of space beyond the limitations of Earth—an experience of the freedom of no boundaries, no pressure, no stress, no pain. The transition of leaving the body at death is very much like the transition of leaving Earth.

So, through your own personal experience as well as understanding the testimony of others who have also made the journey, fear can be transformed into the excitement of an explorer who is able to look beyond and see what's there.

"We can easily forgive a child who is afraid of the dark; the real tragedy of life is when men are afraid of the light."
— Plato

Pictured is astronaut Edgar Mitchell, sixth man on the moon, who had a profound spiritual experience during the Apollo 14 mission. After coming back to Earth, he said, "On the return trip home, gazing through 240,000 miles of space toward the stars and the planet from which I had come, I suddenly experienced the universe as intelligent, loving, and harmonious. My view of our planet was a glimpse of divinity. . . .We went to the moon as technicians, we returned as humanitarians."

CHAPTER EIGHTEEN

"Being" in the Moment
RAM DASS

Ram Dass, also known as Richard Alpert, Ph.D., has motivated millions of Westerners to undertake spiritual practice by using his exquisite ability to communicate Eastern and Western spiritual paths in a highly understandable and entertaining way. He is a former Harvard professor, well-known teacher and lecturer, and the author of *Be Here Now, Grist for the Mill, How Can I Help?* and *Miracle of Love.* This chapter is based on excerpts from a film interview that took place in San Anselmo, California.

"Dying can be used as a profound vehicle for awakening of consciousness because as we make our transition to other dimensions at the time of death, the door between dimensions seems to be more open. This doesn't mean that the door to these other dimensions are closed at other times, just that at the time of death there is a natural shift to non-ordinary, expanded states of consciousness."

— Ram Dass

My Spiritual Awakening

I earned my Ph.D. at Stanford University and went on to teach at Harvard University as a social scientist. Back then, I was very much a behaviorist and a materialist. However, in 1961 and the years that followed, through psychedelic drugs (which were then legal), meditation, and spiritual practices, I had many profound inner experiences that opened me up to far deeper levels of reality than the Western psychological models I had been teaching my students at Harvard. I was able to connect—from the inside out—with another part of my being—one that transcended the level of the body, thinking mind, and personality.

My views on consciousness and on the continuity of awareness after death come through the experiences I've had with the various spiritual practices I've done over the last 30-plus years. I've experienced my consciousness in other domains of reality. I've had experiences in which my consciousness has been pulled out of my body so that my awareness was looking down at my body from the outside. At first, these experiences were frightening, but after a while they became familiar, comfortable.

To help me gain a perspective on what I was experiencing, I began to read a lot of the literature of mysticism. In every religious tradition I studied, I found validation and support. I discovered I wasn't alone in the experience of inner truth.

Awareness and the Thinking Mind

The idea that our thinking mind is not the primary vehicle of our awareness may seem an alien concept to many people. After all, most of us have heard or read René Descartes' famous line, "I *think,* therefore I am." At a certain point, however, one directly experiences that the "I am-ness" of awareness is distinct from thinking. Awareness *precedes* all thinking, so the thinking mind isn't the source of awareness. Awareness works *through* the thinking mind.

Awareness is like a flashlight. A flashlight usually shines on *other* things, on a book or a chair or some other object—not on itself. But when this flashlight of awareness shines back on itself, we become conscious of our own "beingness." To the extent that we experience ourselves as the light of the flashlight—and not as the objects that the flashlight shines *upon*—our awareness, or beingness, opens up into a consciousness that is primary and independent of both the body and the thinking mind. To the extent that we become free from the illusion of *being* these forms, we become liberated from the reincarnational cycle of births and deaths.

The thinking mind is just one mode of awareness of who we are. We don't sufficiently appreciate that we all move in and out of different states of consciousness many, many times every day, all through our lives. For example, this happens when our attention just "goes somewhere" in a sort of momentary lapse of focus, or when we daydream, or when we dream at night. Many of us treat these unusual states of consciousness as irrelevant, as unreal, and in some way, "in error," because they don't work to keep our sense of "somebodiness" functioning efficiently.

I feel that the main reason people are afraid of Alzheimer's disease is because they identify themselves exclusively as being their thinking minds. A woman who'd had a stroke and had lost her ability to communicate recuperated enough to be able to speak again. She told me, "I'd sit there, not being able to talk or write. Although I couldn't communicate, *'I'* was still there."

Death Is Absolutely Safe

There's an ancient story that illustrates another attitude toward the "I"—one that shows the extent to which we can identify not with the thinking mind, but with that part of "who we are" that doesn't die. It is told that there was an invading army in Asia that was devastating the countryside, massacring the local people, and killing all the Buddhist monks in a terrible way—by disemboweling them. One particularly cruel commanding general asked his assistant for a report on how the campaign was proceeding. The assistant said to his commander, "The people fear you and are bowing down in surrender to save their lives. All the monks have fled to the mountains." The commander nodded with pleasure. His assistant then added, "Except for one monk, who's still there. He refuses to leave the temple."

The commander was furious, enraged that anyone would defy him in this way. He decided he would deal with this monk personally. The commander rode up the mountain, threw open the temple gates, and unsheathed his long sword. He saw the monk standing in the middle of the courtyard, apparently waiting for him. The commander strode over and in a fierce, threatening voice, bellowed, *"Don't you know who I am? I could take my sword and run it through your belly without blinking an eye!"*

"And don't you know who I am?" replied the monk. *"I am someone who could have your sword run through my belly without blinking an eye."* It is said that upon hearing the monk's reply, the commander bowed deeply to the monk and left the temple.

For me, that story represents the meeting of worldly and spiritual power. The monk's identity with the "deathless" was so powerful that it disarmed the temporal power of the commander.

Emmanuel is a wonderful spiritual friend of mine—a Being of Light— who is channeled through a woman named Pat Rodegast. Emmanuel once told me, "Death is absolutely safe." The very idea that death could be "safe" allows us to loosen the constraints of our conceptual model about what death is. When we are able to open back up into the awareness of who we really are—of that part of us that death cannot touch—then we will know on an experiential level that "death is absolutely safe."

Emmanuel also once told me that "death is like taking off a tight shoe." I've thought a lot about that image. Most of us, for so many years, have cultivated who it is we *think* we are, our "somebodiness." So when we feel that this "somebody" is in jeopardy, that it is going to disappear or dissolve, we look at it as a loss; we fear the idea of non-existence because we're identified with the "somebodiness." Now, if death is like taking off a tight shoe, then this *"somebodiness"* represents the shoe, and what takes the shoe *off* has to be something *other* than the shoe itself.

Freeing up our awareness and opening up to a greater consciousness— *that* is what takes off the shoe of our "somebodiness." In India, they say that from the point of view of the soul, death is just the "dropping of the body."

It's clear to me that, after the body's death, the Soul or Awareness or Spirit—whatever name you call it—goes on to other planes of consciousness. There are many, many such planes. For example, there are planes of consciousness where we may meet beings we've known who have died before us. Those beings are drawn to us by our mutual love, and they have appearances that we're familiar with so that we recognize them. There's a tendency to be happy at the reunion and to get caught up in wanting to hang on to them, so texts like the *Tibetan Book of the Dead* counsel not to cling to those types of experiences, but to keep moving toward the Light, toward a nonconceptual presence *beyond* form.

As our physical form dies, the mind has a tendency to cling, to be emotionally attached to the life that was just lived. That attachment catapults us into the next form and the next form and the next form. It's all a function of *where* and *what* the mind grabs hold of in the process of dying—especially at the moment of death. In the East, that inertial force of karma is seen as the causal sequence that keeps us in the illusion of separateness. It's all a direct consequence of identifying with form.

Awakening at the Moment of Death

The process of dying can be used as a profound vehicle for awakening consciousness, because as we make our transition to other dimensions at the time of death, the door between dimensions seems to be more open. This doesn't mean that the door to those other dimensions is closed at *other* times—just that at the time of death, there is a natural shift to nonordinary, expanded states of consciousness.

From a spiritual point of view, death can be the highlight of a lifetime. All throughout our lives, we have windows of opportunity to wake up. These catalysts for growth come in various disguises, as both painful traumatic events and times of bliss and ecstasy. Most of the time, though, we awaken a bit, and then we go back to sleep. At the time of death, though, the windows open much wider, and a person who's done spiritual practice throughout life and has already opened up to expanded awareness will experience the process of death with grace and equanimity.

With that grace and equanimity comes lightness, a touch of humor. In the Zen tradition, Zen monks write a death poem before they die. One old Zen master was very close to death, and his disciples were becoming very concerned because he hadn't yet written his death poem. One by one, each disciple said to him, "Master, do not delay—please write your death poem." The Zen master picked up a brush, quickly painted a few characters, and immediately died.

His poem read:

> *Birth is thus.*
> *Death is thus.*
> *Verse or no verse,*
> *What's the fuss?*

There's a similar story about another Zen master who was also very close to death. His students, surrounding his deathbed, brought him a piece of his favorite cake. As the dying Zen master began to nibble on the cake, one of his students leaned forward and asked, "Do you have a final message for us?" The dying man said, "Yes. This cake is *delicious.*" And then he died.

These stories show the quality of lightness that can surround death. In the West, people in the process of dying are more often surrounded by friends and relatives who themselves are "frightened to death"! So the dying person's environment keeps sucking them back into the fear, keeping them trapped.

Who Are We?

It's so easy to fall into the trap of defining the dying person on the basis of their past and present social roles and their self-image. In working with people in the process of dying, it's been my job to not get trapped in this game of false identity. During the times when people are often frightened, I find that I'm able to appreciate and accept the awe and mystery of this natural process. Most of the time, I'm able to maintain a space of peacefulness, even joyfulness, in the presence of death.

The deeper I go into this work, the more I realize that the process involves meeting another person in a place that is boundary-less, where "meeting" dissolves into "being together," into a shared "beingness" with the other person. In that unbounded awareness, two become one—which itself is an expression and manifestation of a very high form of love. I try to keep my consciousness open in a way that allows the person in the process of dying to connect with it. Their consciousness flickers up into what I call "the space of non-dying"; if someone is there to meet them in that space, they can merge into a shared awareness that is beautiful. The contact can be incredible! It is a real gift to be "present" in this way with someone who is dying, because it helps create a supportive environment for them to do their inner spiritual work of preparation.

So, if someone is in the process of dying, the essence of the inner work involves the question, "Who are they, really?" Are they really "a dying person"? Or, are they simply beings, like you and me, who happen to be dying? When we identify with the latter perspective, we begin to experience a way of being in the world in which we don't resist, we don't deny. We don't get trapped in material existence—and we don't push against it. We embrace form, while our consciousness rests more and more in the formless. Our outer bodies and forms may keep changing, but "who we are" ultimately awakens out of form. It is then that one truly begins to move back into the Godhead, into the One, into Brahma, into Christ Consciousness, into Allah, into Yahweh, into whatever you want to call *"It."*

Being in the Moment

Now, with all that I've said, I want to state very clearly that I have absolutely no moral right to tell another human being what for them is a "good death," or how they should prepare for it. If someone chooses to cling to their "somebodiness"—that's up to them. Each person ultimately chooses their own way.

However, it *is* possible to use the time before our death to work through our anticipatory fear of death, to work through a review of our life history, to work with our pain and not to push against it.

Paradoxically, in the period before death, the quality of life can be heightened, even though our bodies are failing. The imminence of death can push our consciousness more fully into the moment. It's a great time to cultivate an ability to appreciate the preciousness of each moment. For many of us, throughout most of our lives, we're so busy planning for the future or thinking about the past that we keep losing the moment. Our mind isn't with the moment. It's not with really tasting the next bite of food. It's not with feeling the air across our foreheads. It's not with appreciating the petal of the flower. But the approach of death breaks through our patterns of "thinking mind."

There was a wonderful woman name Ginnie Pfeiffer who was dying of a very painful cancer. I had visited her several times, but no matter what I said in my attempt to extend some form of help, she rejected my efforts. I finally realized that we weren't going to get anywhere with our intellects. Instead, on my last visit with her, I began to meditate—to empty my mind, to get quieter and deeper and more present. I still saw her suffering, saw that her body was writhing in pain, but although I felt compassion for her situation, my job was not to get caught emotionally, but to continue to deepen my peace. At one point, as my mind grew very quiet, Ginnie turned to me and said, "I am feeling so at peace in the Universe; I wouldn't be anywhere else but here in this moment." She said that—and at the same time her body was writhing in pain! I realized that she was experiencing a sort of contact high from the meditational presence in the room. She had, in a nonverbal way, allowed her awareness to come into a place where we could be together in the moment, where she was no longer the person who was in pain— she was the awareness watching the show.

A big problem that many people confront in the process of dying is that being "in the moment" means learning how to deal with the painful stimuli that are happening in the moment. The body sends so many stimuli, so much information, that it's very hard not to get swept up in it all, to get obsessed with our bodies. Our awareness may be drawn in by a headache, then by a foul taste in the mouth, then by intestinal pains, then by a heart murmur—whatever. However, if we have cultivated the habit of living in the moment during our lives, we'll be better able to handle these stimuli. It is possible to experience pain simply as the stimulation going on in the cells of our bodies, not to isolate it and make it the enemy.

Witnessing the Event

Being fully present in the moment allows us to step back a bit and "witness" whatever is happening. Whatever comes up, we can keep bringing our awareness back into the "ah-so" of the moment. Whether it's thirst or cold or fear, the art form is to not get lost in the ever-changing phenomena. Just keep *witnessing* the phenomena. Stay in the witness, which is absolutely equanimous. The witness isn't cold; the witness is just *witnessing* cold. The witness isn't thirsty; the witness is just *witnessing* thirst.

Now, we can't stay in the witness by clutching and grabbing at it, because in the very act of clutching and grabbing, we lose the witness. The ability to stay in the witness emerges slowly, over time, by being in the "now" of each moment. If one has prepared sufficiently, when the "final exam" of death comes and the phenomena begin to speed up, one is able to stay open and say, "Ahhh, speeding up phenomena," instead of closing down around them. Each moment of living, each moment of dying, is just another moment to be in the moment with.

With practice, we begin to identify more and more with the witness, and not with the stimuli. We identify with the part of our "beingness" that's just noticing how the story is unfolding, instead of getting so lost in the center of the melodrama. Most of us live our lives as if we were the central character in some ongoing TV soap opera. And since, for many people, dying is the biggest drama in town—quite an enticing role—we can get trapped in that drama and forget about using our awareness to witness the ever-changing phenomena. The art form is to dance through the storyline of life and death— to play our parts impeccably—without becoming trapped in them. But the first step out of the trap is to realize that we are trapped in the first place.

The Hospice Movement

The hospice movement has created a very interesting shift in the way we deal with death in our society. Hospice as an institution represents an up-leveling of the medical model to include an awareness of the importance of a humane psychological environment—not only for the person dying, but also for family and friends. In the old medical model, death is seen as the ultimate failure; there's a tendency in Western medicine to try to keep a person alive at any cost, regardless of what it does to the quality of life.

When Dame Cecily Saunders started the hospice movement in England in the 1960s, she brought back into the picture children, pets, family, and friends. She created a new model that provided a wonderful psychological support system that helped the dying person feel that he or she was not going through the experience alone. It was definitely an improvement. But although there are more and more individuals within the hospice movement who are working on themselves spiritually and who relate to clients from that spiritual level, as an institution, hospice has not yet really integrated a spiritual way of working with dying patients. I very much hope that the hospice movement will bring more and more spiritual awareness to the bedsides of people who are dying. If that happens, it has the potential to spiritually transform our whole society.

A Crisis of Belief

For many people, facing death creates a crisis of belief. I think what has happened is that a lot of people have blindly accepted the belief systems offered by social and religious institutions. Those belief systems may make us feel less anxious about death and about the unknown *in the abstract,* but in the face of death or some other intense life crisis, the power of the fear overwhelms the power of the belief system. The belief system crumbles, because the belief isn't rooted in direct experience—so it's not a true knowing. People are then left with the nakedness of the moment. The deepest part of the nakedness of that moment is that we have to admit to ourselves that we just "don't know." Now that isn't necessarily bad. True agnosticism doesn't say, "There is nothing." The spirit of true agnosticism is completely open to the mystery embedded in "I don't know." And in that honest moment of truth of "I don't know," there is the potential to develop a very deep faith. Learning to be at peace with this "not knowing" is a stage in embracing the mystery of life.

Death is a mystery. Instead of seeing that mystery as some terrible thing like, *"Oh my God, not the mystery!"* I suggest that we look at it as a totally creative moment. The mystery is simply the unknown—we just "don't know." But it's okay to be in that place of "I don't know." "I don't know" can be a statement of great wisdom if we can be at peace with "I don't know" as we say it.

"The Way" within Us

We've shared many words, but "The Way" is beyond words. The Way is to be found in the silence. I invite you to begin to treasure this silence, to take all the words we've shared back inside, into a deeper silence within yourself. There is an inner space within you that *knows,* a place where nothing that I have said is really all that strange. You may not *know* that you know, *but you know*. And the way you come to that deeper knowing is through silence, through quietness. Instead of thinking of the silence as boredom or emptiness—which is only the mind *thinking* inside that silence—just go into it. Let it expand. Just be with it. Then find in yourself "what is." And it will be enough.

May you go in peace.

Those who do not know that they do not know
(and do not care to know)
Are ignorant: Pray for them.
Those who do not know that they know
Are asleep: Wake them.
Those who know that they do not know
Are children: Teach them.
Those who know that they know (and truly know),
Are realized beings: Follow them.
— Sufi saying

CHAPTER NINETEEN

The Life of the Open Heart
STEPHEN LEVINE

Stephen Levine is an internationally known workshop leader in conscious living/conscious dying, and is the author of many bestselling books, including *Who Dies?; Embracing the Beloved* (with his wife, Ondrea Levine); and *A Year to Live*. Stephen is a husband, father, and writer who for several years has counseled the terminally ill. He has worked extensively with Ram Dass and Dr. Elisabeth Kübler-Ross, and for seven years he directed the Hanuman Dying Project. This chapter is an excerpt from a film interview that took place in Sausalito, California.

"As one person put it, 'Death is just a change of lifestyles'—
an opportunity to see the cause of suffering, our clinging, and to
discover the surrender that opens the way to our essential wholeness.
Death puts life in perspective. A great gift which if received in love and
wisdom allows the clinging mind to dissolve so that nothing remains but
truth. And we become just the light entering the light."
— Stephen Levine

We think that death is the enemy. But if someone offered you a million dollars to buy your death, the condition being that you wouldn't die for the next 500 years—*no matter what!*—*who* would sell their death? We *count* on our death. Who would take the chance to be in an iron lung for another 450 years? Who would take the chance—having freed their child from death for 500 years—to risk that this child might be crushed in an automobile accident and have to live like that for 485 more years? Who would take the chance of having an enormous septic blood disease that made you feel like you wished that you would die immediately, but the disease lasted for 465 more years?

We *count* on our death. Death makes life safe. If there was no death, there would be very little risk-taking. If there was no death, there would be no sports. People would think twice before leaving their houses or traveling. If you're sometimes frightened or anxious *now* when you wake up in the morning, if there was no death, imagine what it would be like if you knew that whatever intractable pain and permanent injury you sustained that day could not be resolved for 500 years.

Death is a beneficence at the right moment. Talk about abuse, I think there would be no greater abuse than taking a person's death away from them when that was the only available surcease from their suffering.

Death is not the problem. *Living with the heart closed—that's* the problem. We think that if death weren't around, life would be *so* grand—that we could go on forever. However, going on forever, with a life of the closed heart, with a life of abuse, with a life of confusion, with a life of unkindness—is no life at all.

The poet Kabir has said, "If we're alive *now,* we'll be alive *then.*" But very few people are able to *really live* through their deaths. I don't mean they don't *survive* physical death. Some essence of who we are survives death. But people have a tendency to go to sleep on their deathbeds, to fall out of grace because of their fear of pain and suffering and their inability or unwillingness to open their hearts.

What we call enlightenment is just finally, wholly, taking birth—at last taking that other foot out of the womb; at last putting both feet on the ground; at last relating heart-to-heart to other sentient beings; at last listening, fully attending; at last serving others.

When death is not the enemy, then clarity, generosity, and courage become the way of life. Even in the process of dying, it is possible to experience deeper and deeper levels of your true nature. As you go deeper and deeper within yourself, you start to approach the deathless—that which never dies—the uninjured, uninjurable essence of being, which inhabits a body for a while, and then goes on to another. In any case, I know beyond a shadow of a doubt that this is not a belief system. This is how it is—*you survive your death!*

One of the reasons you might believe you are going to die is because you have been convinced that you were born. Yes, this *body* was born—no question about it: Face, head, skull, flesh—all born. But that which existed *before* this body, that which *inhabits* this body *now,* and that which will exist *after* this body dies, is not simply some philosophical niche. The essence of who we are—that which existed *before* this body was born—can be experienced in this millisecond, in this moment.

There is nothing even in the most horrific situation that has the power to permanently obstruct the healing we took birth for. It's true, physical pain *can* be very difficult to deal with, but nowadays, there's much more help available to us. Pain medications can help. Meditation can help by bringing a more merciful awareness to the situation and softening up resistance to pain in the body. Cultivating this kind of awareness doesn't necessarily change the *shape* of the pain, but enormously increases the *space* in which the pain is occurring so the pain becomes less of an emergency. Just the willingness to work *with* the pain softens it—and helps us move into that which we have always pulled away from. We begin to uncover levels and levels of spaciousness within ourselves. Each level, as we go deeper into ourselves, is broader and broader. This is just like the process of dying, in that each stage of the process of death *externally* seems like a closing down of bodily systems, but *internally* we become freer and freer from those systems.

A Deeper Understanding of the Roots of Illness

Zen master Suzuki Roshi was a very grounded person. He was married and lived a balanced life. When it became known that he had cancer, people began to ask him things like, "What's this cancer about?" "What's happening to you?" and "Aren't you in terrible pain?" In characteristic Buddhist style, he would say, "It's all right, you know, it's just suffering Buddha." However, according to some modern holistic notions, we think that illnesses such as cancer are always caused by some kind of imbalance. But was Suzuki Roshi an example of imbalance? No. *The fact is that people get ill, and people die.* The mind creates all sorts of reasons for these things, but the truth of why we get ill is much deeper than thinking that an imbalance caused the illness.

We hear people say, "You are responsible *for* your illness." That's baloney! You are responsible *to* your illness. Responsible *for* your illness means you isolate it, you back up from it. We say to ourselves, "I wouldn't have gotten sick if I had been a nicer person, if my children had been happier, if I'd been happier, if my wife and I had better communication." This is one way "the mind" closes "the heart." But if we can see it all with a little more mercy, with a little more awareness, we will see that that's the same old thing. Closing the heart—that's not *God's* action—that's *our* action. *And it's getting boring—the world is falling apart from that kind of separation!* Being responsible *for* my cancer surrounds it with guilt, surrounds it with fear, and surrounds it with a feeling of helplessness. The very notion that you are responsible *for* your cancer is an *anti-healing* idea and will block healing. It increases the calcified, outer ring of thought that surrounds illness and makes it difficult even for medications to work properly. Being responsible *to* your illness means you can walk to it, you can approach it, and you can embrace it. Ironically, the very concept that you are responsible *for* your cancer is not a *response,* it's a *reaction.* It is a knee-jerk, fear-based, wisdomless reaction to the true nature of how illness occurs, and how the human body and the Great Heart can deal with it.

Being responsible *to* your cancer means that you can start sending mercy and lovingkindness and softness to self and others. Responsible *to* your cancer means "I deserve to heal." Being responsible *for* your cancer means "If I screwed up this bad, maybe I don't deserve to live."

There is also a great tendency on the deathbed to think one has done something wrong to be in this situation—the mind is generally so merciless and judgmental. Our mind tells us that God doesn't love us, that we're a failure. It always concerns me when I see a mother at her child's bedside and she says, "My child was in the fits of the last throes of meningitis, and *God saved my child."* It bothers me when I hear people say things like this because what about *the other* 200,000 children that are sick that day? What about *those other* 40,000 children that starved to death that day? *Did God not love them?* One is not bad, one is not cursed, and one is not punished, by illness. When your child dies, it is not because you did something wrong. And when we are cured, this does not make us the "chosen of God." God does not protect us in this way. The work that's to be done has to be done in our hearts. Find the merciful Jesus in your heart, the merciful Buddha, the merciful sweetness of your own "great nature" that knows better. You haven't necessarily done anything wrong that made you sick.

Forgiving Yourself

Those of you now approaching death, this is the time to forgive yourself. You don't need to drag along your lifelong patterns of rigidity into the process. It's time to let go of the baggage and have mercy on yourself and others. One of the qualities that most softens our path is forgiveness—the cultivation of a merciful heart—for yourself and for other sentient beings, in that forgiveness is a letting go of resentment, but before you can do that, you must first reflect on what it would *even mean* to have forgiveness in your life. In what ways would forgiving yourself and others change your life?

Another thing about forgiveness: You really do forgiveness *for yourself*. It may *also* help somebody else—it's a very kind gesture—but when you forgive, you have more access to your *own* heart. In unforgiveness, you have taken someone and put them out of your heart—and that part of your heart is numbed. I call this numbing the "armoring over the heart." Forgiveness starts to melt that numbness. I have seen people more alive on their deathbed than they'd been in the last 50 years of their lives, because *at last* they started to respond *to* their pain, instead of react *from* it. *At last* there is mercy and lovingkindness. I see people whose quality of life increases—whose connection with their loved ones—their children, their parents, their wife, their husband, their brothers, their sisters, their friends—all increases in depth. I've seen people where the healing was so profound that *everyone* around the deathbed is healed, *including* the person *in* the deathbed, even though they go on to die and did not find physical cure.

The Distinction Between Pain and Suffering

Pain and suffering are not synonymous. Pain is a given in life. If you are neurologically whole, when you knock up against something, your nerve-net picks up sensation. If you knock up against something *hard* enough, you experience pain. If you've got a physical body, you've got physical pain. No one who ever lived experienced it otherwise.

It is the *resistance* to pain, the inability to let it come into our hearts, that creates suffering. Suffering is *not* a given in life—*pain* is. And although pain is a given in life, suffering is to some degree an option in the sense that there is something we can do about it. We can learn to soften to it. We can learn to forgive. We can learn to integrate the confusions of the mind into the wholeness of the heart.

The fact that you have a mind that has desires means that all your desires cannot and will not be satisfied. In fact, even if you could write a list of how to satisfy all your desires a week from Wednesday, by a week from Wednesday, your desires will have changed. It still won't be a wholly satisfying day. This is because at this point in evolution, if you've got a mind, the mind is capable of accepting, inculcating and imprinting conflicting conditioning. The mind says, "Have a chocolate ice cream soda." Great idea! So you have a chocolate ice cream soda. Five minutes afterwards, you say to yourself, "I wouldn't have done that if I were you." No wonder we're so crazy! The mind creates all garden varieties of suffering that so many of us take to our deathbeds.

Now, when we become clearer, it isn't that fear or doubt or anger doesn't arise anymore, but these mental states arise within a greater awareness that is so spacious that they no longer affect you in the same way. What might have been a three-month depression *before* you started forgiveness practice may cycle in miniature form for only 30 seconds. The *same* energy still arises and has the characteristics of regular depression, except that now there's nothing for the depression to hold on to! If you don't hold on to it, what's going to make it stay? It arises, has its moment, and then dissolves. There is neither the attachment of grasping to get more—positive attachment—or the attachment of pushing away to get less—negative attachment. There's simply a sense of "being with it" in a spaciousness that allows whatever arises to unfold.

When we cultivate forgiveness, we are not condoning the actions of people who have been mercilessly cruel to us. We are not saying that abuse or coldheartedness is acceptable behavior in any circumstance—that's not what forgiveness is about. But I *can* forgive someone whose heart could not yet see, someone whose heart was closed—*and that person may be me!* I *can* forgive someone who has lost touch enough with their own great heart to act out and have their pain spill out onto someone else.

Now when I speak about forgiveness, I'm not saying that one should have to forgive a literal "torturer." Most people—thank God—were *not* tortured in the Cambodian "Killing Fields" and were *not* strung up in a prison for 15 or 20 years. *But some were.* And it is absolutely merciless for those people to try to force this type of forgiveness on themselves, because if you try to forgive the person who has caused the most damage in your life without building up incremental capacities to forgive, what you're going to do is end up turning guilt and self-hatred back on yourself. Have mercy on yourself. Don't make this type of forgiveness into another opportunity not to forgive yourself. But when forgiveness *is* appropriate, it will allow a spaciousness and an evolutionary process of growth in your life to continue unabated.

In a very real sense, your true nature, your deathless nature, your Godhead, your essence—whatever you want to call it—is like the sun shining. There is nothing we need to do to make the sun shine, but any number of things, even very minute things—a cloud passing by, a wavering leaf, a shade pulled—can block our reception to the sun. The sun-nature in us—in its true radiance—is always untrammeled, untouchable, unchangeable. But our capacity to receive, to accept, and to experience this sun-nature is very much conditioned by circumstances. When we start to see what those circumstances are, when we start to see how painful it is to live with a closed heart, we start to give ourselves permission not to suffer.

If you are approaching the deathbed and you want to minimize suffering, you're going to encourage forgiveness practice. Forgiveness is a letting go and opening up to that which gives you more access to yourself. You're leaving the world behind. You'll be going to some very interesting spaces. Who needs to drag unneeded baggage along one more moment?

Carrying this old baggage is a little bit like being in the theater and the people behind you will not shut up. And it turns out that the people behind you represent the chattering of your own old resentments, your own old holdings, your own old confusions. That chatter keeps us from the stillness where we discover that there are no boundaries to our beingness, to our true nature.

The Nature of Desire

It sometimes happens that at certain stages of the process of inner exploration, some people get a bit confused because they are searching for a "solid center" within them. The truth is that if you look inside, *there is* no solid center—and you'll go crazy, be pretentious, stiff, and unavailable to love if you try to pretend you have a solid center. Our center is *space.* Our center is the deathless, untrammeled, uninjurable essence of being, which does not depend upon a body for its existence. *In fact, it's the other way around:* We think that our existence depends on the body, when in reality the body depends on the essence of our being. When our essence leaves, the body collapses and instantly becomes a disposal problem. This consciousness, this essence, is unaffected by conditions, but our capacity to experience this essence is very much affected by conditions.

All anger, all fear, all doubt is a reaction, as opposed to a response. A reaction to not having something is frustrated desire. If you had no desires, you wouldn't have fear, you wouldn't have anger, you wouldn't have doubt. These mental states are all based on unsatisfied desires: Desires to have or not to have, desires to be saved—even desires to treat human beings with kindness and to be treated the same way ourselves—these can all give rise to anger, fear, and doubt.

Desire is not "wrong"—as so many people in religious confusion would have us believe. Desire is simply painful. At the very root of the nature of desire is the experience of "not having." The more you want something, the more you don't have that thing that you want. The more you want something, the more the present moment is unacceptable because it does not contain the object of your desire.

The very nature of desire is dissatisfaction. But here's where it gets interesting: What happens when we *get* what we want, whether it be a car or friend or whatever? Let's say that the object of one's desire is coming closer and closer. What's interesting is that as it comes closer, instead of becoming quieter, instead of settling down, my belly is getting tighter, and my blood pressure goes up. The *more* I want, the *less* happy I am. How fascinating. And then it happens. We say, "Oh, I've got it, I've got it!" And in that very moment, we experience a state of mind we call "satisfaction." This state of satisfaction lasts but a brief instant. As soon as we have it, then this object of pleasure becomes something we have a tendency to protect. We now think, *What will happen to it? Will I lose it? Oh, my gracious, I dropped it. It's broken.* So the object of pleasure can instantly become an object of displeasure, of dissatisfaction, when it is withdrawn or destroyed.

What was it that we were trying to get? It *wasn't* the diamond ring we were trying to get. It *wasn't* the car we were trying to get. We were trying to get the experience we call satisfaction. What happened in that instant of satisfaction? *Desire was absent—that's what happened!* You got what you wanted—for a millisecond. The wanting mind, the clinging mind, the agitated mind, opens up like the Red Sea at the moment of the satisfaction of desire—and what shines through is a glimpse of your true nature, what is called satisfaction, that which doesn't die. That same opening to the moment can occur in death if we flow and expand into the process.

So satisfaction occurs in the moment of the absence of desire, when the mind is not congested with desire. It is a sense of the space in which desire floats. It's a sense of your wholeness, of your greatness. It's very interesting, this thing called desire. In fact, some people believe that the very addiction to satisfying desire is connected with a deep and profound homesickness for God. That sense of satisfaction is a taste of the Divine, of the sacred, of your own great nature when it's no longer obstructed by the clouds of desire, fear, and anger; when it's no longer blocked by grief, when it's no longer clinging or conditioned by circumstances.

When conditions no longer block your true nature, love is self-effulgent, just like the sun that just shines and you don't have to do anything to receive its rays. I don't like the term *unconditional love*. A better term for unconditional love is *unconditioned love*. When you start to work on your grief, you start to see what obstructs the sun of your own great nature. Qualities such as forgiveness, softening, mercy, and awareness become your real comrades on the path to becoming healed and whole. If someone becomes more whole before they die, healing has taken place.

The Distinction Between Healing and Cure

I'll share a story about a woman I knew who was dying in a hospital. She had lived her life in considerable separation and rejection of the people around her. She was so unpleasant to everybody that she hadn't seen her grown children in several years. She had *never even met* her grandchildren because her grown children were not about to bring their own kids to visit her and have them verbally abused.

This woman arrives in the hospital in a very advanced stage of cancer. No matter who enters her room, she blames them or complains to them about something. It's *their* fault she's in pain. It's *their* fault she's sick. She's just horrific to her hospital attendants, saying awful, critical things to them, throwing bedpans, screaming at people. In the nursing station, they call her "that bitch on wheels in Room 201." All her power plays are very negative and hurtful. Because of this abuse, the nurses, doctors, and attendants gradually spend less and less time with her, as they don't want to be in her room any longer than absolutely necessary. This woman, clearly unable to contain her pain, is fighting the whole world. It's the only way she knows—let's not judge her.

Her cancer had infiltrated her bones at the base of her spine and spread out to her lower back, pelvis, and the large bones of her legs. One very early morning before dawn, she's in great pain while lying in bed and ringing the bell to call for help, but apparently someone else is being attended to and it's taking a long time for the nurses to get to her room. She later told me, "The pain in my back, in my hips, in my legs was so great, I couldn't stand it. I just let myself go, and I sank under the waves of this pain." This might have been the most surrender, the most letting-go, the most "entering into herself" that she had ever experienced in her entire life.

She then said, "A moment later, I experienced myself lying on a bank of a river in Africa with my water jar broken next to me. My skin was black. A huge boulder had rolled off the hill and hit me in the back. I was dying alone by this river with a crushed back. There was enormous pain in my back, in my hips, in my legs."

She continued. "A millisecond later, there I was, as an Eskimo woman dying in childbirth, with enormous pain in my back, in my hips, in my legs. A moment later, there I was again, lying on my side on a urine-stained mattress, yellow with hepatitis—a young woman dying from the effects of using heroin. Then I was a woman lying on a dirt floor in a grass hut, starving to death, and my infant baby is sucking at my slackened, empty breast. We are both dying of cholera, lying on the floor—with enormous pain in my back, in my hips, in my legs."

She said she didn't know how long these experiences lasted, probably an hour and a half or so. She told me she experienced the "10,000 women in the throes of death." When she came out of that experience, her heart was no longer closed. She said, "It was no longer *my* pain but *the* pain." The pain was no longer just hers—she experienced the universal pain shared by the 10,000 other women dying around the world at the same moment, with similar discomfort in their backs, in their hips, and in their legs.

After this life-transforming experience, she became the heart of the hospital. I have never seen such a healing in all my life. The nurses started spending time in her room on their breaks. Two days later, there she was, meeting her granddaughter for the first time—a little five-year-old girl with bushy red hair who was trying on Grandma's rings. And there were her sons, caring for her on both sides of her hospital bed. The love in that room was miraculous. This woman, who had lived her whole life in separation, in anger, in judgment, was now surrounded by mercy and lovingkindness.

Over the next two weeks, her life completed itself with forgiveness, connecting where she'd been disconnected, touching with an open heart that which was disheartened in herself, in the hospital, in her life. Her body did not improve—she continued to die—but her heart and mind and experience of life radically changed. I would say that even though there was no physical cure—she died two or three weeks later—hers was the most remarkable healing I've ever seen in my life.

Loss and Grief

After someone dies, in the midst of all the confusion and mystery, people very strongly experience the absence of that person. We've seen people who have done everything they could at bedside to prepare for the death—sometimes for months and even years—but I've not met anyone yet who was quite wholly prepared for the enormity of the absence that is created when someone you love very much dies. You may have done a lot of the preparation already, but when you're there, when you see it, when she's dead, when he's dead, when they're dead, it's something else altogether. The first stage of grief is filled with your inability to touch them, to feel them, to smell them, to speak with them, to gather them inside your energy, inside your life.

Another thing that arises in grief is not just the absence of the person who has just died, but the past moments of absence in your relationship.

The times when the heart *didn't* quite connect. The times when it was more important to be *right* than to be a whole human being. The times when we were just scared, when our hearts could not yet see, including the realization that somehow, perhaps inadvertently, we might in some way have contributed to that person's suffering.

So in this first stage of grief, there is often much anger, fear, remorse, self-doubt, and distrust in the process. But as people *allow* all that to be there, as people see that *all* that grief, *all* that anger, *all* that guilt, *all* that fear, *all* that doubt is just a response to loss—a certain mercy, a certain compassion, arises. And also something that is quite stunning. Even in the most abject grief, even in the deepest, darkest moments of your life—*not a single state of mind is new*—unfortunately. Certainly those states of mind didn't exist with the same intensity and duration before, but *none of them are new.* Guilt is not new. Fear is not new. Remorse is not new. Wishing you were dead is not new. None of it is new. What *is* new is that at last you cannot *deny* it. The daily ordinary grief with which we *almost* live our lives, with which we *almost* connect with other people cannot be denied anymore. Denial just can't find any place it can stick because the pain is too great. Grief feels like walking on the floor of the ocean—the whole body/mind system is laboring every moment; every breath is difficult. It's as though you pulled the plug and your life-blood is leaking out.

In many cases, it's in that first stage of grief, in the midst of that profound sense of absence and loss, that the grief of a lifetime catches up with you—*all* the moments of being absent, *all* the moments of not caring for ourselves and our loved ones, *all* the moments of struggling to stay conscious, struggling to stay a human being. But as we open to those moments, as we let those states in, we start to relate to them more and more.

When you love someone, and that someone comes into the room and says, "Gee, I love you," you say in reply, "Gee, I love you, too." When that person is nearby, you feel their energy, feel their love. But in truth, the love you feel is not coming from *them,* it is coming from *you.* The person you love is a connection to the place *inside you* that *is* love. They are a connection to your essence, to your true nature. So when that person is no longer there, when we no longer have a mirror for our heart, the God-essence within ourselves grieves. We grieve the wholeness within ourselves that they were a reflection of. They taught us to love ourselves. They taught us that we were worthy to be loved by somebody as beautiful as they were. And now they're gone from our sight, our smell, our touch.

In the first stage of grief, that sense of loss is not just the loss of a loved one, it's the loss of contact with a love *within yourself.* Our heart's mirror has been broken. Now if our love for the person who has died is not pushed away and the feelings are let in, there is a burning in the heart. This is living with the consequences of love. It burns. But what's the alternative? Not to love? Try *that* one and see how *that* works! See how much life you even *want* to live in the absence of love, in the absence of caring, in the absence of your great genius for living, your great genius for healing.

But as the initial stage of grief and absence starts to melt with the passage of time and as a result of doing inner spiritual work, there are more and more moments when the mind begins to sink into the heart. Instead of the feeling of separation, you start to experience feelings of inseparability. If you've had a loved one die, you've never before had their attention so inseparably as you do now. In your heart, you can now turn to them at *any* moment and internally connect with them. You could never do that in the same way when they were alive, when they were gone on a business trip to Toledo. You can now hold the mirror up to your heart and see your own great nature, your own care for their well-being. In building this inseparability, this doesn't mean that you don't miss them and wouldn't want to embrace and be embraced by them. What it means is that there is something that accompanies this grief that gives it a ground, a workability—the ever-present possibility of healing.

Now, if your daughter died and six months later your friends say to you, "Are you *still* grieving, aren't you *over* that yet," well, *of course* you're still grieving—grief lasts a lifetime. However, as time moves on, your essential interconnectedness and inseparability with that person is maintained, and the grief loses some of its intensity, its duration, its heaviness. But with all that, 25 years from now, if you smell a fresh piece of surgical gauze, or if you hear the dragging of a bicycle chain that sounds like the one your child had before he died, you may be transported back in time to the deathbed of your child. You're back in grief, but the duration is different, the intensity is different.

To think that grief is going to go away is to abuse yourself, to be unkind to yourself. The quality of the grief is going to change—yes. It's going to deepen, yet it may give you *more* access to life because it starts to make your priorities clearer. One of the priorities that becomes very clear on the deathbed is that nothing, absolutely nothing, is worth closing our hearts for a moment longer. When we can live our lives with our hearts more open, with more mercy for ourselves and others, we are then more available to be in the moment; we are then more fully alive.

At the time of death, very few people leave fully alive. What do I mean by this? Out of the hundreds of thousands of people who die each day around the world, how many do you think died with God uppermost in their hearts at the moment of death, with Jesus in their hearts, with love in their hearts? How many people do you think die with that kind of mercy, with that kind of lovingkindness for themselves? We tend to die the way we live, and if we haven't lived in a way that gives us some time to look into what causes us suffering, then we are kidding ourselves if we think we're going to do this inner work on our deathbed, when it's hard to concentrate and there's the pain to deal with and there's this distracting ringing in our ears and we can't digest our food and we've got diarrhea and the smells and the sounds and the tastes are driving us nuts. We're mistaken if we think we'll be able to do it then if we haven't prepared and practiced throughout our lives.

I knew a great Buddhist lama who was on his deathbed in great physical pain. At a certain point, this lama, who had spent ten years in intensive meditation in a cave, had said, "My mind is like a barking dog. My body is a charnel ground." Somebody asked him, "Well, what did you do?" The lama replied, "I had trained all my life to stay clear, so I struggled to regain mindfulness, to again become more present, and then everything was okay."

For this lama, the pain of his illness didn't necessarily go away. He had to gather up all his strength and draw upon the awareness he had cultivated over a lifetime to create enough space to regain his mindfulness. He was then able to accept his death in his heart without pushing anything away. So death's not the problem. It's learning to live our lives with our hearts open—through forgiveness, lovingkindness, and increased awareness. This is what heals us in life, and what we take with us at the time of death.

*"Death is a tax on the soul for having
had a name and a form."*
— Pir Inayat Khan

CHAPTER TWENTY

Dying Before Dying

STANISLAV GROF, M.D.

Dr. Stanislav Grof is a pioneering psychiatrist whose original research has focused on the study of psychospiritual states of consciousness and the development of "holotropic breath work," a therapeutic method of accessing nonordinary states of awareness.

Dr. Grof was president of the International Transpersonal Association, and his books include *Holotropic Mind, Beyond the Brain,* and *Books of the Dead.* This chapter is based on excerpts from a film interview, and an address that was given in Chicago, Illinois.

"For any culture that is primarily concerned with meaning,
the study of death—the only certainty that life holds for us—must be
central, for an understanding of death is the key to liberation in life."
— Dr. Stanislav Grof

W hen the ancient eschatological books of the dead—the Tibetan *Bardo Thodol,* the Egyptian *Pert em bru,* the Aztec *Codex Borgia,* or the European *Ars Moriendi*—first came to the attention of Western scholars, they were considered to be fictitious descriptions of the posthumous journey of the soul, and, as such, wishful fabrications of people who were unable to accept the grim reality of death. They were put in the same category as fairy tales—imaginary creations of human fantasy that had definite artistic beauty, but no relevance for everyday reality.

However, a deeper study of these texts revealed that they had been used as guides in the context of sacred mysteries and of spiritual practice and very likely described the experiences of initiates and practitioners. From this new perspective, presenting the books of the dead as manuals for the dying appeared to be simply a clever disguise invented by the priests to obscure their real function and protect their deeper esoteric meaning and message from the uninitiated. However, the exact nature of the procedures used by the ancient spiritual systems to induce these states remains an unexplored area.

Modern research focusing on nonordinary states of consciousness brought unexpected new insights into this problem area. Systematic scientific study of the experiences in powerful forms of psychotherapy and spontaneously occurring psychospiritual crises showed that in all these situations, people can encounter an entire spectrum of unusual experiences, including sequences in agony and dying, passing through hell, facing Divine judgment, being reborn, reaching the celestial realms, and confronting memories from previous incarnations. These states were strikingly similar to those described in the eschatological texts of ancient and preindustrial cultures.

Another missing piece of the puzzle was provided by thanatology, the new scientific discipline specifically studying death and dying. Thanatological studies of near-death states by people such as Drs. Raymond Moody, Kenneth Ring, Michael Sabom, Bruce Greyson, and Charles Flynn showed that the experiences associated with life-threatening situations bear a deep resemblance to the descriptions from the ancient books of the dead, as well as those reported by subjects in modern experiential psychotherapy.

It has thus become clear that the ancient eschatological texts are actually maps of the inner territories of the psyche encountered in profound nonordinary states of consciousness, including those associated with biological dying. The experiences involved seem to transcend race and culture and originate in the collective unconscious described by psychiatrist C. G. Jung.

It is possible to spend one's entire lifetime without ever experiencing these realms or even without being aware of their existence, until one is catapulted into them at the time of biological death. However, for some people, this experiential area becomes available during their lifetimes in a variety of situations, such as powerful forms of self-exploration including serious spiritual practice, participation in shamanic rituals, or during spontaneous psychospiritual crises. This opens up for them the possibility of experiential exploration of these territories of the psyche on their own terms so that the encounter with death does not come as a complete surprise when it is imposed on them at the time of biological demise.

The Austrian Augustine monk Abraham a Sancta Clara, who lived in the 17th century, expressed in a succinct way the importance of the experiential practice of dying: "The man who dies before he dies does not die when he dies." This "dying before dying" has two important consequences: It liberates the individual from the fear of death and changes his or her attitude toward it, and also influences the actual experience of dying at the time of the biological demise. However, this elimination of the fear of death also transforms the individual's way of being in the world. For this reason, there is no fundamental difference between the preparation for death and the practice of dying, on the one hand, and spiritual practice leading to enlightenment, on the other. This is the reason why the ancient books of the dead could be used in both situations.

"In 1975, I had a very deep spiritual awakening where
my body-awareness completely dissolved as I merged into an
effulgent, shimmering golden-white light. This white light was
similar in luminescence to the white light I experienced in a previous
near-death experience. This profound spiritual awakening showed me
from direct experience that there was no death for the Self. The body
could die, but the Self was eternal, and it would go from one phase to
another phase, unfazed. After this, in meditation, I would regularly
go down the same inner pathway and merge in the same white light
on a daily basis. So in essence, I consciously died every single day.
Over a period of time, I completely lost my fear of death. This
is what I call Divine behavior modification. To this day, I
feel very comfortable merging into the Light and,
in a sense, dying regularly."
— Dr. Gabriel Cousens, psychiatrist, from the video *Experiencing the Soul*

PART VII

The Soul at the Moment of Death

INTRODUCTION

If living life is seen as the greatest art form, then we are *all* life artists of a fashion, living out our lives in ways unique to ourselves. As physical death is equally part of life, how we die is also a highly individual affair. Just as identical twins surfing the same ocean wave do not ride out the wave in identical ways, how skillfully we ride Life's final wave is intimately connected to the quality of our awareness at the moment of our death.

Throughout history and into the present, various death-preparation methods have been developed. These methods can be divided into two categories. The first category includes those practices that are specific and appropriate when physical death is imminent—what can be called "end-of-physical-life" practices. The second much larger category includes those spiritual practices that are more general in nature, which can be practiced throughout life—including the time leading up to physical death.

It is important to acknowledge at the onset that even if one wholeheartedly applies oneself to the available methods and techniques of what contributing author Anya-Foos Graber calls the practice of "deathing" (chapter 23), this does not make our lives problem-free or automatically illuminate all of life's contradictions and mysterious paradoxes. *Preparing for death does not give us absolute assurance that our deaths will necessarily be easy.* Chances are, even if we *have* prepared for death, we will still not be able to circumvent *all* the pain and suffering that may serve our ultimate growth.

Despite the absence of any "magic formula" or guarantee, there *is* great practical wisdom in preparing for our earthly departure—just as there is proven value—but no guarantee—in preparing for childbirth. Becoming familiar with the process of death—even to the extent of learning specific death-preparation methods—has the potential to reduce our natural fear of death, and helps us make a more healing passage when physical life's final "dead-line" arrives.

Part VII, *The Soul at the Moment of Death,* gives us glimpses into some of the spiritual aspects of the process of death as the soul separates from the physical body. We learn that in addition to being a medical/physiological event, death is a multidimensional spiritual experience of profound significance to the evolutionary progress of the soul. We appreciate more fully that from the perspective of the one who is in the process of dying, there is an intrinsic value in cultivating conscious awareness up to and through the moment of death. To an outside observer, the external signs and symptoms leading up to death may appear similar, but from the "inner view" of the person whose inert body is lying on the bed or on the highway, what they are experiencing "on the inside" constitutes a vast and unique inner world.

Physical death can indeed be a positive life experience—for some, even the crowning consummation of a life well lived—*especially* for those who have prepared for death throughout life. At the time before death, although physical cure may no longer be an option, as long as there is breath, inner healing is always available.

We Are the Angels: We Are the Mortal People

Sculptor/artist: Melinda H. White

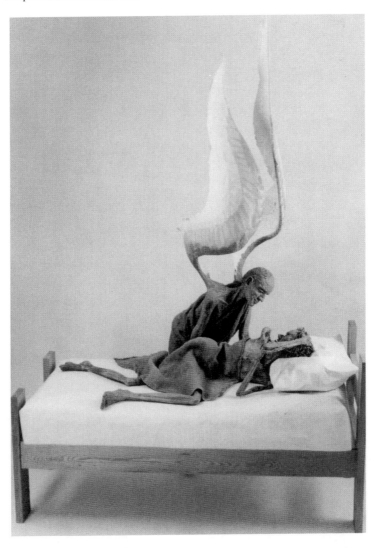

This is a photo of a ten-foot-high sculpture that for many years had its home at Dr. Elisabeth Kübler-Ross's death education training center in Virginia. The work incorporates the artist's experience working in hospice care, and the death of one woman in particular. The dying woman's face depicts the transition she went through from pain and fear, to joy and acceptance. In the face and stance of the angel, we see the attitude of the hospice caregivers observed by the artist. The wings represent both the Divinity in each of us and the angel that was actually reported by the dying woman and her husband shortly before her death. The piece as a whole acknowledges both the pain and beauty of the process of death.

The sculpture is made of papier-mâché, including leaves, cattail plant, and a variety of papers over a wood-and-wire frame.

CHAPTER TWENTY-ONE

Glimpses of Eternity—
My Mother's Last Gift Upon Her Passing
JOAN BORYSENKO, PH.D.

Joan Borysenko, Ph.D., is a medical scientist, psychologist, and international lecturer, with a doctorate in anatomy and cellular biology from Harvard University. Her books, which bridge medicine, psychology, and spirituality, include *The Power of the Mind to Heal; Minding the Body, Mending the Mind;* and *A Woman's Book of Life.* She is the director of Mind/Body Health Sciences, a holistic clinic and center for her ongoing mind/body/spirit research. This chapter is based on a film interview and public address that took place in Chicago, Illinois.

"I looked across at my child, at Justin, and Justin was weeping.
His face was suffused with light and he looked up at me and he said,
'Mom, the room is filled with light. Can you see it?' I said, 'Yes, I see the
light.' And he said, 'It's Grandma. She's holding open the door of eternity
for us so that we can have a glimpse. It's her last gift.'"
— Dr. Joan Borysenko

I had a fascinating mother. She was an absolutely marvelous person, the prototypical Jewish mother, just as I am the prototypical reformed Jewish-American princess. I can tell you that I was a great disappointment to my mother—I did everything wrong. She thought my research and everything else I did was for the birds, particularly when we got into the spiritual dimension, for she thought this was all very silly. My mother was a bit of a Marxist who thought that God essentially was the opiate of the people, and certainly something that she was never going to make the mistake of believing in. Many of her family members had died in the Holocaust. I think sometimes when you face an experience like that, which goes beyond human understanding, either your faith gets deeper or your faith disappears. And for her, faith had totally disappeared.

When she was dying, we tried everything we could to give her some comfort, and, of course, she didn't actually need any—*I* was the one who needed the comfort. I wanted to know that she was at home with death.

One day I was trying to talk to her about these things, and she wasn't interested at all. She loved Miroslav, my husband at the time, and one day he crawled into bed next to her and trotted out all of our favorite near-death experience stories. We figured that these would inspire her, but at the end of three or four really good ones, she looked at him, and with very great love said, "Mir, if it makes you feel better, you can believe in that stuff."

Now, my mother really lived for baseball—she was a great Boston Red Sox fan. At that time, the Red Sox had a third baseman by the name of Wade Boggs who got into big-time trouble—he told his mistress the secrets of his teammates, and then she spilled all this to the media. They had a heyday writing about the terrible humiliation of Wade Boggs.

Three weeks before my mother died, I saw a headline in the paper saying something like, "Why is Wade Boggs coping so well with this wholesale humiliation?" My psychologist's antennae went up. In the article, Boggs explained that his mother had just died, and that after her death she had appeared to him in a full three-dimensional vision. She had explained to him that mistakes are how we learn and grow and that he ought to look at what he had done, not to do it again, think it over, repent for it, pick up his "learnings," and move on—that it was okay. She also appeared in a full three-dimensional vision to Wade Boggs's sister, who was paralyzed with multiple sclerosis. The mother asked her to give the eulogy at her funeral, although the girl couldn't speak—but her vocal cords became unparalyzed and the daughter eulogized her mother.

I called my mother up and said, "Hey, Ma, let me read you this article." After I read the article, there was dead silence on the other end of the phone—this was a very good sign if you were speaking to my mother.

I heard nothing more about this. A few weeks passed, and it was time for what would be her last hospitalization. The ambulance came to take her to Beth Israel—a wonderful hospital where the medical staff really works with the patients and where there is not much of the denial of death. The nurse in the emergency room recognized her and said, "Mrs. Zakon, you are dying. Do you realize that you are dying?" I thought to myself, *What a wonderful gift this is that she knows now, and this is the moment of turning, where the energy goes from trying to hang on to life to finishing up and letting go.*

My mother smiled benignly at the nurse and said, "Dying, I'm dying, do you know what it is to die?" She got up on one elbow and said, "You bet I do! Did you hear about Wade Boggs's mother?"

Everybody has their own epiphany. The rest of my mother's period of dying was really a study of everything that goes into the process.

The entire family was gathered in the hospital room waiting to say good-bye, for we knew that she was going to pass over that day or the next. The day she died, she was having internal bleeding. They took her for tests at nine in the morning, and at four in the afternoon she wasn't back yet. People started to panic, so they dispatched me: "You know the hospital, you've got a white coat—go get her." So I went.

Our worst fears were true—she was lying on a stretcher in the hallway by herself, dying. I said to the doctor, "This won't do. We want her and we want her now." He said, "Another half an hour, her turn will come." I said, "We don't care. She's dying—we have to have her back." The doctor said, "Look, I'm sorry, medical regulations say we have to have a diagnosis." Well, my mother never lost her sense of humor. She looked at him with these poor rheumy watery eyes and said, "You need a diagnosis? Why didn't you ask me? I'm dying. That's your diagnosis."

And you know the interesting thing was that he actually couldn't fight with that logic, and he let her go. I tell this story because each of us has to have our own part in the medical system, and it's always a matter of communication between the patients, between the family, between the person who is dying, to prevent things like that from happening.

As we were going back to her room on that short ride from the basement up to the seventh floor, we did a lot of work. My mother was the kind of person who I think perhaps personified a particular generation, that generation of Jewish women who had lived through the Depression and through the Holocaust and who had to cope with life by not facing their pain. She didn't have much of a vocabulary for emotions of pain, but as she looked at me then she said, "Look, I know that I've made a lot of mistakes. Could you forgive me?"

Those are the most blessed words I could imagine because they opened my heart and enabled me to see the pain I was holding on to, for the ways I had failed her, all the times I had not been there for her, all the times that I hadn't made time for her, all the times that in some way I had judged her life as something I did not want to live. And I was able to look at her and say in just as few words, "I'm sorry, too. I've made a lot of mistakes. Can you forgive me?" In the sacred place, the gateway of death, the words that are spoken carry tremendous power and have tremendous capacity for healing. And there was a tremendous moment of forgiveness that just passed through our eyes at that time.

We got up to her room, and everybody said good-bye to her. My son, Justin, and I stayed with her through the night. Justin was 20 at the time, and he was very close to his grandmother. She had really raised him, as I was a busy graduate student, with hardly any money for baby-sitters. He loved her a great deal, and he found it very easy to look at her and tell her about all of the important differences she had made in his life—very important for a dying person to know, that they have made a difference in some way. He began to sing her wonderful songs, not only from her own tradition but the song she had fallen in love with my father to: "Some Enchanted Evening," which to her was sacred music. She looked up with tears and said, "Do you think Grandpa will be waiting for me?" And it was a wonderful sense of "She's moving now, she's moving over."

Around midnight the doctor asked if she would like a little morphine, explaining that if she took the morphine the pain would get better, but the breathing would get worse. So she took the morphine and said good-bye.

Justin and I started a vigil, sitting on either side of the bed waiting for her to pass over. At about three o'clock in the morning, as we sat there meditating, I suddenly had a vision. I felt luminous, light-filled, and I felt that I was giving birth to the entire world in the form of a baby—I've given birth twice, and know that point of giving birth to life that can feel like a death.

During this vision, I realized that birth was no great picnic for the baby either—that the baby is also dying, and that every death is a birth and every birth is a death. I was equally present in the vision both as the baby and as the mother. The next thing I knew, I had left the consciousness of the mother and I was only in the baby—I was the baby and I was moving through a dark tunnel. I was born out into this tremendous realm of Light—there are no words for what this is like. To say that you come into the presence of love, that it comes both from within you and from beyond you barely begins to sum it up. For me, it was as if my soul had been laid bare, my soul had been seen—I could see every mistake I ever made—and my soul was still pure. The *Upanishads* talk about the self that is immortal and eternal, that cannot be burnt by fire nor crushed by rock nor cut nor injured, that the immortal core of who we are is without blemish, that we cannot lose or sully our souls—and that's what I was shown in that experience.

Then everything about my mother and me became clear: that she had birthed me into this world and that I had just birthed her back out of it, that we were part of a circle of death and birth that went on forever.

I came out of the vision, and when I opened my eyes, I saw that the entire room was filled with light—there was no place where one thing started and another thing ended—it was all molecules of light dancing. I looked across at my child, at Justin, and Justin was weeping. His face was suffused with light, and he looked up at me and he said, "Mom, the room is filled with light. Can you see it?" I said, "Yes, I see the light." And he said, "It's Grandma. She's holding open the door of eternity for us so that we can have a glimpse. It's her last gift." And then he looked at me with eyes filled with so much love, I could feel the light that started in his heart and moved out through his eyes and into mine, and he said, "You must be so grateful to your mother." I realized that he had exactly the same experience I had had, and he said, "You know, she was a very great soul. And she embodied to take a role that was much smaller than the wisdom in her soul, and she did it as a gift for you so that you'd have something to resist against."

This was such a great gift, and a big part of the gift was that when that understanding came out of Justin's mouth, I knew that he had forgiven me for what I had and hadn't done as a mother.

So we had that experience of the sanctity of death, of death as a doorway. During our lives, we go through numerous births and deaths. That's what characterizes all of life—not just the big death at the end when we check out, but all of the little deaths. In the *Bhagavad Gita,* Krishna says, "Just as the dweller in this body merely passes through childhood, youth, and old age, so in death it merely passes into another kind of being. The wise are not deceived by that." Our life is a series of births and deaths; when we are born into this skin as an infant, in a certain sense we die in the life of the spirit. When we die to our baby body, we're born to the body of a child. We die to a body of a child at the time of puberty, and all through life we die through various bodies so that we are reborn on different levels.

I often say, jokingly, that we're one great big cosmic case of multiple personality disorder, that truly the face you see of the person in front of you is none other than your own, that we're all altars of the Divine One. I think sometimes what we think as past-life memories are in fact cellular memories from all our ancestors who have ever come before us, and all of the wisdom from every one of those births and deaths is encoded within us—that we are one soul that is learning to know itself and grow itself. And so the life of each one of us, the death of each one of us, is part of that great wheel, that great circle. It has a lesson to teach us about life. We have to be able to accept the little deaths that we go through and the darknesses in ourselves if we are going to own the light.

"I was told this story by students of mine who are nurses.
They were taking care of a nun who was very close to death.
This woman was in great pain. She was very anxious about dying,
and she was especially anxious about having her rosary beads and other
religious paraphernalia at hand at all times—that was the most important
thing for her. Well, it appears that at a certain point, about a half day
before she died, she left her body, entered into the Light, and had a
classic vision of a spiritual presence. After the experience was all
over, she lost all interest in her rosary beads. Her nurses, who were
my students, asked her, 'Well, how come you don't care about these
rosary beads anymore?' She said, 'I don't need them anymore.
I've seen the real thing.' Then, with a smile on her face,
she very peacefully died."

— Dr. Michael Grosso, from the video *Experiencing the Soul*

CHAPTER TWENTY-TWO

What Counts at the Moment of Death
CHRISTINE LONGAKER

Christine Longaker is the former director of Hospice of Santa Cruz and founding director of the Buddhist Rigpa Fellowship in the United States. She developed the "Spiritual Living and Dying Program" under the guidance of her spiritual teacher, the venerable Sogyal Rinpoche, author of the acclaimed book, *The Tibetan Book of Living and Dying*. This chapter is based on an excerpt from Christine's book, *Facing Death and Finding Hope*.

"Not knowing who we are, not knowing our real essence and our interconnectedness with all life, we have all made mistakes. In this not-knowingness, if we have harmed someone or regret some things we've done, we can ask forgiveness, either from that person or from our God."
— Christine Longaker

Given the extraordinary opportunity for gaining liberation that is presented at death, we need to understand how to prepare meaningfully for death while we are alive. Buddhist teachings emphasize that two things count at the moment of death: how we have lived our life and the state of our mind in that moment.

"How we have lived our life" has two implications. The results of our wholesome and negative actions—and our habits—will follow us when we die. Buddhist teachings describe the principle of karma: Our every action has a consequence, or reaction, on our self. Even though we don't immediately witness the effects of our actions; nonetheless, they are there. All of the actions of our life—including our words and our thoughts—are like seeds that we are sowing, and later in life or after we die, those seeds will mature and bear fruit. The effects of our actions will be our harvest at death, for better or worse, and they will have an impact on our experiences in the after-death states, determining the quality of our next existence.

Those who have survived clinical death and have had a prolonged near-death experience have described witnessing a complete review of everything they had done in life, even scenes they didn't consciously remember. However, they don't just passively watch what they've done; those who entered death's threshold describe experiencing the effect of their actions on others *as though they were now receiving it.*

"Everything in my life went by for review—I was ashamed of a lot of things I experienced because it seemed I had a different knowledge—not only what I had done, but how I had affected other people. I found out that not even your thoughts are lost. It was a total reliving of every thought I had thought, every word I had spoken, and every deed I had ever done; plus the effect of each thought, word, and deed on everyone and anyone who had ever come within my environment or sphere of influence whether I knew them or not."

One woman who had two near-death experiences in her life told me, "After death, when you see the effects of your actions and even your thoughts on everything and everyone, *that is hell.* In all of the seemingly insignificant encounters of your life—perhaps your reaction to a stranger who walks into a shop—you see how you are constantly projecting your judgments, your selfish or negative motivations, and you yourself now feel the effects of them."

It is clear that people who have survived near-death experiences are lucky, for now they have another chance to live, to atone for what they had done, to use their minds and hearts in a positive way, bringing kindness and good circumstances to others. Yet we who hear their message are no different. We can honestly assess our lives, heal our past actions, forgive others and ask forgiveness, and resolve to live in a different way, beginning now.

Another type of seed we are sowing is our habits. Our mindstream is a continuous flow of untamed and negative emotional habits that are the source of much of our suffering in life and untold suffering after we die.

Many years ago, I brought a young Tibetan master, Dzongsar Khyentse Rinpoche, to meet a woman who was dying. When he came into her room, he introduced himself, and she expressed gratitude that he had come to see her. She said, "In the last few weeks, I was resisting my death, but now I think I have accepted it."

He looked at her with a twinkle in his eye and said, *"I don't think so!"*

She laughed and then admitted, "Yes, you're right."

After pulling up a chair to sit beside her, he turned and asked me in a stage whisper, "What should I tell her?" I suggested he tell her about the *bardos,* those periods of transition where we are suspended for a time between two seemingly real states of existence. I expected he would speak about the first bardo of death, when the nature of mind is fully revealed. But what he talked about was the third bardo of death: the bardo of becoming, the period between lives, from the moment when the person's consciousness leaves the body and begins to roam, until it takes rebirth.

Rinpoche proceeded to tell her: "After you die, everything will go on the same as it does now. You will have the same awareness as you have now; you will experience everything just as you do now." As he spoke these words, I reflected on how the dying woman might feel reassured to view death not as an end but simply as a continuation of awareness, independent of the body. But what he said next came as a complete surprise:

"Not only does awareness continue, but after death your habits continue." As I watched her face registering the message, I imagined that we shared the same response: *"Oh, no, not my habits!"*

Death is truly the fruition of all the seeds we have sown in this life, and a continuation of whatever is in our mind and heart from moment to moment. *Death is a continuation of how we are right now, in life.*

The Window of Opportunity

The second thing that counts at the moment of death, "the state of our mind," reveals that how we are when we die is of crucial importance. At death we don't meet anything new. Instead, we experience ourselves naked-ly—both our absolute nature and our ordinary, relative condition. Yet how well do we really know our *true self?* How much have we worked with our conditioned habits, or learned to cultivate compassion and wisdom in our minds and hearts? Here, what I mean by "mind" embraces our whole atti-tude, and the spirit in our heart. Our true mind is not restricted to our intel-lectual or cognitive power, but is a fundamental goodness or "good heart" that is at the core of every being.

Dying is a process of gradual dissolution—of our physical powers, our senses, the gross and subtle elements of which our body is composed, and our cognitive abilities. The external aspect of this dissolution concludes when we exhale our last breath. Yet after this point, an internal process of dissolution still continues, during which our internal energies collapse along with the thought-states of anger, desire, and ignorance that had sup-ported our ego. The conclusion of this inner dissolution is the final moment of death, which most of us will experience as "fainting" into a dark void—a space that is peaceful and free of pain.

When our consciousness awakens from the utter darkness of death, the Ground Luminosity—our true nature of mind—dawns like an immaculate, clear, and radiant sky. The key to this moment is *recognition:* If we recog-nize the Ground Luminosity as our true nature when it dawns, we can unite with it and attain liberation. Therefore, "how our mind is" at the moment of death means, for those who gained stability in resting in the nature of mind during life, simply remaining in that pure awareness while dying, and unit-ing naturally with the Ground Luminosity.

However, since most of us meet death unprepared for this moment, lacking familiarity with resting in our true nature, or in an emotionally con-fused state, we will fail to recognize the Ground Luminosity. By sheer force of habit, we will begin to react emotionally and separate ourselves from the pure experience, thus regenerating our ego's self-grasping, our fear and negativity, and all our patterns of suffering. Even though we have a momen-tary experience of complete freedom, we will resume the mind's habitual grasping and aversion, which propel us helplessly into the confusion and suffering of the after-death bardos and our next existence.

Since the attitude in our minds and our hearts—our very last thought or emotion—is what we wake up to just after the moment of death, then even when we are dying we have the potential to change our habitual grasping attitude, release our attachments, give up our judgments and aversions, and develop a kind heart. In fact, all of the suffering, changes, and losses we experience in our life offer us countless opportunities to "practice dying," training ourselves to let go of our grasping habit and to release and relax into our true nature. And we have many opportunities to heal our relationships, purify our wounded hearts, and transform our response to suffering. Thus, there is no moment in life when we are not preparing for death.

Through spiritual training, we can learn meditative practices that enable us to connect with our inherent wisdom and compassion. When our mind settles deeply in meditation, the conceptual mind and ordinary sense of self may temporarily dissolve. Then we experience the gap or space between our thoughts: a wakeful, clear, radiant awareness unsustained by hopes, fears, or habitual projections. Pursued deeply and sincerely, spiritual practice enables us to purify and release the emotional conditioning and self-grasping ego that separate us from reality. Meditation connects us ever more reliably and profoundly to a natural, effortless awareness in which there is a deep relaxation and spaciousness, an unbounded gratitude, and an all-embracing, joyful compassion.

In the words of Sogyal Rinpoche, "The fundamental message of the Buddhist teachings is that if we are prepared, there is tremendous hope, both in life and in death. The teachings reveal to us the possibility of an astounding and finally boundless freedom, which is ours to work for now, in life—the freedom that will also enable us to choose our death and so to choose our birth. For someone who has prepared and practiced, death comes not as a defeat but as a triumph, the crowning and most glorious moment of life."

"My master, Dudjom Rinpoche, used to say that to help a dying person is like holding out a hand to someone who is on the point of falling over, to lift them up. Through the strength and peace and deep compassionate attention of your presence, you will help them awaken their own strength.

The quality of your presence at this most vulnerable and extreme moment is all-important. . . .I never go to the bedside of a dying person without practicing beforehand, without steeping myself in the sacred atmosphere of the nature of mind. Then I do not have to struggle to find compassion and authenticity, for they will be there and radiate naturally."
— Sogyal Rinpoche, from *The Tibetan Book of Living and Dying*

CHAPTER TWENTY-THREE

"Deathing" and the Failsafe Technique—
At Death and Beyond

ANYA FOOS-GRABER

Anya Foos-Graber is a writer and yoga instructor who synthesized a unique system of conscious dying she calls "deathing." Deathing assists people in the process of dying to leave the physical plane in a spiritually conscious way. She is the author of *Deathing: An Intelligent Alternative for the Final Moments of Life,* and presently lives in Kansas, farming and writing when she is not lecturing on deathing and other related topics. The following chapter was specifically written for this anthology after several lengthy phone conversations with the author.

*"If we can maintain a state of Divine awareness at the moment
of death, and focus on a Divine Being who is 'One with the Father,'
one can 'hitchhike' through the principles of vibrational resonance
and entrainment with the state of consciousness behind the name
that is invoked by this remembrance."*
— Anya Foos-Graber

I'm often asked, "What is *deathing,* and how does it differ from *dying?"* In reply, I draw the analogy between *birth,* the biological process in which the infant propels down and out of the birth canal—which all pregnant females must face, ready or not, informed or uninformed—and *birthing,* in which the mother has prepared herself using methods and techniques that are based on sound physiological, psychological, and spiritual principles.

So *birth* is to *birthing* as *dying* is to *deathing. Deathing* is a term I coined to describe a collection of various techniques that prepare us for death—especially the moment of death itself. Deathing techniques are a synthesis of the collective wisdom passed down by many spiritual traditions around the world, and are based on what happens at the time of biological death and the soul's continuing journey thereafter. Deathing has the potential to transform the often painful evacuation of the soul from the body into a glorious voluntary participation in the cosmic creative process. One then has the possibility of reidentifying with our true Cosmic identity. Deathing can take dying to new heights, just as its counterpart, birthing, can transform birth into a triumphant, light-filled conscious experience.

Unlike my first, unprepared "medicalized *birth,"* the Lamaze-method *birthing* of my second son, Ben Paul, went way beyond simple pain control. Through breathing, visual focus on a spiritual image, and relaxation between contractions, my sense of self slipped into a serene timelessness, even during the labor pains that pounded through me and over me. I surfed these mighty waves and merged the limited "Anya-self" into the birth contractions. I first was able to let go of "Anya." Then my identity expanded to the archetype of the Eternal Feminine. Finally, an "I"—not bound by body or mind—was transported into an awareness of Cosmic Consciousness. All this was happening while my biological body was doing its job of delivering Ben Paul. This unlimited, nonlocalized greater "I" was in ecstasy. An ethereal Light even poured into and filled the delivery room—literally blinding my obstetrician with its sacredness for a short period of time.

The baby was born on my outward breath, just as Ben Paul took his first inward breath. With the umbilical cord still attached and dangling, Ben Paul was placed on my breast, as my consciousness contracted from cosmic consciousness into "motherness," then dipped back down into "Anya-as-mother" in localized form—one might say.

After this powerful experience, Anya was ever-different, unspeakably empowered, just as I had been after the two near-death experiences I'd had as a child, as well as in the myriad out-of-body travels I've had all throughout my life.

In similar fashion, deathing can *also* be an empowering, transcendent event. The veil between dimensions is very thin during the dying process, the moment of death, and shortly after. If we can maintain a high state of Divine awareness, deathing can be the epiphany of a lifetime as the soul is propelled on a direct trajectory back to our Source.

The Failsafe Technique

The best way I know to introduce the primary principle, the most important technique of deathing, is to quote Krishna, from the *Bhagavad Gita,* the Hindu Bible. Krishna says to his disciple Arjuna: "Anyone who, at the end of life, quits the body remembering Me, attains immediately to My Nature—there is no doubt of this. In whatever condition one quits his present body, in his next life, he will attain to that state of being without fail." [Bhagavad Gita, 8: 6]

Now I realize that you may not accept reincarnation, but no matter, the principle of "remembering Me" that Krishna makes reference to *still holds.* Jesus Christ also made reference to the same principle when he said: "No one comes to the Father *except through Me.*" [John 14:6]

Now as the daughter of a preacher's kid, I know how Biblical verses are subject to multiple interpretations, but if we combine Jesus' above statement that "No one comes to the Father except through 'Me' "—with another of his statements—"I and my Father are One" [John 17:11] it seems that Jesus is saying that remembering "Me" is necessary, and even preferable to, remembering an abstract concept such as "God."

Please forgive me if I have uttered a heresy to your way of thinking. I arrived at this view not only from the implications of Jesus' own words and intellectual reasoning: I am also someone who has been blessed with having had many soul flights to other dimensions of reality where I have met many Divine Beings equal in spiritual stature to the founders of the world religions. I have also been present at the bedside of many people as their deathing support person, and I've helped them keep in remembrance of the realized Being closest to their hearts.

I have come to refer to "the remembrance of the name of a realized

Being" at the time of death as the "Failsafe technique." I call it this because *if all else fails,* the invoking of the name of a divine Being is still effective, even if one hasn't practiced the full deathing system that includes breathing exercises, visualization, relaxation, vibration, and withdrawal of consciousness techniques. By focusing at the moment of death on someone who is "One with the Father," one can "hitchhike"—through the principles of vibrational resonance and entrainment—with the state of consciousness *behind* the name that is invoked by this remembrance.

It is said that Mahatma Gandhi trained himself to remember the word *Hari*—his favorite name of the Divine Personage from the Hindu tradition—*at all times,* so that he might reflex to it spontaneously at the moment of death. The very day before he was assassinated, he remarked to his daughter that he wanted her to remember it for him, in case he forgot or was taken by surprise. As the bullet pierced his body, Gandhi died with *Hari* audibly on his lips.

So the importance of keeping one's focus on the remembrance of a Divine Being cannot be overemphasized. This is especially valuable for the many people in our society who are battling negative tendencies during the dying process—which is only exacerbated by "death by hospital"—the medicalized, lonely deaths more often than not experienced in technologically driven hospitals.

You might be wondering, *What is it about the moment of death that makes it so important for the progress of the soul?* Many spiritual traditions teach that whatever one focuses on at this moment casts the "flavor" and atmosphere of what occurs *after* physical death. The way we die—especially the moment of death—has a profound corresponding effect for our state in the afterlife and for future rebirths—as mini-moments compound themselves into maxi-effects. The Failsafe technique can help mitigate the effects of both negative conditions and conditioning.

At the time of death, it is a rare person who can keep their focus on Divinity due to habitual modes of thought and action during our active and busy lives. There's a tendency for our awareness to spin out of control, become too concerned with the physical aspects of death, or be pulled down by negative psychological states.

On the brighter side, at the time of death, conditions are optimal for impressing the "no boundary" divine state of consciousness onto the soul's individual memory field. This cosmic event is the spiritual equivalent of the biological mechanism for reproduction; that is, sexual intercourse. The one spawns bodies; the other propagates the various expressions of consciousness. In this sense, this all-important moment in the deathing process can be considered "cosmic sex."

In everyday life, people speak about making a "good first impression." Well, at the time of death, we have an opportunity to make a good "last impression"—on the cosmic memory banks of the Universal Mind, that is. If it's a *really good* last impression, we may not have to return to human form—the soul will evolve on a higher dimensional octave of creation. When this happens, the soul does not *have to* come back to the Earth plane, but *may choose to come back* out of compassion. For if the incarnated soul is sufficiently purified from the dross of Earthly desires, our soul-essence *will* be able to recognize—and then merge—into what Buddhists call "the first appearance of the Clear Light."

My conception of the mechanism behind how this works is that at the time of death, this unconditional Clear Light appears to the departing soul at the very moment that the physical body and bio-field—the lowest sub-fields that the soul works through—drop away. The releasing of the soul from the cage of the physical body—in exact conjunction with the lifting of the veil to other dimensions of reality at the death moment—provides a fleeting but very real opportunity for the soul to merge in the Clear Light. Although all beings experience this Light briefly at death, few are able to recognize, align with, and merge in It.

When this fleeting opportunity passes, the process of subtle death continues. Our final thoughts and emotions at the time of death affixes its emotional/mental imprint on the cosmic Universal Mind storage system. This holographic "snapshot in time" becomes the template for our next rebirth. Unfortunately, souls have a tendency to take back and get lost in its previous attachments and desires. After varying periods of time in the after-death state, the weight and force of these desires and habits accumulated during Earth life sets in motion another cycle of human incarnation. What type of physical form one takes, and the conditions of the next life, are determined by cause and effect—called "karma" in the East. The divine grace, protection, and mercy of a Divine Teacher can *offset* this karma, and the Failsafe technique can invoke the aid of such an enlightened being.

You may be thinking, *How does Anya know this stuff works?* Well, I've assisted the transit of a number of people in the process of dying, including accidental deaths on highways. And on occasion, I have been able to continue to work with them *after* death on the other side of the veil. I have received sufficient feedback from them that demonstrates to me that my role as a support person using these deathing techniques had auspicious results.

In this connection, I was even blessed to have the opportunity to be the deathing support person for my *own* father. On his inward and outward breaths, I matched my own breathing with his and chanted the name of a contemporary Divine teacher that he was receptive to invoking the presence of. We did this, on and off, for nearly two full days, until he finally slipped into a coma.

After his death, he appeared to both my mother and myself in a waking-dream state and conveyed to us that he was "walking in green pastures with my Lord." Being the son of a Christian preacher, my father might be walking in green pastures with Jesus Christ; he might also be walking in green pastures with the Divine presence of Sathya Sai Baba—the Being we invoked at the time of his physical death. Perhaps both. Either way, I am content knowing that his soul has moved on to "green pastures."

The Failsafe technique is very much needed nowadays in our modern society—where many people die without any preparation or even a support person to help them spiritually. Please understand that I am *not* saying that help is not available on the *other* side of the veil if we do not die in remembrance of God—only that deathing techniques help the departing soul immensely because of the added support and assistance it receives on *both sides*. I feel that our priests, pastors, and rabbis could do a better job at ministering to the needs of the dying if they incorporated deathing techniques, especially the Failsafe technique.

Deathing is a natural and much-needed extension to Dr. Elisabeth Kübler-Ross's five-stage "predeath" psychology. Her pioneering work shows us how to help people navigate through the psychological stages of denial, anger, depression, and bargaining, and finally arrive at the acceptance stage of their deaths. This "predeath" process sets the stage for deathing, which introduces an "at-death and beyond psychology" that helps *the soul itself during* and *after* the process of death.

I am ever hopeful that as we enter the next millennium, our clergy, hospices, physicians, nurses, paramedics, coroners, firemen, policemen—anyone who deals with death on a daily basis—as well as the general public—

will become more aware of the beautiful service we can render to our fellow soul travelers by learning deathing techniques and being support persons for each other.

So, dear kinsmen, my last words of loving advice for your safe passage at the time of death are to consider adding the Failsafe technique to whatever religious or spiritual tradition is closest to your hearts, minds, and souls. If you do, you will speed your evolution and become a member of a new species—*homo noeticus*, knowers of Divine consciousness—as different from most present-day homo sapiens as Neanderthals were from Cro-Magnons!

"I was raised in a family [of] atheists. But in my 20 years as a nurse working with patients with life-threatening and terminal illnesses, I became more sensitive to other nonphysical presences in the room. Throughout the years, I've been present when patients spoke to deceased family members and friends who had come for them, announced the presence of angels, and had visions of Jesus, Mother Mary, and other spiritual beings. I would silently thank these presences for being there and assisting. Not only was the patient not alone, but I no longer felt the 'burden' of providing for all the care needs of my patients. I knew there was assistance, which I could also ask for. Although this knowledge does not curtail all the grief associated with the death of a loved one, it can provide comfort for those left behind. And when it's my time to die, I'm looking forward to seeing who will help and greet me."
—Tani Bahti-Gaines, hospice nurse,
from the video *Experiencing the Soul*

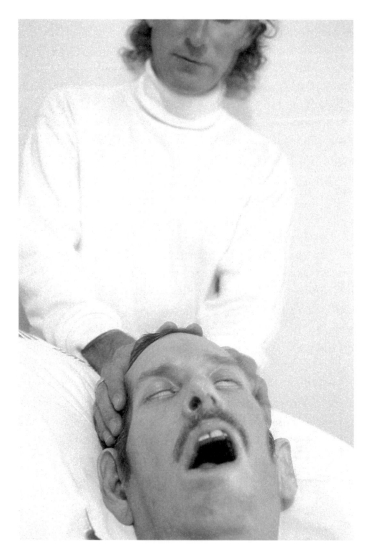

Although this photo may bring up strong feelings and is certainly not a pretty sight, being with Stephen Keyser as his hospice social worker was a very beautiful and sacred experience. Stephen is pictured in a coma five hours before his death. He had prearranged for this photo to be taken because he believed it would help others be less afraid of death. As I cradled Stephen's head with my hands, I was keeping my spiritual focus and praying for his welfare. The spiritual energy in the room was very sacred.

CHAPTER TWENTY-FOUR

The Tunnel of Love—
A "Goodbye for Now" Poem to a Dying Friend

LOUISE L. HAY

Louise L. Hay is an internationally acclaimed metaphysical teacher, counselor, and bestselling author. Her books include *You Can Heal Your Life, Heal Your Body,* and *Empowering Women.* Louise has assisted thousands of people in discovering and using the full potential of their own creative powers for personal growth and self-healing. Her works have been translated into over 25 different languages in 33 countries throughout the world.

At the time of this writing, I have not yet had the pleasure of meeting Louise Hay in person. We have met only by telephone. While speaking, I had a mental image of her appearance as I had remembered it from the photos on her numerous books. Her high cheekbones and refined features conveyed the impression that she was a very "ethereal" person, especially in light of the metaphysical topics in most of her books. With these preconceived notions in tow, we were well into our phone interview for this chapter when to my surprise—midstream in one of her replies—Louise exclaimed with childlike glee, "Oooh! I just found a snail!" I said, "Uh...what did you say, Louise?" She replied, "I said I found a snail." Louise had apparently been weeding her organic garden the whole time I was recording our phone interview, using one of those fancy "no-hands" type phones! So much for my preconceived notions of an otherworldly Louise Hay! She literally was as "down to Earth" as anyone gets!

With great excitement and joy in her voice, this dear lady—I assume still on her knees busily weeding—told me about her passion for composting, her love of earthworms, and how her idea of dining out is to eat out of her own organic garden as much as possible. Then, without missing a beat, she effortlessly segued back to the topic at hand—eloquently quoting author Ken Carey: "The warm rains of New Thought fall gently on the soil of human consciousness"—another "down to Earth" reference to Mother Nature. *Now this is a great woman!*

At the conclusion of our conversation, Louise said, "You know, I'm a simple lady with a simple message: Learn to love and forgive yourself and others. Do your best to live in the now. If we could all do this, life would be so joyous, easy, and simple."

Louise Hay's contribution to this anthology takes the form of a good-bye message she wrote and sent to a loved one who was in the process of dying. I was so moved by the beauty and wisdom found in this poem-letter that I decided to include *it,* rather than our interview. Trust me on this one.

"One of the things we want to do is to make peace with ourselves, no matter where we are and what is going on, and to know that death is not a failure. It is one of the experiences that we have in life. And as I have said many times, when we go, it is our time. And I do think we make an agreement with our souls as to when we will leave."

— Louise L. Hay

Dearest One,

Here are some words of comfort on the perfectly normal, natural process of leaving the planet that you are now going through. The more peaceful we can be with this experience, the easier it is.

We are always safe,
It's only change.

From the moment we are born
We are preparing to be Embraced by the Light—
Once more...

Position yourself for Maximum Peace.
Angels surround you
And are guiding you each step of the way.

Whatever you choose
Will be perfect for you.

Everything will happen in
The perfect time-space sequence.

This is a time for Joy
and for Rejoicing.
You are on your way Home
As we all are.

I have often thought of my own death as:

THE END OF THE PLAY

The final curtain descends.
The applause is over.
I go to my dressing room and remove my makeup.
The costume is left on the floor.
The character is no longer me.
Naked I walk to the stage door.
As I open the door I am met by a smiling face.
It is the new Director,
New script and costume in hand.
I am overjoyed to see all my loyal fans and loved ones waiting.
The applause is loving and deafening.

I am greeted with more love than I have ever experienced before.
My new role promises to be the most exciting ever.

I know
Life is always good.
Wherever I am
All is well.
I am safe.
See you later.
Bye.

OUR MOVIE

In each lifetime
We always come into the middle of the movie.
We always leave in the middle of the movie.
There is no right time.
There is no wrong time.
It is only our time.

The soul makes the choice long before we come in.
We have come to experience certain lessons.
We have come to love ourselves
No matter what they did or said.
We have come to cherish
Ourselves and others.

When we learn the lessons of love
We may leave with joy.
There is no need for pain or suffering.
We know that next time
Wherever we choose to incarnate
On whatever plane of action
We will take all of the love with us.

THE TUNNEL OF LOVE

Our Final Exit is one of
Release, Love and Peace.
We release and let go into the exit tunnel.
At the end of the tunnel we find
Only Love.
Love such as we have never experienced before.
Total all-encompassing, unconditional Love
And deep inner Peace.
All the ones we have ever loved are there.
Waiting and welcoming,
Caring and guiding,
We are never alone again.

It is a time of great rejoicing,
A time of reviewing,
Our last incarnation
Lovingly and only to gain Wisdom.

TEARS ARE GOOD TOO!
Tears are the river of Life.
They carry us through
Experiences that are deeply emotional.

HAPPY ASCENSION
You know I will join you
In what will seem
Like a twinkling of an eye.
— Louise L. Hay

All goes onward and outward,
nothing collapses,
And to die is different
from what any one supposes—
and far luckier.

— from "Song of Myself," by Walt Whitman, American poet-laureate

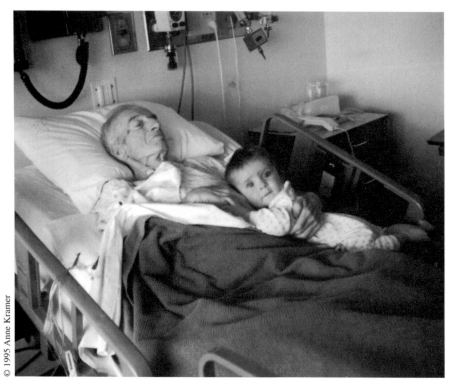

© 1995 Anne Kramer

This photo of 73-year-old Martin Kramer was taken by his wife of 42 years, Anne, as he lay in a hospital bed, dying of cancer. He had been in a coma for eight hours when his seven-month-old grandson, Max, was placed on top of him. Barely opening his eyes, Martin reached down and put his arm around the baby. He passed away that night.

"When I talk about beating a disease, I'm not talking about being cured or being miraculously rescued from death's door. What I'm talking about is giving and receiving love up until the very last minute of your life. That's how you beat the disease."

— Bernie S. Siegel, M.D., author of *Love, Medicine & Miracles*

PART VIII

Science and

the Soul—

The Evidence

INTRODUCTION

As a field of endeavor, traditional science lays heavy emphasis on empirical measurement: The common dictum is, "If it can't be measured, it ain't science." As present-day scientific instruments are incapable of *directly* measuring the soul, consciousness, and nonphysical realms—at least for now—conclusive *direct* evidence for the soul cannot be said to exist. Mounting *indirect* evidence, however, *is* available through ingeniously designed experiments in quantum physics, parapsychology, and other scientific disciplines; the systematic study and analysis of the accounts of people who report transpersonal, transcendent experiences; and the formulation of mathematical equations that theoretically support the existence of a multidimensional "hyperspace" beyond the physical universe.

Supporting this view is physicist David Bohm's brilliant theoretical exposition on the existence of an invisible and more subtle "implicate order" of reality that exists *primary to* and encoded *inside* the material world—the "explicate order."

Encased in matter as it seems to be, could the search for the soul also be "an inside job" that can only be proved *to* oneself, *by* oneself, and *for* oneself, through *direct* experience?

Expressed irreverently—from the perspective of the soul's ultimate liberation from the bondage of mind and matter—could the "way out" be the "way in"? Could the "way in" be the "way out"? Or, as my meditator partner once told me, "Go 'within,' or go 'without.'"

But perhaps our expectations for science are too high—that in matters of soul, the province of science is best limited to theoretical *understanding* of consciousness and the soul, and *not* as a direct aid in helping us *experi-*

ence the soul. In the future, maybe scientific instrumentation will play some role in furthering soul's exploration.

Although a daunting and challenging enterprise, the following scientific pioneers in Part VIII, *Science and the Soul—The Evidence,* have contributed admirably to our theoretical scientific understanding of consciousness and the soul.

CHAPTER TWENTY-FIVE

How Consciousness Creates the Material Universe

AMIT GOSWAMI, PH.D.

Amit Goswami, Ph.D., is a distinguished professor at the Institute of Theoretical Physics at the University of Oregon. He has taught physics for over 30 years and has written several textbooks on the subject. The theme of this chapter is based on Dr. Goswami's book, *The Self-Aware Universe: How Consciousness Creates the Material World,* and was based on an extended phone interview with the author.

"The challenge of the next millennium will be to develop an adequate scientific understanding of consciousness itself. . . .Although there are limitations in our scientific knowledge of consciousness at this present time, the door is always open to directly experiencing this universal consciousness for ourselves."
— Dr. Amit Goswami

I'd like to relate two very important scientific experiments. The first involves the behavior of subatomic particles; the second involves the behavior of human test subjects. The results of both of these experiments close the gap between science and what spiritual teachers have been saying for time immemorial—that consciousness is not bound by the limitations of time/space and material models of the universe.

The first experiment was conducted by Dr. Alain Aspect and collaborators and was published in *Physical Review Letters.*[1] In this experiment, an atom emitted two quanta of light—called photons—that traveled in opposite directions as they left this atom. These photons were then found to *instantaneously* exert an influence on each other's behavior even at a distance. What was particularly extraordinary about the continued interaction between these two photons was that the experimenters determined that there was no possible way that any exchange of signals could have passed through space to account for this interactive effect.

To review, we have two particles that "instantaneously"—literally in "no time"—interact with each other, but traditional science—even quantum theory—is at a loss to explain how this interaction could have occurred without the possibility of any signal being present to effect this interaction. To fully appreciate the extent to which this experimental result rocks the foundation of a purely materialistically based, quantum mechanical model of the universe, Einstein demonstrated that in an exclusively material universe, nothing can travel faster than the speed of light and, when anything travels through space, it *must* take some measurable finite amount of time to do so. And yet, these two subatomic objects affected each other *instantaneously* in space and time—which means "something" would have to travel *faster* than the speed of light to account for the interaction! Could this "something" that influenced the interaction between these photons be *consciousness itself*—a consciousness that belongs to a domain of reality that operates *beyond* the laws that govern time and space—something that literally *transcends* time and space? And could it be that consciousness, existing *outside* of time and space, affects all things *inside* time and space?

The view that consciousness may indeed be the "ground of all being" is supported by another experiment conducted by Dr. Jocobo Grinberg-Zylberbaum and co-workers that was published in the scientific journal *Physics Essays.*[2] In this experiment, two subjects were put in the same room and both asked to silently meditate together, with their eyes closed, for about 20 to 30 minutes—with no outward communication between them during or after the meditation. Before they began their meditation session, the experimenters asked both meditators to inwardly establish a direct feeling of oneness with each other while they were meditating. At the completion of the meditation, they were asked to continue to inwardly cultivate this direct feeling of oneness between them—without the aid of any words or outward actions.

After the meditation session ended, one of the meditators was escorted to a separate room. Both were asked to sit in special type of metallic enclosures that have the ability to block all electromagnetic signals from entering or leaving (Faraday cages). Both subjects were also hooked up to separate electroencephalograms (EEGs)—medical devices that pick up and record the electrical wave patterns of brain activity. Still in their respective Faraday cages, one of the meditators (Meditator One) was exposed to a series of flickering light signals. The sensory stimulus of the lights evoked an electrical response in his brain that was recorded on the graph of the EEG.

The other meditator (Meditator Two) had no knowledge that Meditator One was being exposed to these light flashes. However, at the exact same time that the series of flickering lights were being shown to Meditator One, Meditator Two's EEG reading reflected an almost identical EEG readout—possessing the same unmistakable phase/strength brain-wave patterns on *his* EEG readout—even though Meditator Two's brain was *not* exposed to these light stimulations. As long as the two meditators maintained their direct communication by attempting to feel "one in consciousness," this "transfer-potential" effect was produced again and again, roughly in one in four of all cases studied.

Built into the experimental design was a control group where the pairs did not meditate together, or, if they did meditate together, could not successfully maintain a "feeling of oneness." No correlation in brain-wave function or transfer potential could be reproduced in these control groups.

Let us review this amazing experiment before we examine the implications. First, the meditators were both in separate, isolated Faraday cages, which every scientist would agree completely prevents any physical or material signals from being received or transmitted between the two subjects. Secondly, Meditator Two did not know about the series of lights that Meditator One was being exposed to. Even if he *did* know what was occurring, how could Meditator Two possibly produce the specific brain-wave EEG readings of Meditator One at the exact same time?

The implications of this experiment are staggering. Could it be that consciousness itself was the uniting factor that maintained the contact and transference of experience between two brains, despite the absolute isolation of electromagnetic fields provided by the Faraday cages?

Could it be that consciousness exhibits the property of nonlocality, which means that it operates instantaneously, over any distance, without the necessity of any exchange of physical atoms, physical energy, any kind of signal, through and *even beyond* the boundaries of space-time?

Could it be that consciousness is primary to both mind and matter, and that the apparent separation of objects and subjects that we experience in daily life are but vehicles which consciousness expresses itself *through*?

I believe that the answers to all these questions are a resounding yes! I say this based on the considerable experimental, mathematical, and clinical research that has already been done. I have exhaustively collected and expanded upon much of this research in my book, *The Self-Aware Universe.*[3]

This meditation study supports the view that there are nonlocal, unconditioned, quantum processes that work through our conditioned brains. This means that as human beings, we are simultaneously conditioned and free. To the extent to which we connect with our true quantum nature—that which is beyond the limited "I" or ego—we can lift ourselves out of the prison-house of limited conditioning, and begin to operate on a level of true creativity and freedom. This is what the mystics are referring to when they say we can go "beyond the mind" to an unmanifest place of knowing in which consciousness is one, and we are not bound by space and time considerations.

In quantum physics, the school of thought that holds that consciousness is the ground of all being is nondual, nonmaterial—in the sense that consciousness is not made up of atoms—is called monistic idealism. In this view, there need not be an intermediary third force that unites the mind and the brain, which in the past has gotten us stuck in the mire of dualism. The work of researchers such as physicists Dr. Alain Aspect and Dr. Jocobo Grinberg-Zylberbaum support the view that the consciousness of the observer transforms mere possibilities—wave-form potential—into particles—into the actuality of matter. This is how consciousness creates the material world. To the extent that we consciously or unconsciously access and impact this nonmaterial, unconditioned universal field of consciousness, this is how we create our own reality on the human level of experience.

With all this, it is important to state that traditional Newtonian science is still useful when it comes to measuring and predicting limited areas of reality. These old theoretical models, however, are not complete when we explore the more subtle realities on the quantum levels of reality. Old science is preoccupied with the *object* of inquiry, and persists in the illusion that the observer has no effect on what is observed and only gets in the way of objectivity. *Including* the observer in the equation of life doesn't necessarily mean that we cannot accurately measure in the scientific sense. This new way of scientific exploration will by necessity have to factor in both the subject *and* the object, because we now know enough about the nature of quantum reality to say with confidence that the quantum consciousness *in* the subject, *in* the observer, transforms "possibilities" into "actualities"— changing the outcome of experiments by the very act of participating in the experiment. There are many who believe that we will become fully aware of ourselves as soul only when the knower—the observer—becomes the known. In the words of St. Francis of Assisi, "What you are looking for is what is looking."

The challenge in the next millennium will be to develop an adequate scientific understanding of *consciousness itself.* At the present time, we are only beginning to understand and describe the *attributes* of consciousness. Even in the field of quantum physics, there are many quantum physicists who still ignore data and mathematical proof that point to the primacy of consciousness as the causal factor behind mind and matter. They are still stuck in an entirely materialistic interpretation of the universe.

Although there are limitations in our scientific knowledge of consciousness at this present time, the door is always open to directly *experiencing* this universal consciousness for ourselves—as the realized mystics and spiritual masters have been telling us from time immemorial. In this is our greatest hope for individual and collective happiness.

*"I can't believe that God would choose
to play dice with the universe."*
— Albert Einstein

※ 227

CHAPTER TWENTY-SIX

Religion and the Frontiers of Science
CHARLES TART, PH.D.

Charles Tart, Ph.D., is emeritus professor of psychology at the University of California at Davis and the first holder of the Bigelow Chair of Consciousness Studies at the University of Nevada, Las Vegas. He is internationally known for his psychological work on the nature of consciousness—particularly altered states of consciousness and parapsychology—and as one of the founders of the field of transpersonal psychology. His two classic books, *Altered States of Consciousness* and *Transpersonal Psychologies,* became widely used texts that were instrumental in ushering in these areas of study into modern psychology. He has written more than 200 scientific articles that have been published in such prestigious scientific journals as *Science* and *Nature.* This chapter is based on a film interview that took place in Chicago, Illinois.

"There is hard evidence from over a thousand scientific experiments that supports the view that there is something more than the materialistic model of the universe. This is important for every educated person to know, especially scientists."
— Dr. Charles Tart

I've been trained as a scientist—that's the primary foundation that I speak from. But at the same time, as someone who has been raised in a culture that has doubts and many confusions about whether there is anything after death, I care deeply about the question of survival of consciousness.

In my 30 years of research, I have explored areas that are quite unusual for a Western scientist—questions such as the fundamental nature of the human mind and personality, and how science and religion can coexist harmoniously.

As a child, I was religiously devout. Trying to live a good Christian life was extremely meaningful and joyful for me—one of the centerpoints of my life. Then, as I got older, got more educated, and learned about the scientific worldview, a lot of inner conflict developed because the science I was exposed to seemed to be saying that religion was nonsense. Much of conventional science looks upon religion as just a lot of superstitions that people need in order to comfort themselves because they can't face the facts of existence. This caused me a lot of conflict because I loved science *as well as* religion. I was intrigued by the power of scientific experiments—thinking and then trying things out—that's why I eventually became a scientist. Luckily, I've been able to integrate religion and science in my life without throwing out one or the other.

I've observed, however, that many of my professional colleagues in the scientific world have tried to resolve the conflict between science and religion in two main ways. One way was to hold on to their religion but compartmentalize it in their minds. For example, on Sunday mornings, they might go to church, pray, and repeat certain words, but afterwards, for the rest of the week, they would close that mental compartment as they went about their scientific work with another set of belief systems that contradicted the beliefs espoused in church.

The other main way to deal with the conflict was to completely throw religion out of their lives. They decided for themselves that science was right, and religion was a lot of nonsense and superstition—and probably bad for one's mental health.

As a psychologist, I've come to realize that these two ways to resolve the apparent conflict between science and religion are not healthy. Compartmentalizing religion in one's mind, or throwing it out completely—neither of these ways creates wholeness.

There is hard evidence from over a thousand scientific experiments that supports the view that there is something more out there than the materialistic model of the universe would have us believe. This is important for every educated person to know, *especially* scientists. If one chooses to ignore the available data and insists on identifying with the narrow "scientistic" view that the material world is all there is, one is not actually being a good scientist. And I'm sad to have to say that most scientists are not good scientists when it comes to this issue.

I was fortunate as a teenager when I was working to integrate these two worldviews. I was helped immensely by some books and articles I found in the library about psychic research, especially those that were published by the British Society for Psychical Research. These books and articles were written over half a century ago by some very smart people—some of them Nobel laureates. The thrust of their reasoning went something like the following: Society is experiencing a tremendous conflict between science and religion. In the name of science, religion is being thrown out wholesale. Yet, religions have been around for a long time. Is it *all* nonsense? Since science has been good at answering questions in a lot of other areas, why don't we apply science to the question of religion? So they applied scientific method to rigorously study psychic phenomenon and the spiritual experiences of people around the world.

Now, there *is* some nonsense associated with religion. Certain religious practices and beliefs *are* arbitrary, superstitious, and even psychopathological in the sense that they cause people suffering rather than make for a better life. But is there a core of truth behind the religious experience itself that is valid and real and contributes to our well-being? Speaking as a scientist—and I believe a good scientist who knows his trade well—there is excellent scientific evidence to refute the popular view of science that says that we are nothing but the electrical and chemical signals in our brains— that there is no such thing as the spiritual. Science fails when it does not adequately explain observed facts that have been confirmed and replicated in controlled, well-designed experiments. The first job of science is to take account of *all* the facts. Unfortunately, most conventional scientists ignore the facts. It is sad to take something as vital as our spiritual life and to improperly use science in an attempt to explain it away.

Science has demonstrated that the human mind can do amazing things. I'll just mention a few very briefly. Sometimes the mind can directly communicate with another mind—what we call telepathy. Hundreds of experiments have been set up where there is no ordinary way that people can possibly communicate with each other. And yet, time after time, often enough to be scientifically valid, one mind can send information to another mind or pluck information out of another mind.

Another fascinating phenomenon that has been studied extensively is clairvoyance. Clairvoyance can be defined as the direct perception of the physical world by the mind itself, without the medium of the five physical senses. One classic style of experiment uses a deck of cards that is very thoroughly shuffled, then put in its box and locked in a drawer. No one—not even the experimenters—has looked at the deck of cards before, during, or after it has been shuffled. Nobody in the world knows what the order of the cards are in that deck. And yet, when research subjects in another room are asked the order of the cards, they report more cards in the correct order than is possible by the statistical probability of just guessing.

The working hypothesis behind these phenomena is that the mind can—sometimes, somehow—reach directly out to matter and gather information! I've had enough physical science training to know that this is not accomplished by some kind of "mental radio" or "x-ray vision" that uses any known physical energies. These are simply not plausible explanations.

The mind can do even more than that. Researchers did experiments where they would say to an experimental subject, "An hour from now, I'm going to take this deck of cards, and without looking at the cards, I'm going to thoroughly shuffle this deck dozens of times and then put it in this locked drawer. Would you write down, *now*, what the order of the deck of cards will be, *then?*" And while nobody is perfect at it, some people are able to report more of the future order of the cards than is statistically possible by sheer guesswork.

The results of these types of scientific experiments support the view that the mind can reach into the future. Of course, that's completely impossible in a purely materialistic view of the world. But the evidence itself asks us to revise our everyday perception of space and time.

What is it about the human mind that it can sometimes directly contact another human mind, directly contact the material world, and even contact the future? Neither telepathy nor clairvoyance makes any sense in conventional science's materialistic view of reality. They have no plausible way to explain the evidence, so they ignore or prejudicially dismiss the evidence.

Even more amazing, sometimes the mind can reach out and make things happen! Experiments were done whereby a machine rolled dice on a table while someone stood over against the wall and was told, "Make the sixes come up this time. Thank you. Now make the fives come up. Thank you. Now make the fours come up. Thank you." Although the results weren't consistently spectacular, there were enough extra hits to show that there was something that the person's mind was doing that was able to make the requested numbers come up more frequently than statistical probability tells us they should.

Nowadays, experiments are usually conducted with computerlike devices. For instance, there's an electronic device that randomly flashes green and red lights. When experimental subjects were told to use their minds to make the green light on this machine flash more often than the red light, the green lights then appeared more often. When asked to make the red light flash more than the green light, this also happened.

So speaking very much as a scientist, I can say we have excellent evidence that the human mind is more than the physical brain. And this creates the theoretical plausibility within the scientific method for the survival of consciousness after death. Although we do not have enough *direct* research that *absolutely proves* some sort of survival after physical death, there is at least a plausibility of survival on the basis that the mind can't be solely identified with the brain. So when someone says, "I've had an experience of unity with the universe," maybe this is not just some kind of funny aberration where a person doesn't know where their skin ends anymore. One day we may be able to show scientifically that there *really is* some kind of direct psychic connection to a very real, although nonmaterial, greater reality.

My interest as a scientist has not been limited to this kind of strict laboratory experimentation that shows that the mind can do things beyond what the physical brain and body can do. I've also been very interested in states of consciousness that are different from ordinary waking consciousness—for in altered, nonordinary states of consciousness, we have different and expanded abilities that changes the way we think, the way our emotions react, the way we perceive ourselves, and even the way we totally perceive the universe and reality.

In ordinary consciousness, we are very much aware of the limitations of our body. We are very much aware of the limited space and time immediately around our body within the range of the senses. Ordinarily, that's a wonderful thing. If you're going to walk around in this world, you should have precise awareness of the physical world around you and where your body is in reference to it.

But there are other ways in which the mind can function that open us up to the possibility of experiencing other dimensions of reality, including a spiritual universe. One of these altered states of consciousness is dreams. Our mind does not work in the same kind of pattern in dreams and in sleep as it does in ordinary waking consciousness. Every night, people spend roughly 20 percent of their sleep time in a state in which dreaming occurs. Our culture is so biased toward materialism that we devalue what we can learn in this dream state. We tell people, "Those are *just* dreams, don't worry about them; get out there and increase the gross national product!"— or something like that. We throw away a valuable part of our psychological life. If we paid more attention to our dreams, we could learn a lot about who we are on deeper levels of consciousness.

Now there are many other altered states of consciousness that are important for us to know about and experience. These states of consciousness are commonly experienced by people who are dying, although one does not necessarily have to be dying to experience these states. When people are in the process of dying, they begin to identify less with their body. As certain physiological changes take place, and as people begin to accept the reality that they are dying, they no longer make such an effort to hold on to their everyday, normal personality-selves. The mind then sometimes takes on a whole different configuration, a whole new state of consciousness.

Sometimes the mind of the person in the process of dying can be in a state where it's quite clear to them that death is simply a transition of the outward form, and not anything of particular consequence. If it comes to pass that you have those kinds of experiences, I suggest that you take them seriously and not automatically dismiss them. Don't let people try to talk you out of them by saying, "Oh, you were just hallucinating. You were just dreaming," or automatically accept that "it's just the medicine they are giving you." In fact, scientific studies actually show that during the time of dying, the most profound altered states of consciousness tend to occur in people who take little or no medication, rather than people who are heavily medicated.

So there is something natural about the human mind that can open up to other ways of seeing, feeling, thinking, and perceiving that are literally "meta-physical." Take those experiences as possible glimpses of what consciousness may be like on the Other Side. Modern psychology very seldom talks about this, but I think they are important for those of us who are mortal and going to die—which I guess includes everybody!

A few years ago, I was asked to give a scientific paper at a conference summarizing the evidence on the survival of consciousness after death. I summed up my understanding—after 30 years of research in the field—by making two statements. The first one is this: As part of the process of dying, perhaps after some pain, confusion, and temporary unconsciousness, I really won't be surprised if I regain consciousness after the death of my physical body. On the other hand, there is a certain sense in which I will be surprised if "I" regain consciousness—if "I"—in exactly the form I am now—survives the transition into whatever is on the other side of death. I think there may be a *temporary* continuation of "I"-hood, but a lot of what we think of as ourselves is very much conditioned by our body-oriented habits, including the social reinforcement that passes through our bodies. We're not going to have that on the Other Side. We're going to be in a different kind of consciousness.

So to the extent that we totally identify our deepest self with our ordinary self: "I must have my coffee before I can wake up; I must have things like this, that, and the other"—we are going to make our death even harder. We're going to have to struggle with it more because we're not going to have a physical body after we die. To the extent to which we can realize that we are *in* these physical bodies, it affects what we do—some of it we like, some of it we don't like—we can experience altered states of consciousness in meditation, spiritual experiences, and dreams that show us we're something *more* than a physical body. To the extent that we can loosen up and be more spacious, we can make the transition into death easier. And I suspect it will make for a better existence on the Other Side.

"Do you remember how electrical currents and 'unseen waves' were laughed at? The knowledge about man is still in its infancy."

— Albert Einstein

CHAPTER TWENTY-SEVEN

Evidence Supporting the Spiritual Reality Behind Near-Death Experiences

KENNETH RING, PH.D.

Kenneth Ring, Ph.D., is a pioneering psychologist in the field of near-death research, professor emeritus of psychology at the University of Connecticut, and co-founder and past president of the International Association for Near-Death Studies. He is the author of numerous books dealing with the near-death experience, including *Life at Death, Heading toward Omega, The Omega Project,* and *Lessons from the Light.* This chapter is based on excerpts from a film interview that took place in Storrs, Connecticut.

*"In the future, I believe that the implications of NDE research—
and the message of hope embedded in the NDE itself—will be
widely accepted by our society. . . .Not only will people continue
to undergo NDEs, but more importantly, more people will be pursuing
near-deathlike experiences through meditation and other spiritual
practices. More of us will then come to know that it is only*

our ego's delusion about what is real that keeps us from experiencing
the Light in this very moment, for the Light is the essence of what
we ourselves are. Our challenge is to realize this and
act on it before we die."
— Dr. Kenneth Ring

For centuries, our Western civilization has inscribed in countless souls the frightening image of the Grim Reaper, that horrific symbol of death that forcibly comes to take us away—we know not when, we know not where. However, since the advent of research on near-death experiences (NDEs), the presence of a loving Being of Light, or the otherworldly Light itself, is fast replacing the Grim Reaper as the dominant image of death in our society. Despite this, one of the unfortunate things about the expression, the "near-death experience," is that it implies that this kind of experience only occurs when people survive a near-death crisis of some sort. This is not true. There are *many* ways in which persons experience other dimensions of reality without the necessity of undergoing a life-threatening medical emergency that culminates in an NDE. *Nearly* dying is *only one* reliable trigger of this experience. Other ways include meditation, mystical and spontaneous religious experiences, and out-of-body experiences that are not accompanied by any kind of near-death event.

From a strictly scientific perspective, studying NDErs who have been *nearly* dead provides, at best, *evidence* relevant to the possibility of life after death—it cannot *prove* what persons experience *after* irreversible biological death. Receiving testimony from the irretrievably dead could definitely settle the matter concerning the existence of life after death, but the irretrievably dead are notorious for never sending back their questionnaires!

One thing that *has* been demonstrated is that NDErs themselves do not need scientific proof in order to believe in life after death. For example, an Australian sociologist, Dr. Cherie Sutherland, conducted a study in which she asked NDErs about their beliefs in life after death *before* and *after* their NDEs. She found that *before* their NDEs, approximately 50 percent of them believed in some form of life after death. The remaining 50 percent either did *not* believe in life after death, or they had no opinion one way or the other. However, *after* their NDE, every single person *without exception* believed in life after death in some form. In my own contact with hundreds of NDErs, I've found pretty much the same thing.

For those of us who have not had an NDE, what follows is a very brief sampling of some of the research that supports the view that NDEs are bona fide spiritual experiences that have a reality that is independent of the physical brain.

One of the common features of the NDE is the undeniable sense that the individual's consciousness separates from the physical body. Psychologist Dr. Charles Tart, professor emeritus at the University of California at Davis, wanted to test the hypothesis that "leaving the body" was possible. He found a woman willing to participate as a research subject who claimed to be able to leave her body at will.

The woman's experimental task involved reading a five-digit number that was written on a piece of paper that was placed on a shelf about six and a half feet high—well above what she could see from her laboratory bed. The woman was instructed to "leave her body," float up to the level of the shelf, read and remember the five-digit number, and then report the number the next day to Professor Tart. The woman was hooked up to electroencephalogram and electrocardiogram electrodes so that if she physically got out of bed to view the numbers, the experimenters would know it immediately.

The woman failed to read the number on her first three attempts, which is not that surprising given the novelty of the situation and the difficulty of controlling one's out-of-body state. However, on the fourth session, she correctly reported the number the next morning. The odds against this happening by chance are 100,000 to 1. Again, since her body was secured to the bed, this outcome strongly suggests that some nonphysical aspect of her consciousness—independent of her physical body—enabled her to successfully accomplish her assigned task. To the best of my knowledge, no one has yet offered a credible alternate hypothesis to explain the outcome of this experiment, apart from her somehow being able to read the researcher's mind telepathically, which, of course, would also strain a rationalist's heart to the breaking point. As you can imagine, those who believe in a strict materialistic model of the universe have extreme difficulty in accepting these results.

Another important study along these lines—but specifically with near-death survivors—was conducted by cardiologist Michael Sabom, who compared NDE accounts with actual medical records of what had taken place during heart operations. The NDErs' descriptions of what happened when they found themselves out of body while close to death—what was said and what was done on the operating table—very closely matched both medical records and the eyewitness testimony of nurses, anesthesiologists, and surgeons who were present during these operations.

It should also be mentioned that Dr. Sabom had a control group of non-NDE cardiac patients who were asked the same questions about what they would imagine would take place if they'd had such operations themselves. Their accounts were riddled with errors—for example, they described procedures that would only be found in highly dramatic "TV resuscitations," whereas such errors were *never* made by those who had actually undergone a heart operation and then reported they had witnessed it from an out-of-body vantage point.

Still on the subject of otherwise inexplicable visual perceptions that NDErs may sometimes report, I might mention here that one of my own research projects set out to discover whether NDEs ever take place in blind people and, if so, whether the blind report being able to *see* during these episodes. We found that most of our respondents, including persons who were blind since birth, claimed emphatically that in their NDEs they *were* able to see, not only things of *this* world, but things in the *other* world as well. In some cases, we even have independent evidence that their other-worldly perceptions—which they couldn't have known about by other means—were indeed accurate. Their testimony suggests that whatever limitations or handicaps we may suffer in this life are no longer operative when we are out of our physical bodies and exist in other dimensions. These findings bring a great deal of hope to many people concerning their freedom in the after-death state from handicaps that may have afflicted them grievously in their everyday physical life on Earth.

The study of NDEs in children also lends strength to the authenticity of the NDE as a spiritual experience by providing further evidence of its universality. This body of research shows, for example, that the accounts of very young children—some of them under two years old—were very similar to those of adult NDE reports. This is significant because these children could not yet be influenced by the culture-at-large or programmed by their parents or others with ideas from traditional religious belief systems. The existence of NDEs in very young children suggests that these and other similar spiritual experiences are intrinsic to the human experience. There is every indication that these NDEs or like experiences can happen to anyone at any age, even to the very young.

Another relevant source of evidence comes from a study entitled "Deathbed Observations by Physicians and Nurses"[1] conducted by Drs. Karlis Osis and Dr. Erlendur Haraldsson. These researchers collected and analyzed what they called "deathbed visions"—experiences that were witnessed at bedside by over 1,000 doctors and nurses in a sample of about 35,500 patients who were very near death. Typical examples include a doctor who reports that a few seconds before a patient's death, the dying person says, with eyes closed, "Oh, the Light of God is so beautiful," or "Katie, you've come for me." Only later would it be confirmed by relatives that "Katie" was indeed a deceased relative who was very close to the person who had just died, but about whose death the dying person had not been informed.

Also in this study—and contrary to claims that paranormal experiences are hallucinatory experiences brought on by the side effects of narcotic-based medications—it was found that there were fewer reports of paranormal experiences from patients who were taking narcotics; such accounts were actually *more* common among those who were drug free or taking medicines known not to alter one's state of consciousness.

Since the beginning of NDE research, there have been those who have attempted to deny the reality of the NDE by regarding it as some kind of hallucination. Although such critics will admit that NDErs themselves almost always understand their own encounters as spiritual events that are, if anything, hyper-real, they are inclined to offer alternative theories that attribute NDEs to natural causes. Among the factors that tend to be cited by these critics are biochemical imbalances such as oxygen deprivation or metabolic toxicity; psychological defense mechanisms that serve our biological survival instinct's need to deny death; and genetically programmed neurological patterns that surface at the time of extreme biological crisis when the body's systems are closing down. Other natural causes cited to "explain away" the essential spiritual nature of NDEs include the limbic lobe syndrome, drug side effects, endorphin release, and sensory deprivation.

It is of course true that there *are* mediating biochemical, neurological, and psychological mechanisms associated with NDEs. But are these mechanisms *responsible for* and the *cause of* NDEs, or do they only sometimes *accompany* them? No matter how one views this indeterminate issue, we can at least conclude that, as of yet, none of these alternative theories can adequately explain how NDErs (especially blind ones!) can have verified, accurate out-of-body perceptions of objects and people in faraway locations where there is no rational possibility of any materially based mechanism affording this. Therefore, it seems safe to say that at the present time no neurological, biochemical, or psychological theory of NDEs, invoked singly or together, has been able to account for the kind of verified extraordinary events that occur during them.

I have attempted to share a brief overview of some of the evidence that indicate that NDEs are real spiritual experiences. Nevertheless, when I am with someone who is close to death, I don't cite research in a last attempt to convince the person to change his or her beliefs about life and life after death. However, if the person is open to exploring the topic and invites me to, I *will* talk with him or her about the Light that NDErs have described to me. This Light is, in effect, the heart in the body of the NDE. According to thousands of reports, in this Light is all love, total acceptance, knowledge, complete perfection, warmth, and a beauty beyond our ability to imagine. I've found that just speaking about this Light is often sufficient to reduce or even eliminate a person's fear of death. I've also found that many of our preconceived, traditional religious concepts of an eternal heaven and hell are not particularly helpful frameworks to dwell on in these life-leading-to-death situations.

With all the contact I've had with NDErs, their lack of fear of death, and the sincerity and conviction with which they talk of their experiences have helped to erode—if not completely extinguish—my own fear of death. This phenomenon is not unique to me. We now have research that shows that persons who are merely *exposed* to NDE accounts begin to experience many of the positive benefits of NDEs without having to have an NDE themselves. They develop a deep faith and trust in the inherent goodness of people. Their love for God increases. They find their fear of death has diminished. They discover an increased ability to live more fully and more lovingly. And they are much more clear about what really matters in life—caring for other people and having love and compassion for all things.

In the future, I believe that the implications of NDE research—and the message of hope embedded in the NDE itself—will be widely accepted by our society and by the world as a whole. Not only will people continue to undergo NDEs, but more important, additional people will be pursuing near-deathlike experiences through meditation and other spiritual practices.

More of us will then come to know that it is only our ego's delusion about what is real that keeps us from experiencing the Light *in this very moment*, for the Light is the essence of what we ourselves are. Our challenge is to realize this and act on it *before* we die.

*"I have been totally blind since shortly after my birth due
to too much oxygen in the incubator destroying my optic nerves.
I had a clinical death experience in which I was able to see! I went
sailing up through the roof of the hospital, and then I saw lights out on
the street and the building and everything like that. And I was, in essence,
cavorting through the air, and really enjoying the liberty that I felt,
because I had never been able to get around like that before."*
— Vicki Umipeg, a blind-since-birth NDEr,
from the video *Experiencing the Soul*

CHAPTER TWENTY-EIGHT

The Soul and Quantum Physics
FRED ALAN WOLF, Ph.D.

Fred Alan Wolf earned a doctorate in theoretical physics from the University of California at Los Angeles. He continues to write, lectures throughout the world, and conducts research on the relationship of quantum physics to consciousness. His book *Taking the Quantum Leap* won the prestigious National Book Award. This chapter is based on excerpts from a film interview that took place in Los Angeles, and focuses on the major theme of Dr. Wolf's book *The Spiritual Universe—How Quantum Physics Proves the Existence of the Soul.*

*"At the time of death, or during a near-death experience, it may
very well be that the soul transitions from the material world—which
operates at speeds less than the speed of light—to a world that operates
faster than light speed, the so-called super-luminal spiritual world.
In that transfer, a tunneling effect may take place in much the
same way that it appears to take place in what
astrophysicists call a 'black hole.'"*
— Dr. Fred Alan Wolf

Many scientists question whether the soul exists. Many others in our culture question whether the soul has any relevance in a scientifically oriented, technologically trained modern society. Because science is largely responsible for portraying the world as merely a collection of mechanical parts acting on each other, some people feel a little uncomfortable when a quantum physicist such as myself attempts to understand the soul in scientific terms. Nevertheless, more and more people *are* concerned with questions dealing with the soul, the human spirit, and spirituality.

Is there something about "who we are" that is capable of tuning into the finer, higher vibrations of the soul? This is really a very old question. It started off a great debate thousands of years ago in ancient Greece among the followers of Plato and his student Aristotle.

Plato believed that the physical senses were always going to cloud our perception of the universe. According to Plato, the mere fact that someone is embodied makes our perceptions somewhat distorted, somewhat inaccurate, and somewhat of an illusion. Plato thought that while working at the level of the body and the senses, we can never quite experience things as they are "in reality." He taught that there was a more perfect, nonmaterial realm of existence.

In contrast, Aristotle taught that there is no world outside of our senses. Nowadays, scientists have invented sophisticated scientific instruments such as microscopes and telescopes to *extend* the power of our senses, but the majority of scientists still share Aristotle's basic materialistic worldview.

I believe that the findings of quantum physics increasingly support Plato. There is credible scientific evidence that suggests the existence of a nonmaterial, nonphysical universe—even though it may not as yet be clearly perceptible to our senses and scientific instrumentation. And when we consider out-of-body experiences, shamanic journeys, and lucid dream states—though they cannot be replicated in the true scientific sense—these also point to the existence of nonmaterial dimensions of reality.

Now most of us were not trained to look for and experience our souls. We've been more or less trained to look for things that can be grasped— things that are physical and solid. But the soul is not tangible, physical, or solid. You cannot just reach out and touch the soul. Yet, the soul as an animating principle in the universe is ultimately more important than anything that is physical or tangible.

The question then arises, "How is it that more people do not *directly* experience the presence of their souls?" They may *read* about the soul, they may *believe* in the soul, but if the soul is a reality, why do they feel a sense of soul-loss, an *absence* of the soul in their lives? The answer may be found in the nature of the soul itself.

The soul is alive and vibrant, yet experienced *subjectively.* The world that we see with our everyday eyes—through the filter of our senses—is derived from a more "objective" world. It seems that the "out there" objective world, and the subjectively experienced "soul world," are in conflict with each other. This corresponds to what spiritual teachers have been saying about what happens when living spirit descends into objective matter— *there's a fight!* So if we become too involved with the objective, external processes of life, we tend to lose touch with perception from the level of our soul. It's only when we "go within" into an internal quietness—as in meditation—that we begin to perceive something that is deeper and more meaningful than just the objective "out there-ness." So it's really important for those of us who have lost touch with our souls to spend some quiet time— not in thinking, not in going over the day's list of everything that has to be done—but in being with ourselves in ways that allow a deeper inner reality to bubble up from within our consciousness.

To explore the possible nature of the soul in scientific terms, we can look into the heart of quantum physics. It has to be said at the outset that the study of quantum physics is a very difficult realm to investigate because the objects and forces that are studied by quantum physics are usually infinitesimally small. As we go down to the level of subatomic particles, scientists find that these particles are moving so rapidly that we can't follow them as we would follow an ordinary larger object moving in ordinary space. The movements and properties of these very small objects do not follow the old ways of thinking found in classical physics that were developed by Sir Isaac Newton and others. On this subatomic level of existence, Newtonian physics simply doesn't work. So a new form of physics had to be created to adequately account for the phenomena we observed.

On the subatomic level, particles don't simply move from point A to point B in a continuous fashion. Instead, these particles move in "quantum jumps." Particles virtually leap from one place to another. All visible light is created by these atomic jumping processes. In order to understand how this works, we first have to understand how light behaves in atoms.

We have found that light-emitting electrons inside atoms are instantaneously quantum leaping from one place to another. Although this is some-times hard for the mind to conceive, we know that this is a fact because we have tested and verified mathematical equations with actual experiments in the field. The phenomena observed in these experiments match the theoret-ical equations very well.

Quantum physicists have also demonstrated in experiments with sub-atomic particles that certain fields have a kind of intelligence and seem to be able to do things that ordinary fields can't do. One very strange process that physicists observe is that electrons simply vanish in a puff of light when they interact with certain other particles. In the beginning, we didn't know why this happened. Then we realized that these vanishing electrons were inter-acting with anti-matter. Because anti-matter electrons moved oppositely to electrons, when the opposing particles met, they annihilated each other. When we studied anti-matter more closely, we began to speak about anti-matter as being "bubbles in the absolute vacuum of empty space."

What is this "absolute vacuum of empty space?" Well, how many of you have ever fallen asleep watching television late at night and when you awoke, you heard the static hushing noise from television screen? That noise, produced by the electronics inside the television receiver, is the amplified sound of this "vacuum of space." Many quantum physicists, including myself, believe that the entire universe, the entire creation, was created out of this "absolute nothingness of the vacuum of space." It appears this "vacuum of nothingness" is intelligent, active, and has "con-sciousness." The source of the soul proceeds from—and is present in—this vacuum. Admittedly, the very notion that "some thing" can be created from "no thing" is a very difficult concept for the mind to grasp.

I theorize that the soul emerged into expression at the same time that all the matter in the universe emerged—at the time of the "Big Bang" 15 bil-lion years ago. According to our present scientific model, the universe will continue to exist for another 20 billion, billion years until a time that is referred by scientists as the "Big Crunch."

Between those two points, from the Big Bang, at the beginning of time—to the Big Crunch, at the end of time—all the matter in the universe appears, expands to a maximum point, and then contracts again into noth-ing. And through it all, an ultimate intelligence—call it what you will—guides and directs the various activities of everything in the universe—including all living life forms—in unfathomable, unseen ways.

Some people talk about the Light that is seen at the moment of death and in near-death experiences. From a scientific standpoint, it is difficult to say exactly what is going on. And the reason why we don't know is because we have no idea where the viewer *is* that sees this Light. As an example, right now, you have some sense of being present in your body looking out at the world. But according to what we know from physics, this is an illusion of perception: There is no place inside your body where "you" actually exist. You don't have a particular volume of space or spot that is "you." It is an illusion to think that everything outside that volume of space is "not you"—what we commonly say is "outside of you." The best description we can give for this sense of presence is that you "are everywhere." The main reason that you have more awareness of being in a body is simply because the sensory apparatus of the body commands a great deal of your attention.

Now, much of our attention is linked to our physical senses, and we have the illusion that our human bodies are solid, but our bodies are over 99.99 percent empty space. To show that this is the case, we know that if an atom is blown up to the size of an entire football stadium, the dense part of the atom would be comparable to the size of a single grain of rice placed on the 50-yard line. Now why is that important? Because in an atom, the nucleus accounts for 99.99 percent of all of the matter, or mass, in the atom. Atoms are mostly made of space. So although we experience ourselves as being these solid human bodies, it's more like "who we are" is an awareness or consciousness that lives in space.

Some people may wonder, What is the "Light at the end of the tunnel" phenomenon that sometimes occurs in near-death experiences, and probably at the moment of death as well? Let me offer a possibility here. Although all material objects cannot, by definition, travel faster than the speed of light, there is evidence that the soul, which is nonphysical and therefore not confined by movements in the material world, *can* travel faster than the speed of light. Traveling faster than the speed of light is called "super-luminal speed."

So at the time of death, or during a near-death experience, it may very well be that the soul transitions from the material world—which operates at speeds *less* than the speed of light—to a world that operates *faster* than light speed, the so-called superluminal spiritual world. In that transfer, a tunneling effect may take place in much the same way that it appears to take place in what astrophysicists call a "black hole."

Now this is where it gets really interesting! At the superluminal speed of the soul, we go beyond time and space as we experience it in this physical dimension. We then have the phenomenon of being able to move both forward and backward through time/space. Something like this is described by people who come back from a near-death experience, or just before death. What these people are very likely experiencing are windows into that kind of time/space dimension of reality.

They also report seeing their loved ones that have departed, and also meeting what I call "superluminary figures" such as Jesus, Mother Mary, Moses, Krishna, and many other sacred personages. The specific superluminary figure that appears is usually based on a person's upbringing—Jesus appears to Christians, Krishna to Hindus, and so on. But why do these particular beings manifest in our consciousness? Well, I believe these figures are symbolic representations of our spiritual ideals. For I believe that on a higher level, everyone embodies the archetypal aspects of Jesus, Krishna, Mohammed, et cetera. These archetypes of our ideals serve to heal our sense of soul-loss. They help us remember a part of us that we often forget about in everyday life. The physics of the process of experiencing these beings involves an interaction between our soul and our body-mind. This is nothing less than the "physics of God" that we're talking about!

Some may wonder, *All right, if quantum physics offers evidence for the existence of the soul, where is God in this picture?* Let me offer a speculative but scientifically grounded view of God. First, in speaking about any phenomena— including when we talk about God—scientists prefer to say that something or someone *behaves* in *this* way or *that* way, rather than say that something or someone *does* this or *does* that. So, using this scientific terminology, how does God *behave* in the universe? Well, if we read the Bible, God seems to behave in very paradoxical ways. But there is *one* way that God behaves that seems to be very relevant to this discussion: God *creates.* God is considered the ultimate *Creator* of all that is. If that's the case, is it possible to speak about a "physics of God's behavior" that explains how God creates? I think we can.

Basically, we're looking at a process in which the ultimate source of everything—"God"—or whatever name you want to call it—transforms consciousness into matter. Once this happens, matter inherently acts as a kind of reflection or mirror of the intelligence from which it has sprung. As matter modifies itself over time in an ongoing evolutionary process, new information and intelligence continues to be reflected in an ever-evolving universe.

So what we call "God" continues to create—with infinite intelligence—every billionth of a billionth of second, now, and for billions and billions of years to come. What is created *with* and *in* this perfect Intelligence reflects and modifies everything at every instant and at every level. This happens from the smallest electron to the largest galaxy—including all forms of life in the universe.

Now on a human level, some people are upset when they view their lives and think, *Oh, God, what did I live for? Isn't it terrible that I'm going to die. Life was black when it started. Life was black when I was here. And it's going to be black again when life ends! Oh, God, what's it all about?* In my view, even this blackness and despair has been designed into God's system. You may not completely believe or even remember this in this moment, but on some level, a part of you has actually created all of it! Now, the "you" that created it all is not the person, the personality, the one inside you that identifies oneself as "I'm Joe, I'm Martha, I'm Sam"—that's not the person I am speaking to or about. It's the *greater essence* of "I," this *deeper* presence, the working of consciousness itself that is *in you, in me, in everyone. That* "I"—working through this body—is the *same you* that is reflected in the archetypal images of Jesus, Moses, Mohammed, and Krishna—all of whom remind us of our true essence. The presence of these beings is a reflection of something greater than our "I"-self.

To conclude, when Einstein died, researchers were interested in examining his brain to see whether there was something special about it that made him a genius. Aside from a slightly greater number of glial cells in his visual cortex, there wasn't any significant difference in his brain to sufficiently account for his being a "genius." His brain is still in a jar at Princeton University. So, we're not going to find what makes one person smart and one person stupid by looking at their brains, unless, of course, there's an obvious physical impairment. In the same way, we're not going to find the source of intelligence and the soul in the material world.

I don't see the soul and consciousness as an epi-phenomenon—or product—of matter. It's just the other way around: I see matter as an epi-phenomenon of soul and consciousness. The material world has evolved from the absolute vacuum of space—the home of the soul.

*"If the existence of the soul is admitted on the basis of
the argument that is self-luminous—and knowledge, existence,
and blessedness are its essence—it naturally follows from this
that...there was never a time when It did not exist, because if the
Soul did not exist, where was time? Time is in the Soul. When the
Soul reflects Its powers on the mind and the mind thinks, then time
appears. When there was no Soul, certainly there was no
thought, and without thought, there would was no time."*

— Swami Vivekananda, the first spiritual leader from India to
address the World Parliament of Religions in 1891

CHAPTER TWENTY-NINE

Is There Life After Death?
Science and the Survival Hypothesis

WILLIS W. HARMAN, PH.D.

Willis W. Harman, Ph.D., was president of the Institute of Noetic Sciences and emeritus professor at Stanford University until his death in 1997. His books include *Higher Creativity, Global Mind-Change,* and *New Metaphysical Foundations of Modern Science.* The following chapter is based on a film interview and a public address given at the Institute of Noetic Sciences Conference on Consciousness in Chicago, Illinois.

"Most scientists would claim that there is no satisfactory scientific evidence to support the hypothesis of the continuation of personhood through the transition called death. . . .It is essential to recognize that science in its present form is not in a position to deny the possibility."
— Dr. Willis Harman

The question of whether our personhood in some sense persists through the death of the physical body became an issue in the Western world mainly after the middle of the 19th century, when the prestige and implications of modern science had become such as to seriously challenge the folk belief in some kind of survival of personal consciousness. Interest in the question peaked around the turn of the century and waned to a mere trickle after World War I. There was a slow resurgence of interest beginning in the 1960s, and we seem set for a fresh look at the question in the 1990s.

The question is obviously important to the individual, relating as it does to his or her values and life goals. But it is important to society as well. Our present health-care system spends a major fraction of its resources keeping people physically alive past the point where, with a different cultural outlook on mortality, they would be preparing for a dignified and meaningful death. The concept of survival is central to spirituality and religion. Most important, the fear of nonsurvival—the fear of death as ceasing existence—underlies many other fears, fears which will be even more prevalent as modern society undergoes a paradigmatic transition that is uncharted but imminent.

Most scientists would claim that there is no satisfactory scientific evidence to support the hypothesis of the continuation of personhood through the transition called death. That objection would be based largely on the presumption that discarnate intelligence is simply impossible; consciousness and memory cannot be imagined to exist in the absence of a physical brain. It is essential to recognize that *science in its present form is not in a position to deny the possibility.* That is because the present epistemology (way of knowing, "rules of evidence") of Western science rules out any consideration of consciousness *as a causal reality.* Thus, it does not find in its understanding of causality anything resembling a self or personality, endowed with reason, will, and a valid sense of value—either before or after death.

The eminent British astrophysicist Sir Arthur Eddington made this point with a story of an ichthyologist—a scientist who studies fish—who explored the seven seas with a net of one-inch mesh, and after a lifetime of research arrived at the scientific conclusion that there are no creatures with a diameter less than one inch each!

Thus, we have this basic perplexity. On the one hand, there is a tremendous amount of empirical, anecdotal, clinical, and traditional evidence suggesting that in some sense the essence of the person survives physical death, and that the realm of the afterdeath is not so discontinuous with Earthly life as we might have been led to assume. On the other hand, there appears to be no way within the conceptual systems of contemporary science to make any sense out of this concept.

The Challenge to Scientific Epistemology

The puzzle of consciousness—embodied *or* discarnate—poses the most fundamental challenge to the dominant scientific epistemology. The late Nobel laureate neuroscientist Roger Sperry long insisted that the scientific account of the universe cannot be complete or accurate unless it includes *consciousness as a causal reality*.[1] To include consciousness as a causal force—even though we take that fact to be obvious in our everyday lives—is to abandon the whole idea of a strictly scientific worldview within which everything obeys inviolable "scientific laws" and conscious intention has no place. The quantified relationships of conventional science *do,* of course, describe what happens under those conditions when consciousness as a causal factor is not interfering—and so they are as useful as they ever were for prediction, control, and the design of manipulative technologies. But that science—quantum physics and chaos theory included—is in no way qualified to deny the efficacy of consciousness, whether or not it appears to be embodied.

We will, in time, have an adequate science of consciousness—a science that will be based in the totality of human experience, not merely the phenomenal (that is, in physical sense data). For that we need an epistemology of the subjective. There is good reason to feel that development may not be far off.[2]

Earlier Attempts to Explore Survival within a Scientific Framework

The medieval worldview was characterized by a continuum between this world and the next, such that the question of continuation of consciousness didn't even come up. This continuum had been shattered by the scientific revolution, so that by the mid-19th century there was a near-total discrepancy between the religious worldview within which the survival issue was presumably resolved, and a scientific worldview within which the question was irrelevant.

About this time, considerable public interest developed in the phenomenon of mediumship, wherein a person in an altered state of consciousness appears to be able to receive communications from discarnate entities, and on occasion to evoke such physical manifestations as raps, table tipping, Ouija board influencing, and the like. In the United States, the spontaneous occurrence of such abilities on the part of the Fox sisters triggered a flurry of enthusiasm. Eventually this attracted the serious interest of scholars such as Sir Oliver Lodge and Frederic W. H. Myers in England, and William James in the United States; and led to disciplined investigation and the creation of professional societies, the most prestigious being the Society for Psychical Research, formed in 1882.[3]

The messages came in various ways. Some were utterances by the medium, taken down by a clerical recorder. Others came in the form of automatic writing. A few more were inscribed on closed hinged slates (of the type that were commonly used by schoolchildren) in which a slate pencil had been inserted, and the closed slates are held by the researcher or placed under heavy objects to eliminate any possibility of fraud. (On careful examination, the particles of writing material appeared to have been deposited on the slate face, rather than rubbed off the slate pencil in the normal way. Of course, the idea that writing could take place without a writer to move the pencil was not accepted by skeptics, but there seems to have been adequate critical observers to give the reports credibility).

One of the most consistently performing of the mediums was Mrs. Piper, thoroughly investigated on both sides of the Atlantic by James, Lodge, Myers, and others. On many occasions, she produced information that purported to come from the deceased communicator, and which was rather convincing. In a typical instance, Lodge handed her a watch that had belonged to his uncle, who had been dead for 20 years. "Uncle Jerry," contacted via this connection and asked about his boyhood, recalled (through the medium's voice) several incidents—killing a cat in a place called Smith's field, owning a long snakeskin, and being nearly drowned in a creek—all three of which were totally new to Lodge. Upon questioning two living brothers of the deceased uncle, one remembered the snakeskin but denied killing the cat. The other, however, remembered both the cat and playing in Smith's field, and he gave details of the creek incident.

Myers's investigations in England were outstanding, and toward the end of his life he summarized the evidence for survival in a landmark two-volume work called *Human Personality and Its Survival of Bodily Death.*[4] He and his fellow researchers were consistently frustrated by the difficulties of studying mediumistic communication. He half-jokingly promised his fellow workers that when he died he would devise an experiment that would leave people in no doubt as to his identity and survival. Beginning shortly after his death, and continuing for three decades, there was a remarkable series of communications purporting to come from him (with a few from his colleagues Edmund Gurney and Henry Sidgwick, who had also died by this time) which became known as the "cross-correspondences." These scripts came to a dozen mediums (Mrs. Piper being one) residing on three continents. They comprised fragments of messages, including parts of classical quotations, which were clearly incomplete in themselves, but when assembled at the British Society for Psychical Research office in London, fit together like pieces of a jigsaw puzzle.[5]

Myers's attempt to bring after-death experience into the reach of science did not, it seems, stop with his death, nor even with the cross-correspondences. More than 20 years *after* his death, a sensitive in North Ireland named Geraldine Cummins began to take down through automatic writing, lengthy scripts attributed to the deceased Myers. These were published (with Cummins identified as author, but with a foreword explaining why she believed them to be transmissions from Myers) as two books, *The Road to Immortality* and *Beyond Human Personality.*[6] They contain a fascinating report of his after-death experience and his mapping of the after-death possibilities, the latter being broadly similar to mappings that have appeared before and since from other sources.

All of the work with mediums over these many decades faced the obvious problem that, whatever the original source of the communication, there was no way of telling how much it had been corrupted by bubbling up through the medium's unconscious mind. This problem plagued all of the researchers from Frederic Myers on, and was a source of continual frustration, even when there seemed to be something significantly evidential in the messages received.

As if in response to this problem, shortly after magnetic tape recorders became widely used in the 1950s, messages began to appear on various tape recorders that purported to be from discarnate beings. Some of these were persons who, prior to their deaths, were involved with research on the survival issue. In still more recent times, as other technologies became available, these apparent communications have extended to involve television screens, video tape recorders, and words and images scanned into computer disks; to include real-time two-way communication; and to include photograph-like images as well as verbal messages. All of this would seem on the face of it to constitute a totally preposterous claim, yet some of these communications, collected by researchers in at least six countries, comprise intriguing evidential significance.[7]

The Question Is Still Alive

Thus, there are two developments that together make it plausible that this field of research might take on a new life. One is the recognition that in order to include even ordinary consciousness as a causal factor in phenomena, science will have to be reconstituted on the basis of new metaphysical assumptions—a new "epistemology of the subjective." The other is the emergence of new kinds of data that imply, at least, that progress will be made through the active collaboration of researchers on both sides of the curtain we call death.

One further development adds to the plausibility of growing interest in survival research. Bear in mind that the concept of the unconscious mind has become a widely accepted basis for psychoanalysis and other psychotherapies a full half century before it gained acceptance in strict scientific circles. So, it is not without significance that therapies based on recollection of past lives[8] and on the possibility of spirit attachment[9] are now well established, although the conceivability of neither concept is admitted by the scientific community.

We can begin to see, in outline at least, the kind of answer that is likely to come out of this new research field. Ken Wilber[10] has presented the case that when all the available evidence is brought to bear, it points toward an ontological reality that is a continuum from the material at one end of the spectrum, to Spirit at the other end. The human being is potentially able to become aware of the entire continuum, albeit in Earthly life (and particularly in the modern world), attention is primarily focused on the material. A more adequate science would direct its attention to the entire continuum, not just to the material end. Furthermore, it would include not only scientific (upward) causation—for example, consciousness and behavior "explained" in terms of physical microphenomena—but "downward causation" as well—that is, causation from consciousness and spirit "downward" to the emotional and material.

From that ontological perspective, death appears less an extinction than an awakening to "where one was all along." At death, the center of awareness shifts from the physical to higher planes (with perhaps a period of confusion and/or sleepy resting in between.) We don't go somewhere at death; we are already there. As this new view becomes real in our lives, fear of death disappears. We couldn't non-exist if we wanted to!

"One great scientist, Sir Isaac Newton, came
to the following conclusion about the limitations of science.
He once said, 'I can take my telescope and look millions of miles into
space, but I can put it aside, go into my room, close the door, get down on
my knees in earnest prayer, and see more of heaven and get closer to God
than I can assisted by all the telescopes and material agencies on Earth.'
This profound statement still holds true today. Since Newton's time, no
scientist has been able to develop any instrument for communicating with
the Creator that is equal to the power of going within through prayer and
meditation. As Newton said, prayer took him further than his scientific
tools. He was referring to a process of inverting one's attention
to look and listen to what is within. That looking and listening
to the inner world is another name for meditation."

— Sant Rajinder Singh

CHAPTER THIRTY

Theta Consciousness:
Survival Research with the Living
MICHAEL GROSSO, PH.D.

Michael Grosso received his doctorate in philosophy from Columbia University. He is a distinguished professor of philosophy and humanities and the author of *Frontiers of the Soul, Soulmaker, The Final Choice,* and other books. This chapter is based on an address given by the author in Chicago, Illinois.

*"The argument, as it goes, is: If a conscious subject can
separate from the body before death, it may be able to maintain
that separation after—and thus survive—death."*
— Dr. Michael Grosso

The Renaissance thinker Marsilio Ficino believed that the appetite for immortality is as natural to people as neighing is to horses. The great spiritual traditions assume some form of afterlife. Plato thought that belief in immortality was crucial to moral development. From a psychological viewpoint, C. G. Jung said that modern humanity needs to come to grips with the idea of death, and that we moderns in search of a soul are out of synch with our collective heritage on this score. From a sociological perspective, Ernest Becker tied the pathologies of politics to the denial of death, and concluded that science must provide some kind of answer to our death-denying, power-craving—hence, life-destroying—culture.[1]

Is there a life after death? The question is important for another reason. There is a huge split between popular and mainstream views on the subject. The majority of Americans believe in some form of survival of death. Yet there is a consensus among most educated people in the modern world that there is no postmortem life. (In 1982, a Gallup poll indicated that 67 percent of Americans believed in an afterlife, whereas the percentage of believers plummets among the scientifically educated.) So either the populace or the academic community is deluded. Is there any way to settle this?

Assume, no matter how much new data we gather, that we will remain frozen in deadlock; is there a way to break the deadlock—a way to leap beyond the survival-of-consciousness koan? I believe an option remains, and it is one that has probably served as the basis for achieving conviction about these matters since time immemorial.

Survival research has, for the most part, essentially been based on the idea of studying *traces* of deceased personalities. We study apparitions, ghosts, hauntings, reincarnation memories, mediumistic deliverances—which we then analyze and try to see as supporting or not supporting the survival hypothesis.

I suggest that we supplement the trace approach with a practical, experiential approach—notwithstanding the massive suggestiveness of the types of survival "traces." However, we would no longer study the traces of other, possibly discarnate beings; we *ourselves* would—as Plato defined philosophy—attempt to "practice death and dying." In other words, we ourselves would, here and now, attempt to enter more deeply into the *allos topos*—the "other place."

As Dr. William Roll has suggested, we might study survival by studying the consciousness that may survive bodily death—which he called "theta" consciousness. This would be survival research with the living. Theta consciousness is consciousness, Roll suggests, that would "extend" beyond the body (into what he, following the Iroquois Indians, is fond of calling the "long body").

The long body exhibits itself, according to Roll, in out-of-body experiences and transpersonal and mystical states. The role of theta consciousness would therefore bridge the gap between transpersonal psychology and survival research. Roll also suggests that theta states may correlate with changes in psychophysiology, and cites evidence indicating that transpersonal states are associated with a global decrease of respiration and energy metabolism in the brain and central nervous system. (These are only hints of possible correlations, and what they imply, if anything, is open to discussion.) Ernst Arbman, in his study of trance and ecstasy, reviews data that strongly suggest that what Roll calls "theta states" are physiologically akin to deathlike or near-death states.[2]

A near-death experience might be viewed as an experiment along these lines, imposed by nature. Near-death experiencers claim they "know" their experience was "more real than real" and that there is an afterworld. The pursuit of this kind of subjective conviction may be the best way open to us, if we seek to break the survival of consciousness stalemate. In other words, the best way to break the intellectual stalemate is to induce experiences of theta consciousness, and thus learn to explore the "next " world—*now*. The "next" world we would take as another expression for the Heraclitean depth of *this* world.

A number of researchers are consciously doing this. Roll himself, for example, practices Zen meditation. It may be possible to experimentally induce experiences that could be thought of as a type of practice of death and dying—or in light of modern research, *near* death and *near* dying. Dr. Kenneth Ring has focused on the *aftereffects* of near-death experiences (NDEs)—the psychic sensitivity, enhanced spiritual awareness, feelings of oceanic love, and disappearance of the inhibiting fear of death. Focus on these, Ring suggests, and see where they take us. His approach to the "survival" question, in short, stresses not the traces of other people's possible survival, but the possibility of NDEs being a way to explore theta states among the living. As I would interpret him, the question seems to be: How can we break down the barrier between the "next" world and "this" world of consciousness so that the trace approach, at least from a subjective and existential point of view, *ceases to matter anymore?* This would involve a different kind of *experiment*—a word, let us recall, that stems from a Greek word that means "to experience."

Galileo changed the course of science and history by introducing experiments that actively intervened in nature; the next step in survival research might profit from Galileo's example and try to model itself on the idea of actively "entering" the next world *now*. By using meditation, brain machines, mirror gazing, active imagination, fasting, and other time-honored spiritual and shamanic techniques in combination with modern science and technology, we might learn to experimentally induce, understand, and ratify, for ourselves, the experience of theta consciousness.

If enough people acquired this type of knowledge by acquaintance, we might begin to see a gradual dawning of a new paradigm. Our attitude toward the enigma of death might also change, perhaps dramatically.

*"I wouldn't say that I'm a religious person, even though
I was raised Catholic and was an altar boy in my earlier years.
But something happened that truly opened up my understanding of
the true nature of my spiritual being. This was a temporary night
paralysis I would experience at night and in the early mornings. This
night paralysis led to what I now know to be out-of-body experiences. To
verify I was having these experiences and not just dreaming, I would go
to physical locations that I'd never been, identify what the people were
doing there, and later verify all this—even down to what they were wearing at the time. I would also be able to identify the surroundings because
I had been flying around the neighborhood. I believe that 99 percent
of us travel out of body almost every night, but only about 20 to
25 percent of us have conscious recall of these experiences. If people
could learn how to travel out of body, or know consciously
what it's like to exist beyond the physical, this would be
ideal preparation for transitioning death's door."*
— Albert Taylor, NASA engineer,
from the video *Experiencing the Soul*

EPILOGUE

ELIOT JAY ROSEN

My role as editor has been not unlike that of a restaurant maître d': The preface and general introduction initially greeted you as you entered; you were escorted to your table by the title and description of each chapter found in the table of contents; you were given a taste of what was on the menu in the Part introductions preceding the eight major divisions of the book; and finally, you were introduced to each of the 32 guest contributors by way of brief biographical sketches preceding each chapter.

I'd like to conclude this book by stepping out of my role as editor and share—on a more personal, heartfelt level—some pivotal events in my own journey of soul.

When I was 18 years old, I left my suburban home outside New York City to attend Albany State University where I was studying philosophy of religions and psychology. Soon after my arrival, I was intermittently plagued by what could be described as a deep existential despair. I found myself feverishly searching outside myself for something or someone to fill what felt like a meaningless void.

What set the stage for this state of mind was my mother's death when I was 12 years old, which left a gaping hole in my heart. And only a few months into my undergraduate career, I was traumatized by the tragedy of finding my college roommate's decomposing body sprawled out on the kitchen floor. The little blue pills he had used to commit suicide were scattered everywhere. Only at his funeral was I told by his mother that Alan had attempted suicide several times before we had met.

Thinking that a change of scene would ease the pain of this loss and diminish the harrowing images of death that continued to haunt me, I took my semester break in a beach town in sunny Florida. A day after my arrival, I was walking alone on a deserted beach late one night when I spontaneously fell to my knees on the sand and cried out: *"God, if You really exist, please help me! Show me You're real, for I can't take this pain anymore."* Immediately after this poignant cry of the soul left my lips—as I gazed up at the starry sky in fearful wonderment and felt the powerful ocean waves crashing around me—an inexplicable feeling of peace shot through me. It was as if this involuntary outburst was an arrow sent from *my* heart into a reservoir of Divine mercy reverberating in *God's* heart, and that this same arrow, dipped now in God's love, had met its intended mark as it returned to again pierce *my* heart. Although this incredible peace lasted only a few minutes, within my soul I knew that my sincere plea for Divine intervention would be forthcoming.

When I returned to the university, I joined the Student Psychology Club. The guest speaker one evening was an elderly gentleman who had spent many years in India with a saintly person. At the conclusion of his talk, he allowed us to touch the white silken robe that he had brought with him that had been worn by this holy one. As I touched the hem of his garment, I was transported into a bliss beyond space, time, and description. The impact of this spiritual experience so profoundly affected me that within a few months, I made a pilgrimage to India to continue my spiritual journey. The purpose of the trip was to learn how to have these types of spiritual experiences "on my own"—and not as a by-product of coming in contact with a vibrationally charged object.

My month-long visit to India halfway around the globe was quite an eye-opener for a 19-year-old, but the object of my search remained unfulfilled. Looking back, it is ironic that I eventually found what I was looking for in my own backyard—in another holy land sometimes referred to as "the Gold Coast of Florida," but not before I almost killed myself on a self-imposed "cleansing" diet of fruit and vegetable juices. At the time, I thought that purifying my body with these fresh-squeezed juices would increase my spiritual receptivity. The problem, however, was that I hadn't a clue on how to safely conduct the radical extended juice fast I had embarked on.

My weight had dropped to an alarming 80 pounds, and I was near-bedridden before I broke my fast. Although I didn't know it at the time, I desperately needed the supervision of a qualified natural health practitioner. At a certain point, I was so weak that while I was pulling the blanket over my shoulders, I popped out of my body and found myself "in the Light." I had the immediate knowledge that my body had stopped breathing, and two questions immediately arose in my consciousness in quick succession while I was out of my body. My first question was, "If I'm not breathing, how is it I'm still aware and conscious?" My second question was, "If I'm not breathing, who just asked that question?" The answers to both these questions led me to the inescapable conclusion that "I" had an existence that was separate and independent from "my body." Soon after this near-deathlike experience, a kindly person gave me a book called *What Is Spirituality?* written by Sant Kirpal Singh. In the book, the author described with great precision and beauty exactly what I had been seeking—a way to practice a scientific method of meditation under the guidance and protection of a competent spiritual teacher. I began to attend weekly spiritual meetings where these teachings were discussed, and local practitioners meditated together.

My outer search had ended—but the inner journey did not really begin until I was formally initiated into the inner science of Light and Sound meditation by Sant Darshan Singh, the spiritual successor to Sant Kirpal Singh. To my surprise and delight, to practice this "science of the soul" there was no necessity to leave the religion of one's birth or the normal activities of contemporary modern life. Another aspect that I appreciated was the high standard of ethical purity required on this path. It was also refreshing to find that there were never any financial charges asked for the teachings. The spiritual teacher himself lived entirely on his own income and did not accept gifts in any form—material or otherwise.

On November 29, 1975, the night before I received meditation instructions, Sant Darshan Singh blessed me with his presence on the inner planes of consciousness. I wrote this poem immediately after this profound experience:

> *If eternal time is consumed in the enormity of space,*
> *And space in turn subdued by endless time,*
> *How fragile then, this moment in time, in place,*
> *How small and mortal appears our human race.*

Is there no Great Heart to enfold me—
Some saving harbor amidst the teeming ocean of life,
To assuage my longing cries
For a transcendent love that never dies?

Glorious vision and celestial strains
Bursts through the timeless vault of space behind closed eyes,
Leaving my pillow wet with grateful tears.
Effulgent melodies of the Inward Beyond
Rekindles the memory of His existence.

Life's fearful trembling now fade
As the pretense of an authorless creation is lifted!
For yet another lifetime, the homeward search for the
Divine Beloved begins again.

The loneliness I had felt all my life now began to melt into a longing to become closer to God. The progressive unfolding of my soul had begun. Life's highest purpose was re-remembered.

Although our individual approaches to the Divinity within varies, and you may *already* be committed and content in your chosen spiritual path, I encourage all those that may still be searching to learn more about how to transcend physical consciousness and enter into higher realms of God-consciousness. The great mystics and saints—both past and present—have told us that by practicing meditation under the guidance of a fully competent spiritual teacher, our souls are nourished by a ravishingly beautiful inner Light and an ever-enrapturing inner Sound. These spiritual teachers say that this inner Light and Sound emanate from God Himself and serve as connecting lifelines through which our souls travel through the inner planes of consciousness until we finally merge back in God.

The Power of Prayer and Meditation

It is said that prayer is a process in which we offer up our heartfelt pleas to God, and that meditation is the process through which we receive His *response* to our prayers, begin to experience His direct presence, and ultimately merge back in our Creator. If we wish to attain lasting happiness that is not dependent on ever-fluctuating external conditions, then prayer, meditation, and living an ethical life based on the principles of love and forgiveness are tried-and-true methods that open the floodgates of our receptivity to Divine grace. Our souls will then be able to contact an inexhaustible storehouse of peace, love, and knowledge that emanate from our Creator—even while we are embodied in these biological forms. We will literally experience ourselves as "being in the world, but not of it." [Paraphrase of John 17:15-17] We can be in line at the grocery store or caring for our children or working at our jobs, and we can simultaneously be filled with His Holy presence.

It is my prayer for all of us that we continue to "seek first the kingdom of God," in the faith that if we do so, "... all other things shall be added unto (us)." [Matthew 6:33]

I will conclude this epilogue with an excerpt from a poem by the great mystic and poet Jala'u'din Rumi, whose words capture the essence of the Divine journey ahead when he declares:

"Take the grinding stone of love and
Grind thyself to dust,
With the staff of hope and the sandals of true living
Go on the pilgrimage to Union.
With the vision of the one without a second,
Rise above all religion to the Universal religion.
He alone is a true man who worships at the shrine of HU-MAN-NESS."
— Jala'u'din Rumi

APPENDIX A

Resource Listings—Taking the Next Step

The contributors to this book invite you to contact them to find out more about their work. Some of these individuals have also listed research and charitable organizations that you may wish to explore further.

Dr. Joan Borysenko—For anyone interested in Joan's writings, research, and public workshops, please contact Mind/Body Health Sciences at 393 Dixon Rd., Boulder, CO 80302 (USA). For information on The National Emotional Literacy Project for Prisoners, a nonprofit organization dedicated to providing prisoners with tools for healing and rehabilitation, write or call The Lionheart Foundation, Box 194, Boston, MA 02117. Phone/fax: (617) 267-3121.

Dannion Brinkley—Dannion can be reached at P.O. Box 1919, Aiken, SC 29802 (USA) or (205) 831-6551. Dannion wishes interested readers to find out more about Compassion in Action ("the *real* C.I.A.," says Dannion), a group of specially trained volunteers that help hospices serve the terminally ill. Write Compassion in Action, P.O. Box 84013, Los Angeles, CA 90073 (USA). To locate the local hospices in your area or to become a hospice volunteer, call the National Hospice Organization at (800) 658-8898, or write the National Hospice Foundation at 1901 N. Moore St., Arlington, VA 22209 (USA) to make a tax-deductible donation.

Dr. Diane Cirincione/Dr. Gerald Jampolsky—The Center for Attitudinal Healing (T.C.A.H.) was founded by Jerry and provides psycho-social-spiritual services on a free-of-charge basis for people who wish to develop a spiritual perspective on life's challenges—especially for those who are experiencing life-threatening illness. There are over 100 affiliated T.C.A.H. centers around the world. To locate the T.C.A.H. nearest you, or if you wish assistance in creating a T.C.A.H. in your area, call (415) 331-6161 or write The Center for Attitudinal Healing, 33 Buchanan Dr., Sausalito, CA 94965 (USA). The Internet address is: www.healingcenter.org.

His Holiness the Dalai Lama of Tibet—To assist the imperiled people of Tibet and the exiled Tibetan government now operating in India, you may send tax-deductible donations made out to The Tibet Fund, and mail to: The Office of Tibet, c/o Representative of His Holiness the Dalai Lama, 241 E. 32 St., New York, NY 10016 (USA), or call (212) 213-5010.

Ram Dass—For information on the spiritual teachings, books, and audio- and videotapes of Ram Dass and others, please call (415) 457-8570, or write the Hanuman Foundation, 524 San Anselmo Ave., San Anselmo, CA 94960 (USA). The Hanuman Foundation also supports other benevolent organizations that help AIDS patients, hospices, and others in need.

Betty J. Eadie—For information on Betty's books, public talks, and her ongoing benevolent work, please write Betty J. Eadie, P.O. Box 25490, Seattle, WA 98125 (USA).

Dr. Amit Goswami—Dr. Goswami can be reached by writing to him in care of the Institute of Theoretical Physics, University of Oregon, Eugene, OR 97403 (USA). Dr. Goswami is in the foundational stages of forming a Ph.D. tract institute for the study of consciousness. Anyone interested in this program—students, faculty, financial supporters, etc., should feel free to write him at the above address.

Anya Foos-Graber—For information on Anya's writings, public talks, or to order her book, *Deathing: An Intelligent Alternative for the Final Moments of Life* (Nicolas Hays, 1989) she can be reached through Nicolas-Hays Publishers, c/o Ms. Betty Lunsted, Box 612, York Beach, ME 03910 (USA).

Alex Grey—A full-color, deluxe-size edition of Alex's extraordinary art is available in the book *Sacred Mirrors: The Visionary Art of Alex Grey,* which can be ordered directly from Inner Traditions International at (800) 246-8648, or purchased through your local bookstore.

Dr. Stanislav Grof—For information on Stanislav's books and trainings, please write 20 Sunnyside Ave., Suite A-314, Mill Valley, CA 94941 (USA), or call (415) 383-8779. Several years ago, Dr. Grof and his wife, Christina, created the Spiritual Emergency Network, a telephone hotline for people in psychospiritual crisis. The Spiritual Emergency Network phone number is (408) 426-0102.

Dr. Michael Grosso—For information on Michael's writings, books, and continuing research please write to him at 26 Little Brooklyn Rd., Warwick, NY 10990 (USA). He also may be contacted by e-mail at: mgrosso@warwick.net.

Bill Guggenheim—For information on the After-Death Communications Project (ADC Project), and to share your own after-death experiences with Bill for his continuing research, please write to him at P.O. Box 916070, Longwood, FL 32791 (USA).

Dr. Willis Harman—At the time of Dr. Harman's death in 1997, he was president of the Institute of Noetic Sciences (IONS), a nonprofit research, educational, and membership organization that works closely with numerous partner organizations and a global network of colleagues in the sciences, business, health-care, education, and various other professional fields. For information about membership, call (800) 383-1394, or visit their website at: www.noetic.org.

Louise L. Hay—To find out more about Louise's books and lectures, please write to her in care of Hay House, Inc., at the address below. Louise has created the nonprofit charitable organization, the Hay Foundation, which "gives a helping hand to where it is needed most" by financially supporting small diverse organizations that supply food, shelter, counseling, education, hospice care, and financial assistance to those facing the challenges of life (battered women, AIDS patients, the homeless, etc). All of the profits from this book, *Experiencing the Soul,* are generously being donated to the Hay Foundation by Hay House, Louise's publishing house. Please send your tax-deductible donations to the Hay Foundation, P.O. Box 5100, Carlsbad, CA 92018-5100 (USA), or call (760) 431-7695.

Dr. Brent Hinze and **Sarah Hinze**—To find out more about Sarah and Brent's books and speaking engagements, and about Royal Child Studies, a nonprofit organization dedicated to awakening hearts to the sacredness of each human soul, write to them in care of: Royal Child Studies, P.O. Box 31086, Mesa, AZ 85275-1086 (USA), or call (602)898-3009. E-mail: shinze@juno.com.

Dr. Jean Houston—To find out more about Jean's books, workshops, and trainings, write or call the Foundation for Mind Research, P.O. Box 3300, Pamona, NY 10970 (USA) , or call (914) 354-3288. Jean would like you to consider supporting the Kashi Foundation, a nonprofit interfaith spiritual community providing spiritual care, comfort, and education for individuals living with AIDS and those in need. This foundation can be reached at (800) 226-1008, or you can contact them by writing to the Kashi Foundation, Dept. 106, 11155 Roseland Rd., Sebastian, FL 32958 (USA).

Stephen Levine—For a schedule of Stephen's workshops or a catalog of the healing, wisdom-filled books, audio- and videotapes of Stephen and Ondrea Levine, please write to Warm Rock Tapes at P.O. Box 108, Chamisal, NM 87521 (USA), or call (800) 731-HEAL. Stephen would like you to consider supporting the Hanuman Foundation Dying Project, an organization that assists people in the process of dying. Please write to the project at 524 San Anselmo Ave., San Anselmo, CA 94960 (USA), or call (415) 457-5406.

Christine Longaker—To find out more about the Rigpa Foundation Spiritual Care Education and Training Program, a program that provides support groups for professionals and seminars for people dealing with spiritual care issues for the dying; or to find out more about Rigpa, a nonprofit foundation that disseminates the Buddhist teachings of Sogyal Rinpoche, please write or call Rigpa at 449 Powell St., 2nd Floor, San Francisco, CA 94102 (USA), or call (415) 392-2057.

Sri Daya Mata—To learn more about the teachings of Paramahansa Yogananda, the yoga meditation techniques he taught, and the spiritual and humanitarian work of the Self-Realization Fellowship, the international society he founded; to request prayers from the society's Worldwide Prayer Circle; or for a catalog of books and recorded talks by Yogananda, Sri Daya Mata, and others, you may write, call, or fax: Self-Realization Fellowship, 3880 San Rafael Ave., Los Angeles, 90065 (USA), or call (213) 225-2471. Fax (213) 225-5088.

Dr. Edgar Mitchell—For information on Edgar's books and activities, you may write him at P.O. Box 5400337, Lake Worth, FL 33454 (USA).

Dr. Raymond Moody—For information on Raymond's workshops, books, and unique psychospiritual services, you may write to him at P.O. Box 417, Anniston, AL 36202 (USA).

Anne Puryear—For information on the books, activities, and services of Anne and her husband, Dr. Herbert Puryear, and the Logos Center, an inter-faith church, metaphysical school, spiritual community, and holistic healing center, write or call the Logos Center, P.O. Box 12880, Scottsdale, AZ 85267 (USA), or call (602) 483-8777.

Dr. Kenneth Ring—Kenneth is one of the early pioneers in near-death study research. If you are interested in learning more about near-death experiences—whether you've had an NDE or not—he recommends that you contact the International Association for Near-Death Studies (IANDS). IANDS has dozens of local chapters in the United States and around the world. Write the International Association for Near-Death Studies, P.O Box 502, East Windsor Hill, CT (USA), or call (860) 528-5144.

Dr. Elisabeth Kübler-Ross—Elisabeth is now retired after 40 years of dedicated service to humanity. Due to a stroke, she can no longer answer her mail. If you wish to honor her life and work, she asks you to support Amnesty International, a human-rights organization that works to preserve and restore the inalienable rights and freedom of all people, including political prisoners and victims of race, gender, religious, and political discrimination. To find out more, or to contribute financially, call (800) 266-3789, or write Amnesty International, 322 8th Ave., New York, NY 10001 (USA).

Joseph Sharp—In the spirit of the theme of "sacred individuality" and following your own unique calling, Joseph encourages you to choose an unorthodox way of expressing your benevolence. Choose an outrageous, "off-the-beaten path" person or organization who could benefit from your caring, and give them your love, time, and/or financial resources. This could be the eccentric homeless person down the street you see every day as you travel to work, a lonely elderly person, or a fledgling nonprofit organization whose mission you believe in. To contact Joseph, he can be reached via e-mail at: jhsharp@ix.netcom.com.

Sant Rajinder Singh—To receive free literature on meditation and the spiritual teachings of Sant Rajinder Singh, call (800) 222-2207, or write Science of Spirituality, 4S-175 Naperville Road, Naperville, IL 60563 (USA). For updates on Sant Rajinder Singh's free public meditation programs in the U.S., and his tour schedule around the world, please call (630) 955-1200, or visit his website at: www.sos.org.

Dr. Charles Tart—Dr. Tart's personal website is full of interesting articles and the latest updates in cutting-edge research. His address is: www. paradigm.sys.com/ctart. Dr. Tart encourages readers to find out more about the Institute of Transpersonal Psychology (ITP). ITP helps people develop a spirituality that's effective for contemporary life, using science and scholarship in constructive ways toward these ends. For information, write to ITP at 744 San Antonio Rd., Palo Alto, CA 94303 (USA), or call (650) 493-4430.

Melinda H. White—For more information on Melinda's art, and/or to order a six-postcard set of *We Are the Angels: We Are the Mortal People,* write 38 Southwind Drive, Burlington, VT 05401 (USA), or call (802) 864-3660.

Dr. Harold Widdison—Harold is always interested in hearing from individuals who have had spiritual experiences, which helps his ongoing research. He can be reached at 3445 N. 4th St., Flagstaff, AZ 86004 (USA), or call (520) 779-1585. He also encourages readers to support Compassionate Friends, a nonprofit, self-help organization that offers friendship and understanding for bereaved parents, siblings, and grandparents who are grieving the death of their children. For the local chapter nearest you, or for information on how to form your own local chapter, write Compassionate Friends, P.O. Box 3696, Oakbrook, IL 60522-3696 (USA), or call (708) 990-0010.

Dr. Fred Alan Wolf—Fred encourages interested individuals to support the Internet Science Education Project (ISEP), a nonprofit California foundation dedicated to supporting and stimulating public interest in the most important scientific issues of our times. ISEP's website address is: www.hia.com/hia/pcr.

Marion Woodman—To find out more about Marion's books and activities, write 251 B Sydenham St. London, Ontario, Canada NGA1W4. She also wishes readers to support their local cancer society wherever they may live. In Canada, please support the Canadian Cancer Society at 10 Alcorne Ave., Suite 200, Canada M4V3B1, or call (416) 961-7223.

APPENDIX B

About
For A World We Choose Foundation
(A tax-deductible, nonprofit educational and charitable organization)

In the formal mission statement of **For A World We Choose Foundation** it states that "as an organization, we provide a wide spectrum of nontraditional educational and experiential opportunities that successfully integrate the life-enhancing effects of applied scientific knowledge with the transformational benefits of consciousness-expansion methods and technologies." In "plain English," this translates into the following activities and projects:

Future Plans:
The Spiritual Center for Living

Many of us in modern society not only need to redefine and enlarge our understanding of *what death is,* but need added practical knowledge on how this natural process can be more intelligently and compassionately facilitated in the most spiritual and loving ways possible.

When created, the Spiritual Center for Living will be a rurally based residential center dedicated to educating and aiding people-in-the-process-of-dying (PPDs), their caregivers, and anyone else—even those who are young and healthy—in ways to prepare for a more healing passage.

Working in conjunction with medical care provided by local hospices, this residential training center will expand on the existing hospice model by adding hard-to-find individualized spiritual training and support in preparation for this often difficult time of life.

We encourage people of all ages—even the young and healthy—to attend our traveling Conscious Living/Conscious Dying Workshops so that they can work *throughout* their lives to "prepare for a more healing passage." If you are interested in a workshop in your area, please contact us at the addresses and phone numbers listed at the conclusion of Appendix B.

If you wish to get involved in the Spiritual Center for Living, including supporting its creation by making a tax-deductible donation, please write or call us.

The Spirit of Life Tour

The Spirit of Life Tour is an interactive, multimedia educational/entertainment workshop offered to community groups; public schools; hospices; self-help groups; nursing homes; colleges; hospitals; places of worship; schools of medicine, nursing and social work; and other interested organizations and groups. The content and format of the presentations are modified for the specific needs and goals of the respective audiences, but all presentations include nondenominational, uplifting educational speakers on health and spirituality; artistic performances by spiritually oriented musicians and artists, free literature, and carefully chosen books, videos, and audio tapes available for purchase.

Local organizations and performers are sometimes invited to share the forum with our "traveling troupe." Please mail us information on the specific mission and activities of your organization. For performers and speakers, send an audio- and/or videotape that represents your talents.

To secure stable and continual funding for these presentations, we hope that socially and spiritually conscious corporations and benevolent foundations will supplement our own revenue sources to support our benevolent work.

All donations for the Spirit of Life Tours are 100 percent tax deductible.

Education Outreach

Other ongoing activities of For A World We Choose Foundation include the sponsoring and organizing of lecture series, conferences, and experiential workshops in the private and public sectors (including the public school systems); continuing to produce and disseminate life-enriching videos, books, and tapes that further the benevolent mission of our foundation; and networking, supporting, and sponsoring any other organizations and individuals who are in alignment with our foundation's principles, goals, and mission.

Any individuals or organizations who wish to find out more about these activities may write to Eliot Rosen, Director, For A World We Choose Foundation, P.O. Box 1072, Studio City, CA 91614 (USA), or call (888) 554-2560. Fax: (818) 769-8810. Our website address is: www.naturalusa.com/fawwcf, and our e-mail address is: fawwcf@worldnet.att.net

To order the companion videos, *Experiencing the Soul* and *Conscious Dying: Preparing Now for a Healing Passage* (both approximately one hour in length), send $24.95 to the above address (plus $3.00 for shipping and handling per tape; quantity discounts available). Make checks payable to: For A World We Choose Foundation.

ENDNOTES

General Introduction
1 Roger Bacon, as quoted by Dr. Charles Tart, personal communication.
2 C. G. Jung, *Memories, Dreams, Reflections,* Vintage Press, 1989.
3 Ibid.

Chapter 2
1 Raymond B. Blakney, trans., *Meister Eckhart* (New York: Harper & Row, 1941), 243.
2 Natalie Goldberg, *Long Quiet Highway* (New York: Bantam Books, 1993), 183.
3 Jon Kabat-Zinn, *Wherever You Go, There You Are* (New York: Hyperion, 1994) xvi.

Chapter 3
1 The Foundation for Inner Peace, *A Course in Miracles,* second edition, 1996, Viking/Penguin Publishers.

Chapter 25
1 Aspect, A.; Dalibard, J.; and Roger, G. 1982. "Experimental test of Bell inequalities using time-varying analyzers." *Physical Review Letters* 49:1804.
2 J. Grinberg-Zylberbaum, Delaflor L., Attie, A. Goswami, "Einstein, Podolsky, Rosen Paradox-Transferred Potential, *Physics Essays,* vol. 7, 422–428, 1994.
3 A. Goswami, *The Self-Aware Universe: How Consciousness Creates the Material World* (Tarcher Putnam, 1995).

Chapter 27
1 Osis, K., "Deathbed Observations of Physicians and Nurses" (Parapsychology Foundation), 1961.

Chapter 29

1 R. W. Sperry, "Structure and Significance of the Consciousness Revolution," *The Journal of Mind and Behavior*, vol. 8, no. 1, Winter 1987.

2 W. Harman and C. DeQuincy, *The Scientific Exploration of Consciousness: Toward an Adequate Epistemology,* published by the Institute of Noetic Sciences.

3 B. Inglis, *Natural and Supernatural: A History of the Paranormal* (Prism Press, 1992).

4 F. W. H. Myers, *Human Personality and Its Survival of Bodily Death* (Longman, Green, 1903).

5 R. Haywood, *Beyond the Reach of Sense: An Inquiry into Extra-Sensory Perception* (E. P. Dutton, 1961).

6 G. Cummings, *The Road to Immortality* and *Beyond Human Personality* (Psychic Press, Ltd. of London, 1952).

7 M. Macy, *When Dimensions Cross* (Noetic Sciences Review, Spring, 1993, 17–20).

8 W. Lucas, *Regression Therapy: A Handbook for Professionals,* (Noetic Sciences Review, Spring, 1993, 20–22) and I. Stevenson, *Children Who Remember Previous Lives* (Univ. of Virginia Press, 1987).

9 W. Baldwin, *Spirit Releasement Therapy* (Noetic Sciences Review, Summer 1993, 36–39).

10 K. Wilber, *The Great Chain of Being* (Journal of Humanistic Psychology, vol. 33(3), Summer 1993, 52–55).

Chapter 30

1 E. Becker, *The Denial of Death* (The Free Press, 1973).

2 E. Arbman, *Ecstacy or Religious Trance* (Scandinavian University Books, 1968).

About Eliot Jay Rosen

An expert in the field of death and dying, **Eliot Jay Rosen** was the former head of the social work department at Hospice Hawaii. He is the present director of the nonprofit organization For A World We Choose Foundation.

As a student, he received his master's degree in clinical social work from California State University at Sacramento. His book-length master's thesis, "The Health Risk Factors and Policies of the National School Lunch Program," was a pioneering exposé on the under-recognized health dangers of the U.S. government-administered school lunch programs. He went on to author four legislative reform bills for the Hawaii State Senate and House to help improve school lunches.

As a health and mental health professional, he is a licensed independent social worker in both Hawaii and New Mexico. He is also a certified nutrition counselor and licensed massage therapist.

As an educator, Eliot was on the teaching faculty of the Elisabeth Kübler-Ross Hospice, Grief Counseling, and Death Education Program at Northern New Mexico Community College.

As a writer, his credits have primarily been in the fields of health, mental health, and spirituality. He has been published in national magazines such as *Whole Life Times, Yoga Journal, Meditation Magazine, Evolving Times,* and others. As a ghost writer, his writings have been presented at the United Nations Third International Conference on Health and the Environment.

As a spokesperson, Eliot has appeared on numerous television and radio shows speaking on the subjects of conscious living/conscious dying, holistic health, and practical spirituality.

As a spiritual aspirant, Eliot was initiated by Sant Darshan Singh (1921–1989) in 1975, and presently seeks spiritual guidance from the present living spiritual teacher, Sant Rajinder Singh.

In addition to the above, Mr. Rosen's professional milestones have included being personal assistant, nutritionist, massage therapist, and vegetarian chef for actor/director Danny DeVito and other entertainment industry stars; and he has produced and hosted the Los Angeles-based radio show *Health-Choice.* He has also performed as a professional drummer throughout the United States. He currently lives in the Los Angeles area.

Feel free to write to Eliot with respect to whatever you have read in this book, or for more information on For A World We Choose Foundation, the nonprofit organization that is receiving all the royalties from this book. (See Appendix B for more information.) To find out more about both *Experiencing the Soul* and *Conscious Living/Conscious Dying* workshops offered in behalf of For A World We Choose Foundation, contact:

Eliot Rosen, Director, For A World We Choose Foundation,
P.O. Box 1072, Studio City, CA 91614 (USA)
(818) 760-6762 • fax: (818) 769-8810 • e-mail: **fawwcf@worldnet.att.net**
Website: **www.naturalusa.com/fawwcf**

To order this book's companion video, *Experiencing the Soul,*
see page 281.